JCMS Annual Review of the European Union in 2006

Edited by

Ulrich Sedelmeier
and
Alasdair R. Young

General Editors: William Paterson and Jim Rollo

Blackwell
Publishing

First published 2007 by Blackwell Publishing Ltd

British Library Cataloguing-in-Publication Data applied for
ISBN 978-1-4051-5980-7

The publisher's policy is to use permanent paper from mills
that operate a sustainable forestry policy, and which has been
manufactured from pulp processed using acid-free and
elementary chlorine-free practices.
Furthermore, the publisher ensures that the text paper and cover board
used have met acceptable environmental accreditation standards.

For further information on Blackwell Publishing, visit our website:
http://www.blackwellpublishing.com

CONTENTS

Editorial: 2006 A Quiet Year?

ULRICH SEDELMEIER
London School of Economics
ALASDAIR R. YOUNG
University of Glasgow

After the dramatic events of the past couple of years, 2006 has been relatively quiet for the European Union (EU). While 2004 saw the dramatic enlargement of the EU and the signing of the Constitutional Treaty and 2005 saw its rejection by Dutch and French voters, 2006 did not bring major changes either in the EU's membership or institutions. Given that 2007 has already (by mid-May) seen the accessions of Bulgaria and Romania and the intensification of discussions on what will replace the Constitutional Treaty, 2006 might be seen, as Jörg Monar (this volume) suggests, as something of an '*intermezzo*'.

Although 2006 may have been a relatively quiet year for the EU in structural terms, there were a number of significant developments across the breadth of the EU's policy waterfront. This emphasis on the business of governing rather than on the form of governance might reflect the maturation of the EU as polity and the predominance of 'normal' politics. In terms of internal policy, 2006 saw agreement on the Services Directive and the REACH (registration, evaluation and authorization of chemicals) Regulation (Howarth, this volume); a decision to expand the euro area to include Slovenia (Johnson, this volume); renewal of the inter-institutional agreement on budgetary discipline (Pollak and Puntscher Riekmann, this volume); and the application of the mutual recognition principle to both civil and criminal law matters (Monar, this volume). There were also several decisions taken to change the functioning of the EU's institutions, including reform of the comitology procedure to give the European Parliament a greater say and agreement to increase the transparency of Council decision-making under the co-decision procedure (Dinan, this volume). Externally, the EU successfully co-ordinated a peacekeeping mission to Lebanon (Lavenex and Schimmelfennig; Ojanen and Vuohula, this volume); it also expanded its external efforts to reduce migratory flows and reinforced its co-operation on external border protection (Monar, this volume); and was particularly active in the wider world (Allen and Smith, this volume).

As this policy activity suggests, the EU's political institutions continued to function well despite enlargement and in the absence of treaty reform (Dinan, this volume). This reinforces our snap impression in last year's editorial (Sedelmeier and Young, 2006) that the non-ratification of the Constitutional Treaty has not precipitated a crisis in EU decision-making. This is not to say that decision-making is always easy or efficient. Particularly in policy areas where the decision rule is unanimity there can be blockages (see, for example, Monar, this volume) and problems of policy coherence (Allen and Smith, this volume). In external relations there were movements towards developing an External Action Service in the absence of treaty reform (Allen and Smith, this volume). By contrast in justice and home affairs, some Member States resisted selective institutional changes in the hope of maintaining pressure for adoption of a more comprehensive version of the Constitutional Treaty (Monar, this volume). For the most part, however, problems with reading agreement do not stem from only the new Member States. For example, with regard to the EU's relations with Russia, problems stemmed not only from Poland impeding a common EU policy, but also from Germany's active unilateral policy (Allen and Smith; Ojanen and Vuohla, this volume). It might be that one consequence of the enlarged EU is that larger Member States, at least, may be more inclined to pursue foreign policy unilaterally or in privileged groups (Allen and Smith, this volume).

One way in which enlargement does seem to have further complicated EU decision-making is because of the sheer number of states; governments change in one Member State or another every few months. For example, seven governments fell during 2006 (Henderson and Sitter, this volume). Compounded by cabinet reshuffles, this means that there is considerable turnover in the membership of the various configurations of the Council of Ministers (Dinan, this volume). This volatility will compound the deleterious impact of size on the collegiality of decision-making and make any socialisation of members more difficult.

An effective, but undramatic year for the EU made it harder for us as editors to identify an appropriate subject for the Keynote Article. We identified a common theme – the concern about competitiveness – that linked a couple of the big, if not spectacular, events of 2006: the suspension of the Doha Round of multilateral trade talks and the adoption of the services directive. Colin Hay, in the Keynote Article, argues that there is a widely held conception of competitiveness in the EU that accepts that increased competition leads to increased competitiveness. He contends, however, that that conception rests on the assumption that all markets for goods and services are analogous to those for cheap consumer goods – that is, both highly price sensitive and highly demand price elastic. This assumption, he argues, leads the EU to privilege strategies of cost and price containment to the detriment of other strategies for enhancing competitiveness, resulting in an 'obsessive competitiveness disorder'. The pervasiveness of the competitiveness discourse is also central to David Howarth's article on the EU's internal developments, in which he argues that the framing of the REACH regulation in competitiveness terms contributed to the weakening of health and environmental objectives.

Our decision to invite Lisa Conant to write the Review Article on the politics of legal integration was motivated in part by the idea that, as in the 1970s, political paralysis might spawn, or be off-set by, judicial activism, in which case it would be particularly useful to have an overview of the 'state of the art'. In addition to contrasting the approaches of legal scholars and political scientists to the study of the EU's legal system, Conant provides an overview of the debate in international relations theory regarding the development of a supranational legal system; summarizes the subsequent scholarship extending the analysis into the domain of comparative politics; and discusses an emerging literature that situates legal integration within a domesticated context, which generates questions that reach beyond the classic concerns of integration theory.

Reviewing the concrete legal developments in 2006, Michael Dougan identifies several important European Court of Justice (ECJ) decisions that address key aspects of the relationship between the Member States and their citizens: *Watts*, on the obligation of national authorities to pay for healthcare received in another Member State; *De Cuyper*, concerning a Member State's competence to restrict unemployment benefits to claimants not resident within its territory; and *Family Reunification Directive*, in which the ECJ finally addressed the legal status of the Charter of Fundamental Human Rights. Dougan (in this volume), however, cautions against attempting to discern a shift in the 'legal policy' of the ECJ on the basis of a small survey of rulings.

A striking feature of 2006, particularly in contrast to 2005, is how far the EU has retreated in the lives of the EU's Member States. The EU was not a significant issue in any of the nine elections held in EU Member States during 2006 (Henderson and Sitter, this volume). This was the case even in Austria, which held the Council's rotating presidency at the time (Pollak and Puntscher Riekmann, this volume).

There also seemed to be increased acceptance of Economic and Monetary Union, or at least reduced criticism of it, spurred by improved economic growth in the euro area, which made meeting the Stability and Growth Pact's criteria easier (Verdun, this volume). This increased acceptance, however, proved short-lived given the comments of France's newly elected president (*Financial Times*, 9 May 2007). The European Central Bank was extremely active during 2006, raising interest rates an unprecedented five times in the course of the year (Verdun, this volume). These increases compounded reservations about the value of the euro relative to other currencies, with critics claiming that its high value was hurting the competitiveness of euro area firms.

Stronger euro area growth has had an important and positive impact on the non-euro area economies, which continued to grow faster than those in the euro area (Johnson, this volume). Despite their more rapid growth, a number of non-euro area Member States had problems moving towards meeting the convergence criteria, especially those concerning inflation and deficits (Johnson, this volume).

With regard to the EU's external relations there were signs of increasing concern about enlargement beyond those to whom the prospect of membership has already been extended and particularly about the EU's 'integration capacity' (Lavenex and Schimmelfennig, this volume). The numerous problems encountered in the on-going enlargement processes during 2006, however, were due primarily to problems in candidate countries, including unresolved territorial issues and resurgent nationalism, rather than to the EU's increasing concerns about its capacity. 2006 provided further indication that the EU's European Neighbourhood Policy has trouble dealing with regional conflicts and non-co-operative authoritarian regimes, confirming doubts about its potential to promote peace and democratic change (Lavenex and Schimmelfennig, this volume). Further afield, the EU was very active, although the lack of strategy continued to be evident (Allen and Smith, this volume). External events – such as the war in Lebanon, tensions with Russia, trade disputes with China and the USA – encroached significantly on the EU's agenda during 2006 (Pollack and Puntscher Riekmann; Ojanen and Vuohla, this volume).

In these contributions, you will notice further movement towards more reflective approaches. The articles, therefore, do not aim to be comprehensive, rather they explicitly identify a few key developments in each issue area and explore their implications. We conclude with a note of clarification. As this is the *Annual Review of the European Union* in 2006 Bulgaria and Romania are treated as applicant countries and Slovenia is treated as a non-euro area country. For the 2007 *Annual Review* Bulgaria and Romania will be addressed in the article on the 'Political Developments of the EU Member

States' and Slovenia in the article on 'Economic Developments in the Euro Area.' Beyond the traditional thanks to the contributors, we would particularly like to thank Lisa Conant and Amy Verdun, who both delivered babies and still delivered their contributions. Yenay Esmée Verdun was born on 20 December 2006 and Myles Everett Conant was born on 25 March 2007.

Reference

Sedelmeier, U. and Young, A.R. (2006) 'Editorial: Crisis, What Crisis? Continuity and Normality in the European Union in 2005.' *Journal of Common Market Studies* 44(s1), pp. 1–5.

JCMS 2007 Volume 45 Annual Review pp. 7–16

The Austrian Presidency: Pragmatic Management

JOHANNES POLLAK
SONJA PUNTSCHER RIEKMANN
Institute for European Integration Research, Austrian Academy of Sciences

Introduction

When Austria took over the Council Presidency on 1 January 2006, the European Union (EU) found itself at a crossroads following the French and Dutch rejection of the Constitutional Treaty in 2005. The ratification crisis was, however, only one of those unexpected events which jeopardized the new three-year programme for the six presidencies from 2004 to 2006, invented to ensure greater coherence and consistency in the leadership of the EU. While such a programme limits the scope of activity and priorities of a given presidency, it is no substitute for active leadership in critical cases. Hence, a presidency has to be evaluated, first, with regard to the management of the routine matters handed over by previous presidencies; second, with regard to its own priorities; and, third, by its responses to crises. How a presidency manages to deal with these dimensions is influenced by the nature of internal EU challenges, international developments and the domestic politics of the country holding the presidency.

The EU faced a series of considerable internal challenges during the Austrian presidency. Shortly after the negative French and Dutch referendums on the Constitutional Treaty, the European Council decided to start a period of reflection that, after several months, had not produced impressive results. Moreover, though governments considered the conclusion of the financial perspective for 2007–13 a success, in January 2006 the European Parliament (EP) overwhelmingly rejected the compromise worked out among the EU leaders and demanded a substantial re-allocation of certain budget lines and an overall increase in the total amount. These rather bleak internal conditions greeted the Austrian presidency.

The external developments affecting Austria's performance included considerable foreign policy predicaments: the Russian–Ukrainian gas dispute, the illness of Israeli Premier Arial Sharon, the electoral success of Hamas in Palestine, the 'cartoon crises', Iran's re-enforced nuclear ambitions and last but not least the protracted negotiations in the World Trade Organization (WTO). Given the Member States' poor record in finding common positions in response to external events, the potential for renewed cleavages was significant. One objective of the Austrian presidency was to rebuild the mutual trust between the Member States in order to keep divergences at bay.

During its first presidency in 1998, Austria defined its role modestly as an 'honest broker'. This time it expanded the motto by describing the presidency as 'a service for Europe'. According to the Austrian government this service included several broad priority areas, reflecting a mix of European and national issues, among them the discussion of the Constitutional Treaty's future and the rebuilding of confidence in the European project among EU citizens, economic growth and employment, enlargement with a focus on the West Balkan countries and fostering the global role of the EU as a strong and reliable partner.

In the following, we focus on whether and how a few examples from the three main areas – internal challenges (the constitutional question), external developments (the Russian–Ukrainian gas crisis) and Austrian domestic politics (the elections in October 2006) – influenced Austria's presidency in dealing with routine matters (the inter-institutional agreement following the agreement on the new financial perspective), its own priorities (the Western Balkan countries), as well as internal and external events.

I. Routine Matters: The New Financial Perspective

After the last-minute deal on the financial framework for 2007–13 in December 2005, the Austrian administration heaved a collective sigh of relief. After the considerable divergences between the Commission's proposal (1.20 per cent of Gross National Income, GNI), the EP's wish (1.18 per cent of GNI) and the European Council's inconclusive June 2005 meeting, the Member States reached a political agreement to reduce the expenditure ceiling to 1.045 per cent of GNI shortly before the start of the Austrian presidency. A lot of technical tasks, however, had to be accomplished in the first months of 2006. The budget deal required a new inter-institutional agreement between the EP, the Commission and the Council and various legal acts for its implementation in different policy fields. Given the considerably divergent expectations and interests, the negotiations on the inter-institutional agreement were expected to be sensitive.

Talks with the EP started in January and, according to the Austrian Finance Minister, were to last only two to three months. In agreement with the other Member States Austria time and again emphasized the need for sound financial management and more effective budget implementation. On 18 January, the EP rejected the December deal struck by the heads of state and government. Thus, the first 'budget trialogue' that started on 23 January was marked by vast disagreements since the Commission also called for improvements in and corrections to various aspects of the European Council's deal. From the very beginning the Austrians supported a tough line, sticking to the December 2005 result. Since the other Member States shared this position, a formal mandate for further negotiations did not seem necessary. Agreement on this rather extraordinary Austrian request was only possible because as a net contributor, it enjoyed the trust of the other Member States.

On 15 February, the Commission sent the EP and the Council additional proposals on renewing the inter-institutional agreement on budgetary discipline. The Commission's seven complementary proposals with a view to the second trialogue on 21 February were extensively criticized by the Member States during the COREPER meeting on 16 February, which also confirmed that the Austrian Presidency was going to have very little margin of manoeuvre in negotiating with the EP. The Member States were especially critical of the Commission returning to matters such as national statements of good budget management, the procedure for review of the financial regulation and the role that the EP could play in recasting the own resources system.

In a statement following the second trialogue meeting on 21 February, the Council and the EP pledged to boost contact ahead of the next three-way budget meeting, scheduled for 21 March. The Austrian Presidency was represented at the three-way talks by Austrian Finance Minister Karl-Heinz Grasser, who again pointed out that he had little room for manoeuvre in the negotiations with the EP. The EP, however, wanted to improve on the Council deal. It demanded increased funding for various programmes (life-long learning, Erasmus, Leonardo, foreign policy and consumer policy), greater budget flexibility, a well-defined role for itself in the review process for the EU budget and a pledge from Member States to certify that EU funds have been properly managed. The EP urged the Council to act rapidly, warning that if not, the Budget Committee might decide at its meeting on 6 March to look at the option of cancelling the 1999 inter-institutional agreement, thus risking a crisis. Although the positions of the Council and the EP were far apart,

Austrian Foreign Minister Ursula Plassnik maintained that the negotiations had taken place in a constructive atmosphere and recalled the presidency's intention to conclude an agreement in April.

Before the third trialogue meeting this optimistic view seemed to be jeopardized by the Council's rejection of the EP's wish to participate fully in the budget review exercise scheduled for 2008–09. In addition, the main stumbling blocks – the total amount of spending and the degree of budgetary flexibility – remained virtually unchanged. After the meeting on 21 March, which took place in a much better atmosphere than the first two meetings,[1] it was clear that both institutions were pinning their hopes on the last meeting scheduled for 4 April. In a press conference after the third meeting, Austrian Finance Minister Grasser recognized that the Member States should finally agree to increase the total amount of spending by €1.8 billion (0.21 per cent), whereas he called the EP's request for €12–13 billion (1.5 per cent of GNI) unrealistic. By proposing a slight increase in overall spending, he provoked criticism from the other Member States, thus signalling to the EP that its demands were excessive. After eight hours of negotiations, the last trialogue meeting reached a definitive agreement on the financial perspective for 2007–13 and on the text for a new inter-institutional agreement on budgetary discipline and the improvement of budgetary procedures. The compromise saw a €2 billion increase in the total maximum amount of EU spending, setting the limit at 1.048 per cent of GNI and the involvement of the EP in the procedures amending the EU budget in 2008–09.

From the very beginning of the negotiations it was clear that the Austrian Presidency was acting under constraints established by the December 2005 deal. Both the Council and the EP seemed totally inflexible in their demands from January to March 2006. While the repeated statement of objectives by both institutions surely was part of the negotiating game and failure not highly likely, the final compromise was reached because of the meticulous preparations of the Austrian Presidency. As a matter of fact, Austrian officials had contacted the EP informally in 2005 and prepared the ground for nego-tiations on the inter-institutional agreement in ten meetings that sorted out technical issues. The Austrian Ministry of Finance had started preparations 18 months ahead of the presidency establishing close contacts with the Com-mission. Support by the Council secretariat was crucial for the success as much as the fact that Austria as a signatory of the 2003 'letter of the six', demanding a reduction of the EU budget to 1 per cent of the Community GNI,

---

[1] This improved atmosphere was due to the decision of the EP to not examine the Budget Committee's draft resolution denouncing the 1999 inter-institutional agreement in protest against the Council's lack of willingness to negotiate.

enjoyed considerable trust from the other Member States. Moreover, since budgetary affairs were perceived as a highly technical and routinized matter, they gained only marginal public attention and could therefore not be exploited in the upcoming Austrian elections in the autumn.

II. Austria's Own Priorities: The Integration of the Western Balkans

One of the top priorities of the Austrian Presidency – set at the end of 2004 – was to confirm the European perspective for the Western Balkan countries other than Croatia, negotiations with which Austria had managed to link in October 2005 to negotiations with Turkey. Although a number of European Council meetings, particularly the June 2003 Thessaloniki declaration, had reiterated support for their European perspective, these statements had been somewhat guarded and the Austrian presidency's aim was a declaration that explicitly mentioned the future membership of Serbia, Montenegro, Macedonia, Albania and Bosnia Herzegovina. This priority was remarkable given the Austrian public's pronounced scepticism about further enlargement, which only 29 per cent support. This scepticism may be due to the start of the Turkish accession negotiations, an issue to which the Austrians are particularly hostile. Public scepticism was certainly fuelled by the Commission's highly critical monitoring reports on Bulgarian and Rumanian accession, presented on 16 May (see Henderson and Sitter, this volume). The government had to strike a balance between responding to hostile public opinion and the need to support the Balkan countries in view of its specific economic and security interests in the region. During the presidency, Chancellor Schüssel repeatedly referred to the 'absorption capacity' of the Union, especially with an eye on the negotiations with Turkey. In mid-March, Foreign Minister Plassnik announced that the Gymnich meeting on 10–11 March should deal with the Balkans, which must not be allowed to become a zone of insecurity between Austria, Italy and Greece. One of the objectives of the meeting was thus to bring the Balkans back onto a European track.

On 11 March the 'Salzburg Declaration' of an informal meeting of the foreign ministers of the EU Member States, the acceding states (Bulgaria and Romania), the candidate states (Croatia and Turkey) and the potential candidate countries of the Western Balkans reaffirmed the European perspective for the Western Balkans. The European Council on 15 to 16 June endorsed the Salzburg Declaration. Although the substance of the Salzburg Declaration did not go beyond the conclusions of the 2003 Thessaloniki summit, the struggle over wording and definitions proved arduous. In particular, offering an explicit membership perspective to these countries was not to everybody's liking. If it had not been for the Austrian insistence on the declaration – with the support of, for example, Hungary and Slovenia – changed circumstances would have sidelined the Balkan issue. The generally sceptical mood, especially in France and the Netherlands after the negative referendums on the Constitutional Treaty and the reluctance of some Balkan countries to comply with certain EU demands, dampened the mood for further enlargements (see also Lavenex and Schimmelfennig, this volume).

The 33 foreign ministers (plus the EU Special Representative for Bosnia Herzegovina, the Special Representative of the UN Secretary General for Kosovo and the Special Co-ordinator of the Stability Pact for South Eastern Europe) pledged to promote enhanced regional co-operation, mainly through the development of a regional free trade area, for example by extending the existing Central European Free Trade Agreement. Tangible results of the new Balkan strategy concerned mainly visa facilitations. The visa fees for the new biometrical passports would have risen enormously and provided for a nearly insurmountable obstacle, for example, for student exchange. Thus, on 4–5 May a Viennese conference on 'The Role of Internal Security in Relations between the EU and its Neighbours' agreed to suspend the increase of visa fees for the countries of the Western Balkan. In addition a 'Convention on Police Co-operation for South Eastern Europe' was signed.

Despite a certain 'enlargement fatigue', the Austrian presidency successfully brought the Balkans back on the EU agenda. The specific Austrian domestic situation with a largely eurosceptic population hardly influenced this pet project of the presidency. The fact that the first steps towards bringing the Balkans back in were made in the field of security co-operation might have helped to convince the other Member States to follow the Austrian initiative. Again, the meticulous and timely preparation and the careful development of existing initiatives like the Thessaloniki Declaration proved crucial.

III. Internal Challenges: The Constitutional Treaty and the European Citizens

After the rejection of the Constitutional Treaty in France and the Netherlands, the constitutional debate appeared stranded and was confined to a so-called period of reflection. Austria's contribution to this period was rather loose and incoherent. The Netherlands made it clear that a discussion about the constitutional text was not desirable before their local elections in March. By contrast, France declared its willingness to talk about the issue, but it was obvious to all Member States that for any progress on the issue they would have to wait until after the French presidential elections in April 2007. Thus, the Austrian Presidency set itself the modest goal of keeping the constitutional issue under discussion. The opening conference 'The Sound of Europe' took place on 27 January and coincided with the 250th anniversary of Mozart's birthday. According to then Chancellor Wolfgang Schüssel, its aim was to restore the much needed trust among the Member States and between governments and European citizens. Thus, the purpose of the conference was not to find a solution to the constitutional impasse but rather to lift spirits. Unsurprisingly, the speeches reiterated the need to concentrate on issues affecting the everyday life of the citizens. This approach was complemented by a specific conference on subsidiarity – a pet theme for Austrian politicians who often complain that the EU is assuming too many decision-making powers – with the original title 'Europe Begins at Home'. Hence it was quite convenient that the spring European Council meeting traditionally focused on issues like growth and employment, education, energy and welfare.

A debate about how to proceed with the Constitutional Treaty only began at the meeting of the foreign ministers in May. The ministers agreed a two-track approach, which was reflected in the presidency conclusions of the European Council on 15–16 June. On the one hand best use should be made of the possibilities offered by the existing treaties in order to deliver concrete results that citizens expect. On the other hand, the German Presidency of 2007 was expected to present a report assessing the state of discussions with regard to the Constitutional Treaty. The background for this two-tiered approach stems from the provision in the Nice Treaty that a smaller Commission has to be installed in 2009. Without the ratification of the Constitutional Treaty a specification for the envisaged rotation principle sketched out in the Nice Treaty needs to be found. In addition, the EP elections in 2009 are expected to provide impetus for a 'relaunch' of the constitutional momentum. In order to revive the constitutional process, the EU leaders agreed to issue a declaration on 25 March 2007 to commemorate 50 years of the Treaties of Rome, which would set out Europe's values and ambitions and confirm their commitment to deliver them. In his concluding speech to the EP on 20 June, Chancellor Schüssel emphasized the willingness of all Member States to stick to the substance of the Constitutional Treaty. But he also made clear that new (unspecified) initiatives were needed, because resubmitting the same text for a second referendum was not an option. The Austrian Presidency had, however, not taken into consideration the EP's initiative on reviving the constitutional debate with the help of 'Citizen's Forums' (based on the Duff/ Voggenhuber Report PE 364.798v02-00, adopted 19 January 2006), nor had it spelled out a programme to implement the Commission's 'Plan D'. By way of a general assessment regarding the Austrian handling of the constitutional stalemate, we hold that due to the inconclusive position of the Heads of State and Governments on how to proceed with the Constitutional Treaty little was to be expected. Thus, the contribution of the Austrian Presidency was a rather indirect one following no clear plan beyond the attempt to keep the discussion about the Constitutional Treaty on the agenda.

IV. External Challenges: The Energy Question

Energy provides an excellent example of how the EU's internal developments can be driven by external events. So far, the EU's activities in the energy area have been limited to the internal liberalization of the gas and electricity markets. The gas crisis between Russia and Ukraine in January 2006 brought energy security to the top of the EU's agenda. Following the breakdown of talks between Ukraine and Russia on the price of gas exports, on 1 January Russia cut off gas supplies to Ukraine. Although Gazprom decided to allow gas for only the EU to transit the pipelines in Ukraine, gas supplies to EU customers, who depend on Russian gas for one quarter of their supplies, were disrupted for two days. The EU criticized Gazprom's unilateral act and the Gas Co-ordination Group (established already in 2004) convened its first meeting during the crisis. On 4 January, Russia and Ukraine reached a deal that also secured the flow of gas to the EU.

The Hampton Court Summit in October 2005 had already instructed the Commission to devise a strengthened common EU approach to energy supplies and the Commission presented a Green Paper on Energy in March. Since Austria had forged close links with the Commission well ahead of the start of its presidency, work on the Green Paper could be accelerated. Based on this Green Paper, the presidency suggested new steps towards a common European energy policy focusing on sustainable resources. Its list of priorities and recommendations included the conclusion of the negotiations of the Energy Charter Transit Protocol and the ratification of the Energy Charter Treaty, the drafting of an agreement on energy with Russia, the use of the European Neighbourhood Policy to further the EU's energy policy objectives, the diversification of sources of energy supply, the promotion of renewable energies and a more efficient use of energy. Although the Member States welcomed the Green Paper, it was substantially changed before it was adopted by the spring European Council. The presidency conclusions emphasized horizontal co-operation instead of a European regulator and included neither a European Energy Supply Observatory nor the plan for strategic energy technologies.

Following the gas dispute, the Austrian Minister for Agriculture and the Environment, Josef Pröll decided to include the biomass action plan, adopted by the Commission on 7 December 2005, on the agenda of the Agriculture Council of 23 to 24 January in order to devise a plan to reduce dependence on fossil energy sources. This decision was based on two strategic considerations related to Austrian domestic politics. First, Austria styled itself as the leader in the use of alternative energy sources and second, it could emphasize its opposition to nuclear power. Thus this initiative responded to domestic criticism of the government for being lukewarm on environmental protection and tepid in its opposition to the 'nuclear renaissance' in Europe.

Moreover, on 16 March, Vienna hosted a conference entitled 'Energy Paths, Horizon 2050' that debated possible options for sustainable energy supply by 2050, with particular emphasis on technological choices. The biggest success in the energy field was the agreement on concrete figures concerning emissions, renewables and energy sources at the spring summit. Concerning the relations with Russia – the EU–Russia summit took place on 25 May – the presidency's aim was to keep the energy question under discussion. While it was made clear to President Putin that the topic would remain on the agenda under the Finnish presidency, it was equally clear that Russia would not sign the Energy Charter. Nonetheless, the presidency managed to start a process in this important policy area – a surprising development since the failing ratification of the Constitutional Treaty deprived the EU of the legal basis for creating an Energy Community.

Conclusion: More Pragmatism than Vision

The second Austrian Presidency was characterized by three interrelated features. First, the general perplexity after the voters' rejection of the Constitutional Treaty in France and the Netherlands continued well into the first six months of 2006. Second, external events once more showed the need for a coherent and efficient European common foreign policy. Third, Austria again proved to be a technically well-organized if somewhat uninspired 'honest broker'. For the successful management of routine affairs, external crises and its own priorities two points proved crucial: the meticulous preparation that started well ahead of the presidency and the forging of close links with the Commission, the EP and the Council Secretariat.

Apart from these basics, the political separation of the domestic and the supranational level seems to be important. While it was clear that the constitutional stalemate would persist, this issue did not seem to influence the daily policy-making nor did it impact on the EU's capacity to react to external challenges. Moreover, the presidency's routine work was only marginally, if at all, influenced by the Austrian elections in the autumn of 2006 or by the

eurosceptic mood of the domestic public. At the same time though, euroscepticism seems to have prevented the government from utilizing the presidency to profile itself *vis-à-vis* the national audience. Today, however,
presidencies generally appear to steer a somewhat clumsy course between
meeting their European tasks and downplaying the scope of their decisions
domestically. The resulting dilemmas are enhanced by the fact that presidencies are largely handled as the exclusive task of the executive, whereas other
national institutions, such as parliaments and political parties, are largely
onlookers, rather than transmission belts between the EU's politics and its
citizens.

JCMS 2007 Volume 45 Annual Review pp. 17–24

The Finnish Presidency: Efficiency Before Eloquence?

HANNA OJANEN
EERO VUOHULA
The Finnish Institute of International Affairs

I. Mastering the Unforeseen, Fumbling the Foreseen

At the conclusion of the second Finnish presidency of the European Union (EU) in the second half of 2006, the Finnish Foreign Minister Erkki Tuomioja noted that the Presidency had consisted of 65 per cent unforeseen events and 35 per cent anticipated events; and overall, it had been more successful with the former than the latter (Tuomioja, 2007).

There are several reasons for such a surprising conclusion. Above all, some of important issues like the services directive, REACH and the EU Battle Groups had been largely agreed prior to the Finnish presidency. Therefore, the ambitions on the legislative front and European Security and Defence Policy (ESDP) were not particularly high. Due to the expiration of the Partnership and Co-operation Agreement (PCA) with Russia and the fact that that relations with Russia is a special field of interest and expertise of Finland, the presidency's main efforts concentrated on concluding the mandate for the negotiations on the PCA. However, these efforts were impeded by the dispute between Poland and Russia on meat imports (see Allen and Smith, this volume). Another anticipated item on the agenda, enlargement, proved to be more strenuous than before. Against this background it can be said that the successful handling of the unexpected war in Lebanon 'saved' the Finnish presidency and it can be considered a 'successful' presidency. The Finnish presidency would appear as one in which political leadership was the most prominent in sudden crises and least prominent in issues EU's on the long-term agenda.

II. Style and Substance that Matched Expectations

The expectations on the Finnish presidency were not particularly high. It was seen as a transition presidency, with the German presidency already looming large in people's minds. Although the first Finnish presidency in 1999 had been widely applauded, Finland was not expected to achieve much at a time when the EU still found itself lacking direction after the rejection of the Constitutional Treaty in France and the Netherlands in 2005. The low expectations thus were due both to the general lack of inspiration within the EU and Finland, a small member country lacking a prominent presence on the mental map of other EU governments.

The domestic image of the Finnish politicians in charge was not flattering, either. In the national media, it was noted that they often appeared as dead standing pine stubs on international arenas (*Helsingin Sanomat*, 2006) and the efforts to add some colour to the December European Council by bringing in Santa Claus were ridiculed.

Finnish politicians have hardly ever had a high profile in Europe. Yet, compared to the 1999 presidency, there was a change in style in that now, pro-European attitudes were harder to detect and more emphasis was put at the level of discourse on national interests. Prime Minister Matti Vanhanen represents the Centre Party, traditionally less European and internationally minded than the Social Democratic Party of the then Prime Minister Paavo Lipponen. In Vanhanen's view, in contrast to that of his predecessor, Finland does not need to be in every nucleus or core of the EU countries; belonging to the core is not an end in itself. At the very beginning of his premiership he stated in an interview that the EU had only instrumental value for him and that he did not feel comfortable waiving the EU flag or listening to the EU anthem. His statement caused quite a row and he subsequently toned down his rhetoric. Overall, there was less enthusiasm in Finland towards the presidency than in 1999, both among the political elite and the general public and the upcoming parliamentary elections in March 2007 made politicians even more wary of overt EU-mindedness. The Preliminary Programme of 26 May was accordingly a very routine paper without much European *élan* that did not articulate any new plans or specific goals.

Another difference was the impact of team presidencies, the new setting in which the framework of the programme had been drawn up early on in co-operation with the Austrian government and published in December 2005 (Finnish Prime Minister's Office, 2006). One of the main goals of team presidencies is to increase coherence. On enlargement, however, Austria and Finland held very different views. On topics where the countries were closer to one another, the team programme may have further contributed to lowering the level of ambition of a single country's input.

Nonetheless, there was also strong continuity between the two Finnish presidencies. It is striking to note how the themes of the 1999 Finnish Presidency (Finnish Ministry for Foreign Affairs, 1999) resemble those of 2006: a globally active and influential Union; an enlarging Union; a transparent and efficient Union; a stable, competitive and employment-creating Union; a society based on information and knowledge; social and ecological responsibility; an area of freedom, security and justice. Also the EU's relations with Russia and enlargement to Turkey were central during both terms. These were themes that Finland was expected to take up.

Two characteristics are particularly distinctive of Finland as the country holding the presidency: first, the considerable role geography plays in shaping its priorities and mindset in general and, second, the pragmatic orientation that emphasizes deeds rather than words and leads to matters being presented in a down-to-earth way. Pragmatism, however, seldom combines with vision or innovation. As the Prime Minister confessed in his speech at the European Parliament (EP): 'I have to say that I am dull and proud of it [. . .] if it is dull for decisions to be taken in an orderly fashion and on schedule' (Vanhanen, 2006a).

III. The Foreseen: Russia and EU Enlargement

Russia and the Northern Dimension

Finland's role in EU–Russia relations changed with the EU's eastern enlargement. Finland is no longer the only EU member to border Russia and thus to have a claim to special expertise on EU–Russia relations. Many new EU member countries share such expertise, but bring a much more critical view of Russia into the EU. The Finnish presidency's aim of strengthening the EU's policy towards Russia was thus both particularly timely and more difficult to achieve.

Negotiations on a new PCA were expected to begin during the presidency, with the central item on the agenda of the EU-Russia Summit on 24 November being agreement on the principles, general coverage and structure of the mandate for the negotiations. The presidency realized this aim, as there was no disagreement on structure or contents. The formal adoption of the mandate was postponed, however, by the Polish government's threat to veto the PCA negotiations unless Russia ended its restrictions on imports of Polish meat, which it justified on quality grounds. The disappointment of the Finnish presidency was augmented by the illusion created by the positive atmosphere after the well-handled informal EU summit between EU heads of state and government and Russian President Putin in Lahti on 20 October.

In the run-up to Lahti, Prime Minister Vanhanen appeared to have managed to unify the EU position at least in that he expressed rather clearly to President Putin the EU's concerns about the human rights situation in Russia directly during a working dinner. This was met very favourably by the media. Most observers considered it the first time that the EU leaders in unison raised the difficult issue of human rights face to face with President Putin. As there were signs that President Putin might wish to finalize a number of international agreements prior to the end of his second term in 2008, with the PCA and accession to the World Trade Organization (WTO) among the most important, the news on the United States lifting its opposition to Russia's accession to the WTO added momentum to begin quickly the talks on a new, qualitatively improved PCA. A concrete result of the EU–Russia summit was an agreement to abolish by 2012 the excessive fees that Russia has charged western airlines over-flying Siberia to Asian destinations; this had been an issue for 13 years.

Another important issue at the summit was the reform of the EU's Northern Dimension (ND) policies, which had been launched under the first Finnish presidency in 1999, but which ran into problems as a result of opposition to engaging with Russia because of its actions in Chechnya, failure to consult neighbouring states and a lack of concrete results on those projects that were pursued. For Finland, the Northern Dimension is a part of Finnish and EU policies towards Russia, a platform to discuss practical projects with the EU's backing in the Baltic Sea area and in north-west Russia along the Finnish border. This time, however, considerable changes were made to the structure of the Northern Dimension. In particular there was much greater engagement of neighbouring states. A special high-level meeting between the EU, Russia, Norway and Iceland held after the EU–Russia Summit endorsed a declaration and a political framework document that transforms the ND from being an EU policy towards Russia into a joint policy framework in which the EU, Russia, Norway and Iceland are all equal partners. The Finnish presidency presented this transformation as a great success. The clearer link to EU–Russia co-operation and the new permanent status of the ND (which had previously taken the form of three-year action plans) may contribute to further projects in north-west Russia in the fields of environment and the social and health sector, in the future probably also logistics and energy efficiency.

EU Enlargement and the Case of Turkey

As in its first presidency, Finland had to deal with enlargement, but the overall attitude towards further enlargement was now more negative (see also

Lavenex and Schimmelfennig, this volume), with some Member States –
including France, Germany, the Netherlands and Austria – wanting to slow
down the process. Finnish public opinion has been critical of further enlargement, but the government has been among the staunchest advocates since its
1999 presidency, which saw candidate country status granted to Turkey.

Accession negotiations with Turkey had started in October 2005. In the
second half of 2006, there was increasing criticism of Turkey's lack of
progress in implementing its obligations under the Additional Protocol of the
Ankara Agreement, which threatened the continuation of accession negotiations. Finland made an unsuccessful attempt at finding a solution that would
lead to Turkey opening up its ports and airports, at least in part or for some
time, to Cypriot vessels, while also making direct trade with northern Cyprus
possible. As a result of the inability to obtain agreement from the Turkish
government, accession negotiations on the eight chapters relating to the
customs union would not be opened until Turkey meets its obligations and no
chapter will be closed before that. A political agreement on the development
of the northern part of Cyprus was achieved, but the details of implementation
were left for later (see also Lavenex and Schimmelfennig, this volume).

As mandated by the June European Council, an in-depth examination of
enlargement was due at the December European Council. Prime Minister
Vanhanen's point of departure was that no new conditions – notably 'absorption capacity' – should be imposed on candidates and that the existing commitments should be kept. This position largely echoed that of (Finnish)
Commissioner for Enlargement, Olli Rehn. Each candidate would be treated
equally and progress in the accession negotiations would depend on each
country's individual merits only. Concerning Turkey, Finland stressed that its
future was inside the EU and that there should be no derailment of negotiations. The EU's door would be open, but the corollary of openness was a
rigorous application of the conditions. The overall agreement on enlargement
reached at the December summit was, however, slightly less optimistic. The
EU was very cautious about any new commitments and wary about giving
untimely promises on timetables. Nonetheless, the European Council confirmed the existing decisions with regard to Turkey and the western Balkan
countries.

IV. The Big Unforeseen: Middle East

The real test of the Finnish presidency was the sudden crisis in Lebanon.
Everybody was caught unprepared for the quick escalation of the conflict to
a full-scale war between Israel and Hezbollah in which large parts of Lebanon

were devastated. Another surprise for the presidency was the prominent role it had to assume in the efforts to manage the crisis. The EU quickly managed to reach a united position on the basis of UN Security Council Resolution 1701. The EU's leadership was seen essential in mobilizing the troops to strengthen the peacekeeping operation (UNIFIL) sufficiently.

Prime Minister Vanhanen did not hide his satisfaction when he presented his mid-term review of the Finnish presidency to the chairpersons of the Foreign Affairs Committees of the Member States' parliaments, stating: 'So I think the EU has done well in Lebanon. I know it has claimed on many previous occasions that Europe's hour has finally come, all to no avail, but I still feel that the EU can now have a stronger role in the Middle-East, in re-launching the peace process between Israel and Palestine, making progress with the roadmap' (Vanhanen, 2006b). Yet, it was the Foreign Minister Erkki Tuomioja who was seen as the man behind the Finnish success. The national press even reprimanded the Prime Minister for his lack of presence during the crisis.

The negotiations to strengthen the UNIFIL operation were one of the most demanding tasks of the presidency. Beforehand, the expectation was that the emphasis in EU crisis management would be on developing civil-military co-operation, a pet project of Finland together with the United Kingdom and Austria. Among the main achievements in the area of ESDP during the presidency were the full operational capacity of the Battle Groups (from January 2007) and the Civilian Response Teams reaching the preliminary stage of capability by the end of 2006.

V. Achievements and Disappointments in the Field of EU Legislation

Most legislative processes take years and presidencies often affect the complicated decision-making procedures only marginally. They can delay or speed them up to some extent, but parliamentary procedures are particularly difficult to influence. Nonetheless, the Finnish presidency claimed credit (at least in the domestic media) for both the Services Directive and the chemicals legislation REACH even though the substantial work to find the necessary compromises were done during the previous presidencies (see Howarth, this volume).

In justice and home affairs (JHA), Finland sought to simplify decision-making. Its proposal was to use the '*passerelle*' of Art. 42 of the Treaty on European Union to decide, unanimously, to switch to qualified majority voting (see Monar, this volume). At their September meeting, however, the JHA Ministers failed to find an agreement. The efforts, however, were seen as most useful in preparing the ground for more success later on.

Constitutional Treaty

When the Finnish presidency was being planned, the expectation was that the Constitutional Treaty would enter into force during the presidency, in November 2006. It would then have been the task of the Finnish presidency to ensure a smooth transition to the new institutional arrangements, especially in the area of external relations where Javier Solana, as Secretary-General of the Council, EU Foreign Minister and Vice President of the European Commission, would have taken over the chairmanship of the External Relations Council.

In June 2006, however, the European Council decided to continue the pause for reflection which followed the failed referendums in France and the Netherlands in 2005. Finland was willing to sound out positions among the Member States during its presidency, but this intention was not necessarily welcomed at first by the succeeding German presidency, which intended to take the debate on the Constitutional Treaty forward. Nonetheless, the Finnish Minister of European Affairs, Paula Lehtomäki, produced an (at this stage confidential) report on her consultations with her counterparts, and it was very much appreciated by the German presidency to whom it was left to draft a comprehensive report on the options to be followed.

In conclusion, it would seem that the expectations of the Finnish presidency were highest with regard to EU–Russia relations, where special knowledge and expertise was expected from Finland, while they were lowest on the issue of the future of the Constitutional Treaty. Yet, Finland apparently made very useful, behind the scenes, progress on the latter issue, probably greatly benefiting from its low-key style that did not antagonize anyone as well as from the very absence of high expectations. The successful handling of the EU's response to the conflict in Lebanon will most probably be counted as a success. After all, while failures are often attributed to particular presidencies, successes are not; they always have several mothers and fathers.

References

Finnish Ministry for Foreign Affairs (1999) 'The Finnish Presidency of the EU', available at: «http://presidency.finland.fi».

Finnish Prime Minister's Office (2006) Finland's EU Presidency, available at: «http://www.eu2006.fi».

Helsingin Sanomat (2006) 15 December.

Tuomioja, E. (2007) Speech in the UPI-FIIA EU Presidency Series, Helsinki, 2 February.

Vanhanen, M. (2006a) Speech at the European Parliament, 18 December; available at: «http://eu2006.navio.fi//news_and_documents/speeches/vko51/en_GB/178743/».

Vanhanen, M. (2006b) 'The Finnish EU Presidency – A Mid-Term Review'. Speech in Helsinki, 28 September, available at: «www.vnk.fi/ajankohtaista/puheet/puhe/en.jsp?oid=169451».

Keynote Article: What Doesn't Kill You Can Only Make You Stronger: The Doha Development Round, the Services Directive and the EU's Conception of Competitiveness*

COLIN HAY
University of Sheffield

Introduction

If competitiveness is, in Paul Krugman's (1994) now famous terms, a 'dangerous obsession', then the European Union (EU) has long suffered, as it continues to suffer today, from a particularly acute obsessive competitiveness disorder. In this article I reflect on the form of this contemporary obsession, establishing the distinctiveness of the European conception of competitiveness. I do so by considering two key events affecting the EU in 2006: the suspension of the multilateral trade round on the Doha development agenda (DDA) and the eventual adoption of a revised version of the Services Directive. In each I detect a highly conserved understanding of competitiveness, shared by EU trade negotiators, the Commission and even by a number of ostensibly dissenting voices. I show that this contemporary discourse of competitiveness is not in fact dangerous in Krugman's terms – being predicated neither upon a zero-sum conception of trade nor on the assumption that competition between nations is analogous to that between corporations for market share. Yet it is dangerous nonetheless. For in anticipating the efficiency gains arising from heightened economic integration, it tends to assume that all markets for goods and services are analogous to those for cheap consumer goods – that is, both highly price sensitive and highly demand price

* I am extremely grateful to Anand Menon, Vivien Schmidt, Uli Sedelmeier, Daniel Wincott and Alasdair Young for their combination of encouraging and incisive comments on an earlier iteration of this chapter. The responsibility for any flaws in the argument is, of course, mine alone.

elastic. This assumption leads the EU to privilege strategies of cost and price containment to the detriment of other strategies for enhancing competitiveness. As such, I argue, it is cost competitiveness specifically, rather than competitiveness more generally, that is the dangerous obsession in Europe today. In so doing, I show how the privileging of price competitiveness threatens the viability of the distinctive social and economic paradigm to which the EU ostensibly remains wedded in its conception of a 'European social model'.[1]

I develop my argument in two parts, dealing with the DDA and the Services Directive in turn. In this first I show that it takes an exceptionally cynical reading of the stance adopted by the EU before and following the suspension of the Doha Round to detect in it evidence of the protectionist disposition to which Krugman alerts us – and this despite the Commission's consistent appeal throughout the negotiations to the language of competitiveness and despite the centrality of Europe's protectionist common agricultural policy (CAP) to the negotiations. There is, I suggest, no evidence that the DDA was suspended by virtue of the EU's weddedness to a zero-sum conception of trade. Indeed, there is plenty of evidence that a positive-sum conception of trade led it to see considerable benefits in a multilateral trade deal. These, in turn, were understood principally in terms of the efficiency gains anticipated to arise from heightened cost competition.

Important though this acknowledgement of the EU's positive-sum conception of trade liberalization is, it is no refutation of the thesis that competitiveness has proved a dangerous obsession for the EU in recent years. In fact, as I aim to show in the second part of this article, it has – though for rather different reasons to those identified by Krugman. Here my focus is on the contested Bolkestein Directive on the internal market for services. As in the stance adopted with respect to the DDA, the public discourse in and through which both the original and significantly revised Services Directive were framed is clearly predicated on the efficiency gains anticipated through the heightened competition engendered by market liberalization. The case for service market liberalization, then, does not rest on the problematic assumption that the competition between nations is analogous to that between corporations. It does, however, rest on an equally problematic and largely unacknowledged assumption – namely that markets for services are analogous to those for cheap consumer goods and are both highly price sensitive and demand price elastic.

---

[1] The revised version of the Services Directive, for instance, is introduced in precisely such terms – as an attempt to 'preserve' the European social model (European Parliament and Council, 2006, p. 1).

As a direct consequence, and like much of the Lisbon-engendered discourse of competitiveness, the discussion of the relative merits (and demerits) of market liberalization has been framed almost entirely in terms of a narrow and restrictive conception of cost/price competitiveness. And whilst elements of both the DDA and the Services Directive have certainly been challenged, the framing of the debate in such terms has not. Such a fetishization of strategies of cost/price containment as the principal means to the end of competitiveness, I suggest, may have a series of deleterious economic consequences. In particular, it may serve to ratchet down both prices and wages in a market which is both far less integrated internationally (and hence less prone to the pressures of international competition in the first place) and significantly more demand inelastic than that, say, for most consumer goods.

If such an assessment is indeed warranted, then there is a powerful *prima facie* case for suggesting that a dangerous obsession not with competitiveness *per se* but with cost competitiveness specifically may serve to undermine a long-standing European model of growth and the much-vaunted 'European social model' with which it remains explicitly linked by the Commission. This model has been predicated on a highly skilled, trained and dedicated workforce producing quality goods in relatively price-insensitive markets. It is threatened as never before by the perceived imperatives of cost competitiveness. It is principally in this respect that competitiveness may prove to be a dangerous obsession for Europe's policy-makers.

I. What Doesn't Kill You Can Only Make You Stronger: Competitiveness in the Doha Round

On the face of it, there could be no better test case for Krugman's thesis as to the dangerous obsession of competitiveness than that provided by the stance of the EU in the recently suspended Doha Round. For not only was this as clear an instance as it is possible to imagine of a genuinely multilateral negotiation of the terms of global trade, in which one might expect the preferences of the key parties to be laid bare; it is also one in which a significant proportion of the EU's publicly stated position was framed directly in terms of the language of competitiveness.

The Doha Round, of course, got off to a fairly inauspicious start. Picking up many of the unresolved issues from the previous Uruguay Round, it was scheduled to begin in 1999 at the Ministerial Conference of the World Trade Organization (WTO) in Seattle. Yet disruption by anti-globalization protestors and the misgivings of many developing nations led to its start being postponed until the more secure surroundings of Doha in Qatar in

November 2001. Its agenda, set to a considerable extent by the EU itself (Kerremans, 2005), was rather different in both breadth and substance from previous rounds and came to be characterized by its emphasis on development. Ostensibly, it sought to promote development through trade liberalization, extending the remit of negotiations in the Uruguay Round beyond agriculture and services and refocusing such negotiations in terms of a number of specific millennial targets and goals. What was clear even before the start of the round was that reform of the EU's protectionist CAP was likely to prove a condition of any agreement. Indeed, the broadening of the agenda of the Doha Round was a clear and explicit attempt by the EU to allow 'benefits in other areas to offset the anticipated political costs associated with concessions on agriculture' (Young, 2007, p. 123; see also Allen and Smith, 2001). More than any other single issue, agriculture has shaped the content and trajectory of the negotiation process since 2001.

That the EU's trade negotiators went into the July 2006 Geneva Ministerial Meeting of the Doha Round – whose agenda they had done much to frame and for whose focus on development they had sought to take principal credit – committing themselves so boldly and publicly to securing a deal which might bolster the competitive position of the EU (Mandelson, 2005, 2006a) is actually rather paradoxical. Of course, in one sense it seems to provide considerable grist to the Krugmanite mill; indicating that the EU went into these negotiations with the clear aim of shoring up its perceived competitive advantage and wedded to a seemingly rather zero-sum conception of global trade. To those keen to detect in the EU's stance a protectionist disposition there is, of course, nothing paradoxical about that. What is paradoxical, however, is that the EU trade negotiators were apparently so shameless in declaring both *publicly* and *before the negotiations had even begun* their seemingly rather narrow and parochial commitment to securing a deal favourable to Europe. What makes this doubly paradoxical is that they should have done so having argued so consistently and strenuously for a better deal with the developing world and presenting the resulting 'development round' of the WTO as an appropriate response to the concerns of NGOs and anti-globalization activists about the unfair terms of north–south trade (see, for instance, Mandelson, 2006a, 2006b).

Of course, however politically misguided it might seem to reveal one's hand in advance of delicate international negotiations in this way, none of this is likely to come as too much of a surprise to followers of EU trade policy. For, acutely conscious as one can only imagine EU trade negotiators to be of having to legitimate their conduct with respect to an internal European audience whilst conducting delicate international negotiations with other trade delegations, their public statements are unlikely to be highly consistent between audiences. As has been widely noted, EU Trade Commissioners typically speak with forked tongues, Peter Mandelson being no different in this respect than his predecessors (see also Meunier and Nicolaïdis, 2006). Yet this very observation is itself suggestive of the potential analytical purchase to be gained by contrasting the internal and external face of EU trade diplomacy (see also Jabko, 2006).

In fact, as is often the case, the most telling insights into the motives and preferences of the EU trade negotiators going into the Geneva Ministerial Meeting in July 2006 are to be found in the internal strategy documents and press releases which *followed* the suspension of negotiations. Particularly significant here is the strategy document, *Global Europe: Competing in the World* (Commission, 2006). Launched in October 2006 as the contribution of the Directorate General for External Trade (DG Trade) to the EU's Growth and Jobs Strategy, it gives a very interesting and unusually detailed insight into the relationship between its external trade policies (both multilateral and bilateral) and its internal strategies to promote European competitiveness through the continued liberalization and deepening of the internal markets for goods, services and labour. There is not in fact a great deal new in the strategy itself. Indeed, it merely echoes themes that had been consistently articulated by Mandelson during his tenure as Trade Commissioner (see, in particular, Mandelson, 2005). But that is what makes this document, and the various briefings and press releases which accompanied its publication, particularly interesting. For, arguably, it spells out more clearly than anything else the assumptions underpinning the EU's stance with respect to the DDA.

The most immediately striking feature of this strategy is the manner in which it is introduced. The headline in the press release from DG Trade accompanying its publication states, 'new strategy puts EU trade policy at the service of European competitiveness and economic reform' (DG Trade, press release, 4 October 2006). This, again, seems like a remarkable thing to concede publicly – even to a largely internal audience. And such a concession is rendered no less remarkable by its timing – coming in the immediate context of the recently suspended multilateral trade negotiations which the EU's trade negotiators were at the time strenuously seeking to revive. For, in effect, it seems to indicate that the EU's motivations in a delicate international trade round supposedly prioritizing development had consistently been driven by narrowly European considerations. Whilst it is not at all difficult to project onto *other* trade delegations very similar motives, publicly declaring such preferences is surely tantamount to inviting upon oneself the lion's share of the responsibility for the suspension of the Doha Round.

Yet closer scrutiny reveals this reading to be a somewhat premature, if nonetheless quite understandable, misinterpretation of a rather more complex

– and, indeed, strangely contradictory – position. For whilst the implied subordination of EU trade policy to considerations of European competitiveness might seem almost inevitably to commit the EU to a zero-sum conception of trade, the finer grained detail of the text (and supporting documents) strongly suggests otherwise. Thus, the executive summary of the new strategy proceeds as follows:

> This policy review [. . .] sets out a strategy for opening new markets abroad for EU companies to trade and ensuring that European companies are able to compete fairly in those markets. It also commits Europe to ensuring that its own markets remain open, arguing that in a global market, with global supply chains, Europe needs to import to export. It cannot argue for openness from others while sheltering behind barriers of its own. (Commission, 2006, p. 1)

Similarly, in the main body of the strategy document itself we read, 'progressive trade opening is an important source of productivity gains, growth and job creation [. . .] rejection of protectionism at home must be accompanied by activism in creating open markets and fair conditions of trade abroad' (Commission, 2006, pp. 5–6).

A number of points might immediately be noted about this. First, the ostensible subordination of trade policy to EU competitiveness notwithstanding, there is a very clear commitment here both to the notion that trade liberalization results in efficiency gains and to the multilateral promotion of trade liberalization that follows from this understanding. Whatever else it is doing here, competitiveness is not a synonym for a zero-sum conception of trade. Indeed, throughout his tenure as Trade Commissioner, Mandelson has repeatedly referred to the 'progressive advance of trade liberalization' through multilateral and bilateral means as providing 'the engine room of the world economy for six decades' (for instance, Mandelson, 2006b). In this respect, like previous trade commissioners, he would seem to understand Ricardian economics very well.

So how precisely is the notion of competitiveness being used here? In a word, strangely. The argument seems to be that the kind of multilateral trade liberalization to which the EU was ostensibly committing itself in Geneva (and, indeed, throughout the Doha Round) is, in and of itself, good for European competitiveness. This argument in turn seems to rest on the assumption that such multilateral trade liberalization will, on the one hand, present new opportunities for European exporters to show themselves to be competitive internationally in newly opening markets and, on the other, will expose European producers at home to greater competitive challenges from the developed and developing world as domestic markets are further liberalized (Commission, 2006, p. 6; Mandelson, 2006a). In other words, such multilateral trade liberalization is good for European competitiveness because it increases the *need* for European producers and service providers to show themselves to be competitive if they are to survive. Trade liberalization, it seems, is good for competitiveness, because without it there is likely to be less pressure for European businesses and service providers to prove their competitiveness internationally.

This is, of course, all rather tautological – for competitiveness is only a virtue in a context in which one needs to compete. Seeking out opportunities to compete in order to show that one is competitive is to turn a potential virtue into an obsession. And promoting an intensification of the terms of international competition in order to test one's competitiveness is to turn an obsession into a compulsive obsession. There is also a potentially alarming conflation here. Placing oneself in a situation in which one needs to be competitive (or more competitive) is no guarantee of competitiveness.[2] Indeed, the EU's strategy here seems rather taking Friedrich Nietzsche's famous truism (1997, p. 6), 'that which does not kill us makes us stronger' as an invitation to engage in ever more dangerous pursuits.

Yet there is another element to this. Recall that the press release announcing the *Global Europe* strategy linked trade policy not only to European competitiveness but also to structural economic reform. Trade liberalization is not only good for European competitiveness in the sense that it provides the opportunity and increases the need for Europe to prove itself competitive; it is also good, in the Commission's view, in that it provides a powerful stimulus for structural economic reform. But it is not just any structural economic reform that it is likely to promote, but specifically that advocated by the Commission – in other words, the Lisbon strategy.[3] In Mandelson's own terms, 'the road to Lisbon runs through open global markets' (Mandelson, 2006c). This is a very important point and is a further sense in which the EU's external trade policy is linked to the attainment of internal policy objectives

---

[2] This is, of course, a rather Krugmanite sentiment. For much of his critique of US policy-makers, in particular, is that they obsess unnecessarily about competitiveness when they might, more profitably, be concerned with productivity. That competitiveness is an unnecessary concern is a reflection of the fact that the US economy (in 1994, as now) is not especially open. Competitiveness, as he suggests, is only a virtue to the extent to which one competes (1994, p. 7). By the same token, then, opening one's economy further in the hope that it might provide a boost to competitiveness is, at best, a rather perverse strategy predicated on the mistaken assumption that competitiveness is a virtue in itself. Trade liberalization may well be a good thing, but to justify it in terms of the boost to competitiveness that the rigours of heightened competition *may* instil is bizarrely circular. It is also to confuse the heightened need for competitiveness with the attainment of such a goal.

[3] Whether such structural economic reform also includes reform of the CAP – and the system of agricultural subsidies with which it has come to be associated – is an interesting point to which I return presently in some detail.

framed in terms of competitiveness. The argument here parallels that above. The resumption and successful completion of the Doha Round, it is assumed, would expose European producers and services providers in domestic markets to more intense international price competition. Such pressures, in turn, will entrench and lock-in the need for the structural reforms contained in the Lisbon process. In short, multilateral trade liberalization is to be welcomed since it will have the effect of disciplining Europe's more reform-averse governments into accelerating the necessary process of structural reform contained in the Lisbon agenda. Indeed, one might go further still: trade liberalization renders the – at this point, still *contingent* – Lisbon agenda *necessary* (cf. Watson and Hay, 2003); in so doing it depoliticizes it.

Two points might immediately be noted here. First, this is certainly just as tautological as the more general argument about competitiveness. The attainment of the Lisbon goals is presented as a good in itself. Consequently, anything which increases the need for such reforms (and hence makes their attainment more likely) is to be welcomed. But recall that the Lisbon agenda was justified in the first place in terms of Europe's failure to 'meet the challenges' posed by the competition to which it was already exposed. In such a context, it is surely strange to present, as a justification for opening further Europe's domestic markets to international price competition, the boost to the Lisbon agenda that it is assumed will follow. It is once again also to conflate the need for a public good (in this case structural economic reform) with the delivery of such a good.

Second, note the emphasis here on cost competitiveness. The opening of Europe's markets to the developing world, in particular, is repeatedly justified in terms of its benefits for the consumer – in the form of cheaper goods and, to a lesser extent, services.[4] Here a classic Ricardian account of the efficiency gains of free trade is invoked consistently:

> It is easy to forget in the midst of a give and take negotiation, that we all benefit from progressive and careful liberalization. It is a development tool that brings its own efficiency gains. (Mandelson, 2006b)

Consumers will benefit because cost competitiveness pressures will intensify, with the price of goods and services falling as a consequence. Indeed, it is precisely such pressures which presumably translate themselves into the imperative of labour-market flexibilization and the 'modernization' of the European social model enshrined within the Lisbon agenda. Passages like this

---

[4] That the benefits for consumers of services are emphasized rather less is perhaps a reflection of the fact that EU services markets are, by comparative international standards, already quite open. To the extent that this is true (or assumed to be true), the anticipated efficiency gains (and hence the associated price reductions for the consumer) are rather less than in other markets.

show that the public face of the EU's trade diplomacy is non zero-sum and indeed highly conventional, in Ricardian trade theoretical terms. Yet they also show how heavily dependent the EU's understanding is on the assumption that all markets for goods and services are analogous to those for goods (typically cheap consumer goods) with a high demand price elasticity. Finally, they suggest the extent to which the reform trajectory on which Europe is currently embarked (as reflected in the Lisbon strategy in particular) is predicated on the conflation of competitiveness and cost competitiveness. It is to the potential dangers of that strategy and the fetishization of price competitiveness on which it seemingly rests that we turn in the next section in considering the Services Directive. But before doing so it is first important to consider a potential objection to the analysis thus far presented, before concluding this section with a few more general comments about the stance adopted by the EU towards the DDA.

The most obvious objection to the above analysis is that, in discerning a single discourse of competitiveness in the EU's negotiating stance with respect to the DDA, it overlooks the unevenness of the EU's position. In particular, the analysis mirrors the EU's own strategy by placing too much of its emphasis on what might be seen as the Commission's offensive and very public discourse of trade liberalization in *non-agricultural* sectors, ignoring as a consequence its defensive and more protectionist negotiating stance with respect to agriculture. Judged by its deeds rather than its words, it might well be argued, the EU simply failed to address the panoply of trade-distorting subsidies and tariffs insulating European agriculture from free and fair market competition. In short, there is a danger of being taken in by the EU's official discourse which was itself a key part of a strategy to divert attention away from its continued strongly protectionist disposition with respect to agricultural markets.

This is a compelling and, to some extent, a familiar argument – and, up to a point, it provides an important corrective to the above analysis. But we need to proceed with some caution here. Yes, the CAP is significantly trade-distorting, protectionist even. And, yes, had the Doha Round come to a successful conclusion in Geneva in July 2006 the CAP would have remained significantly trade-distorting. But it is simply wrong to infer from this that DG Trade and the EU's trade negotiators in the Doha Round were animated by a zero-sum conception of trade in general or even in agriculture more specifically. Far more problematic still would be to assume that the CAP persists precisely *because* the EU is wedded to a zero-sum conception of trade, believing trade between nations (and, indeed regions) to be analogous to that between corporations and hence defending the CAP because of its contribution to a European conception of competitiveness. Such an inference is simply wrong. To the extent that EU trade negotiators, in the Doha Round as

before, have sought to defend export subsidies, protected markets, high tariff
levels and tariff and regulatory peaks in agricultural markets, they have not
done so by invoking a zero-sum conception of trade.[5] Indeed, at no point in
the Doha Round has DG Trade contested the idea that reform of the CAP and
the ultimate elimination of trade-distorting subsidies, tariffs and regulations is
a good thing. Moreover, ongoing (if incremental) CAP reform is seen as a
good thing precisely because, as in the more general discourse elucidated
above, it will encourage European farmers to be more competitive.

That is all very well, it might be countered, but if the practice of EU trade
negotiators has not been to give up such protectionist measures easily in
multilateral negotiations on trade then the EU speaks with a forked tongue.
We should not so easily be taken in by its public – and legitimatory – rhetoric.
Again, there is clearly something to this argument. But it is wrong to see the
unwillingness (more accurately, the incapacity) of EU trade negotiators to
offer to dismantle the CAP in anticipation of the efficiency gains which might
follow from a more genuinely free trade regime as an index of their weddedness to a zero-sum conception of trade. The reasons for the CAP's persistence
are rather different – and, in fact, not so very difficult to appreciate. They are
bound up with path dependence. Quite simply, whatever the net efficiency
gains anticipated from trade liberalization and however much the dismantling
of CAP might provide (or be seen to provide) a powerful incentive for
productivity gains in European agriculture, the transition to a post-CAP
environment is likely to result in a very significant contraction of the European agricultural sector (as any Heckscher-Ohlin model would surely
predict). And the costs of the structural adjustment entailed are likely to be
considerable. In this context, the incremental and phased reduction of tariff
levels, the adoption of regulatory impediments to market access and so forth
are perfectly rational responses to a problem of institutional dysfunctionality.
Moreover, as a strategy, it is entirely consistent with the conception of competitiveness that I discern in the EU's negotiating stance in the Doha Round
and, accordingly, with the anticipation of considerable efficiency gains from
trade liberalization – in agriculture, as elsewhere.

[5] Though the issue falls well beyond the remit of the present article, the same might also be said of those
Member States – such as France and Spain – that have been most consistent in their defence of an
ultimately protectionist CAP. Of course, it might be objected, that whether they have explicitly made
reference to a zero-sum conception of trade or not, the effects are much the same – protectionism and
trade-distortion have persisted. But the point is that it is perfectly possible and, indeed, quite rational to
accept that there are potential (and, indeed, sizeable) efficiency gains to be had from trade liberalization
without rushing to eliminate all protectionist measures in all sectors as quickly as possible. Moreover, to
argue that the defence of protectionism in agriculture by states like France and Spain is not in and of itself
evidence of a basic misunderstanding, on their part, of the benefits of trade, is by no means to defend their
protectionist stance. It is, however, to offer a more informed perspective on the obstacles to CAP reform.

As this suggests, whilst the very notion of putting EU trade policy 'at the service of European competitiveness' cannot but raise Krugmanite suspicions about the motives of EU trade negotiators with respect to the DDA, such suspicions are simply not borne out by a more detailed analysis of the EU's stance before, during and after the Geneva Ministerial Meeting in July 2006. Strange and paradoxical at times though its publicly stated understanding of the relationship between EU trade policy and European competitiveness have certainly been, it is predicated clearly and consistently on a classic Ricardian view of the potential efficiency gains to be achieved through free trade. It is also predicated, more problematically, on a view that such efficiency gains arise primarily through the intensification that trade liberalization brings of the cost competition between both producers and service providers. Yet, in each respect it is highly conventional. As such, it would take an extremely cynical reading of the EU's stance in the Doha Round to detect in it evidence of the kind of protectionist disposition to which Krugman alerts us. There is no evidence that the DDA was suspended by virtue of the EU's weddedness to a zero-sum conception of trade. Indeed, there is plenty of evidence that the Commission was, as it remains, powerfully committed to a positive-sum view of trade and to a conception of further trade liberalization as a useful disciplining device in the internal promotion of labour-market and other structural economic reforms.

Yet this is by no means to exonerate the EU of all responsibility for the suspension of the Doha Round. Two points might here be made. First, ultimately, there is only so much one can infer about the strategies of parties in a diplomatic negotiation from their public pronouncements. In the absence of evidence to the contrary, I have (naïvely perhaps) assumed EU trade negotiators to be true to their word and, more importantly, to the conception of trade and competitiveness that has ostensibly informed their position. It would take a more cynical reading than my own to hold the EU's understanding of trade responsible for the suspension of the Doha Round, but some degree of cynicism may nonetheless be warranted. Second, to exonerate their understanding of trade and competitiveness is one thing, to exonerate their conduct in the negotiations is another. EU negotiators certainly brought much to the table at the Geneva Ministerial Meeting, but they also demanded much from the US and the developing world in return. Moreover, the briefings they gave immediately prior to the meeting itself – which seemed to anticipate failure and to begin the task of apportioning responsibility – indicated that they were pessimistic from the outset about the prospects of reaching a deal. Citing, as has become their norm, the inevitable inflexibility of their bargaining position which comes from having to speak for an entire region (see Meunier, 2005), the EU's negotiators were also highly intransigent once negotiations had stalled. But if the above analysis is correct, it would be wrong to attribute this to the prevalence amongst EU negotiators of a zero-sum conception of trade.[6] More likely is that most if not all parties accepted the efficiency gains to be achieved by reaching a deal, but failed to reach a common understanding of how those efficiency gains were to be distributed. Trade may well not be zero-sum, but the distribution of the efficiency gains it yields most certainly is.

II. The Bolkestein Directive: Servicing Europe's Competitive Imperative

My argument thus far is that there is more to the potentially dangerous obsession of competitiveness than the problematic analogy between competition between nations and that between corporations for market share to which Krugman draws our attention. Indeed, rather more pertinent to the question of whether competitiveness is a dangerous obsession amongst European policy-makers today, I suggest, is the common assumption in the competitiveness discourse that all product and service markets are analogous to those for cheap consumer goods characterized by a high demand price elasticity.

If the Doha Round provides something of a test of Krugman's assumption that the language of competitiveness almost invariably entails the appeal to a zero-sum conception of trade, then the development and revision of the Bolkestein Directive on the internal market in services provides an equivalent test of this alternative thesis. For it gives us a rare insight into the assumptions of EU policy-makers about the nature and character of the process of competition, at least in service markets.

Named after its principal architect, the former Commissioner for the Internal Market, Frits Bolkestein, the directive on services in the internal market (to give it its full title) was intended to rejuvenate the flagging Lisbon agenda by reducing barriers to cross-border trade, cross-border provision and direct investment in services. This it sought to do by eliminating, in essence, all non-proportionate or discriminatory regulations of individual Member States pertaining to the provision of services unless justified in terms of a demonstrable public interest. Particularly contentious in this regard was the so-called 'country of origin principle'. This would have allowed service providers effectively to test the waters in other markets by providing, prior to

---

[6] It is, of course, possible that the Doha round was suspended by virtue of the commitment of *other* parties to the negotiation to a zero-sum conception of trade – the most obvious candidate perhaps being the US. Clearly, this issue cannot be adjudicated without a detailed consideration of any and all such parties' understandings of competitiveness – and that, alas, falls well beyond the remit of the present contribution.

establishment and for a limited period of time, services to customers within those markets on the basis of the laws pertaining in the service provider's country of origin. In so doing it would have allowed the now notorious 'Polish plumber' to provide services in France under the legal conditions pertaining to the provision of services in Poland. As is well documented, the threat posed both to the Paris sewers and to the employment prospects of indigenous Parisian plumbers by the somewhat clichéd depiction of the Polish plumber became a key focus for opposition to the Constitutional Treaty in France in particular (see, for instance, Brouard and Tiberj, 2006; Schmidt forthcoming; Taggart, 2006). The country of origin principle became a similar focus for opposition to the Directive within the European Parliament and the Council of Ministers and was ultimately dropped from the revised version of the directive adopted on 12 December (see European Parliament and Council, 2006).

Limits of space prevent a detailed assessment of this case (but see Howarth, this volume). It is, moreover, important to state from the outset that my interest in the Services Directive is not prompted by an attempt to gauge the degree to which it has been diluted in the process of revision and redrafting. For what it is worth, the suggestion that the original directive has been 'castrated' (Anderson, 2006) is, I think, somewhat overstated, though significant changes have undoubtedly been made.[7] Yet one thing is clear – however much the scope of the directive has been circumscribed by a long list of specific exemptions and however much the removal of the now infamous country of origin principle has been taken as a decisive victory by the directive's opponents from left and right, the underlying rationale remains highly conserved in the final negotiated compromise. It is that underlying rationale that concerns me here. Both the original and revised versions of the directive draw on a common set of assumptions about the benefits of market liberalization and the heightened competition to which it gives rise. These assumptions are consistent, distinctive and, I suggest, problematic. Yet since it is the revised version of the Services Directive that will ultimately enter into force (some time in early 2010), it is to this alone that I will refer in what follows.

[7] Three important points might here be noted. First, the degree to which the eventual compromise reached dilutes or castrates the directive is difficult to gauge in the abstract, since it will depend so significantly on the specific legal interpretation of the right to establishment (see also Nicolaïdis and Schmidt, forthcoming). Second, this notwithstanding, the impact of the initial directive was always going to be highly uneven, both territorially and sectorally. Its impact was always going to be far greater in highly regulated economies sharing (land) borders with less regulated Member States and in those services markets that are most price-sensitive. Third, as this in turn suggests, the scale of the anticipated impact of the original directive was always dependent on the degree to which Europe's service markets were assumed to be price sensitive. The more price sensitive they were assumed to be, the greater the impact the Bolkestein Directive was projected to make and the more that potential impact might be seen to have been lessened in the process of reaching a compromise.

The premises and objectives of the Services Directive are in fact succinctly stated at the outset and they are, again, framed very clearly in terms of competitiveness (European Parliament and Council, 2006, pp. 2–4). They can be summarized in terms of a series of quotes from the text itself.

- 'A competitive market for services is essential in order to promote economic growth and create jobs in the EU' (p. 3).
- 'A wide range of Internal Market barriers [. . .] undermine the global competitiveness not only of EU service providers, but also of the EU manufacturing sector, which increasingly relies on high quality services' (p. 3).
- 'A free market which compels Member States to eliminate restrictions on cross-border provision of services while at the same time increasing transparency and the information required, would give consumers wider choice and better services at lower prices' (p. 3).
- 'The [current] fragmentation of the internal market has a negative impact on the entire European economy, in particular on the competitiveness of SMEs and the movement of workers and prevents consumers from gaining access to a greater variety of competitively priced services' (p. 4).
- 'The establishment of a genuine internal market is a matter of priority for achieving the goals set out by the Lisbon European Council of improving employment and social cohesion and achieving sustainable economic growth so as to make the EU the most competitive and dynamic knowledge-based, employment-boosting economy in the world by 2010' (p. 4).
- 'Removing [internal] barriers to [trade in services] [. . .] is a basic condition for overcoming the difficulties encountered in implementing the Lisbon strategy and for reviving the European economy, particularly in terms of employment and investment' (p. 4).

What is immediately striking about this list is how similar the rationale offered for internal service market liberalization is to that offered for external trade liberalization in the context of the DDA. Internal service market liberalization, just like external trade liberalization, is good for consumers, is good for competitiveness and is good for the prospects of resuscitating and realizing the goals of the Lisbon agenda. And internal service market liberalization is good for very similar reasons – consumers can expect to benefit from cheaper services and greater choice; the intensification of internal competition will result in increased international competitiveness (since service providers will need to be competitive in order to survive in such a market); and the efficiency gains arising from trade liberalization in a sector which already accounts for 77 per cent of EU GDP (Commission, 2006, p. 8) will go a long way to realizing the Lisbon goals for employment and growth, to say nothing of their implications for labour market integration.

Yet there are serious reasons to doubt the optimistic projections contained in both the original and adopted versions of the Services Directive and, indeed, the claim that the full implementation of the Directive could boost EU employment by 0.6 million. For all of the above rests on a series of common assumptions both about the character of service markets and the competition between service providers to which they give rise. These are, at best, crude and simplistic, at worst entirely inappropriate.

So what are these assumptions? Well, they are essentially three-fold. Markets for services are assumed to be highly price sensitive and both price and demand elastic. They are price sensitive in that consumers are assumed to shop around and generally to choose the cheapest provider of a given service; they are price elastic in the sense that any reduction in price is assumed to result in an increase in demand; and they are demand elastic more generally in the sense that there is not assumed to be a finite demand for a given service – there is a *prima facie* case for suggesting that supply and demand co-vary (and that the coefficient of co-variation is high).

The basic problem with these assumptions is that they are largely transposed from the analysis of product markets (like those for cheap consumer goods). Yet even were we to accept such assumptions as entirely unproblematic for product markets, which they are not, it is clear that they fail to reflect a number of key features of almost all service markets. Three in particular stand out:

1. Such markets are highly labour intensive, such that the cost of a given service is likely to be related very closely to the price of labour;
2. Many service markets, notably those for corporate services, but also those for legal services, are not especially price-sensitive – convenience, proximity to the site at which the service is to be provided and the reputation of the service provider are typically more significant factors in determining demand;
3. Many such service markets are highly price inelastic – reducing the price for which the service is provided is likely to have little or no consequence for the volume of demand for the service, which is essentially fixed.

Of these three factors, it is the third which is arguably the most significant. For it means that markets for products and markets for services (whether price-sensitive or not) are by no means directly analogous. We cannot assume that just because heightened price competition in markets for consumer goods, for instance, may result in increased consumption, increased growth and increased employment, the same will occur in markets for services. Yet the Services Directive rests on precisely such a supposition.

So what happens to the rationale for internal service market liberalization when one replaces the offending assumptions with more realistic ones? In short, much of its appeal disappears. Consider its impact in services markets which are price-sensitive.[8] The Services Directive is, of course, designed to intensify price competition between service providers; and it is entirely realistic to think that this will be its principal effect. But the consequences of heightened cost competition are unlikely to be as benign or beneficial as the Commission assumes given that: (i) close to 70 per cent of all EU employment is in services; (ii) service provision is labour-intensive; (iii) labour costs are the principal factor determining the price of a given service; and (iv) many service markets, like that for insurance, exhibit a minimal price elasticity of demand. Substitute these assumptions for those which underpin the Services Directive and an altogether different and rather more alarming prospect emerges.

Service sector liberalization does indeed intensify price competitiveness, leading to a reduction in effective prices. Since labour costs represent such a high proportion of the price of a service, price reductions squeeze wages. Since such a high proportion of EU employment is in the service sector, a sectoral fall in wages is likely to translate into a significant aggregate drop in consumer demand for both goods and services. And, in the kind of flexible labour-market now being built in Europe, excess capacity in the service sector is likely to result in redundancies, further suppressing demand as well as driving down wages.

This is depressing enough in itself. If anything, however, it understates the extent of the potential problem. For it fails to take account of the low price elasticity of demand which characterizes many service markets. Arguably, in such markets, public authorities should be striving strenuously to maintain, even to increase, the price for which services are provided. For, to encourage price competitiveness in markets characterized by a high demand price inelasticity is in fact to suppress potential GDP. If the quantity of the service demanded does not rise (or does not rise significantly) as its price falls, then heightened price competition merely reduces the financial value to the sector

---

[8] As noted above, the rationale for the liberalization of the internal market for services seems to proceed from the assumption that all services markets are highly price-sensitive. This is, of course, a crude exaggeration, but arguably rather less crude an exaggeration than the assumption that such markets are demand price elastic. It is nonetheless important to note that many services markets – like that, say, for fine dining – are far more quality-sensitive than they are cost-sensitive. It is tempting to see such markets as largely immune from the impact of the Services Directive. But this is too simple – for market liberalization may well serve to increase the relative salience of price in the shaping of consumer preferences. Insofar as this is indeed the case, the assumption that all service markets are highly price-sensitive may tend to become something of a self-fulfilling prophecy.

of the provision of the service. Moreover, in a situation in which reductions in price are likely to be reflected in reductions in wages, it is also likely to suppress further potential demand. Once again, it seems, the dangers of fetishizing cost competitiveness are cruelly exposed.

One further factor completes this depressing picture – demographic change. As its populations age and its birth-rates fall, Europe, as is now almost universally accepted, faces a significant worsening of its already precarious fiscal balance (see, for instance, Gros, 2005). Indeed, it is precisely for this reason that so much of the Lisbon agenda is focussed (quite rightly) on measures designed to improve employment rates amongst those of working age. But it is not just rates of employment that are important here; certainly no less significant, arguably more so, are the aggregate levels of earnings of the working population. For it is these, rather than employment levels, that ultimately determine the overall fiscal take.

In this respect, the Services Directive is doubly problematic. First, if the above scenario is right, service market liberalization is unlikely to deliver the anticipated increase in aggregate employment levels. Second, even if it were accepted that the Services Directive will boost employment levels across the EU, it is difficult to see how it can do anything else but suppress wage levels. And by holding down potential earnings in this way, it merely exacerbates Europe's problem. If the ratio of net welfare recipients to net welfare contributors is rising, then the last thing Europe can afford is a set of public policy commitments that suppress the earnings – and hence the fiscal – potential of those in employment.

There is, of course, a potential objection to this, just as there was to the analysis of the EU's stance with respect to the DDA. Put simply, doesn't the dilution – if not the outright 'castration' – of the original Bolkestein directive indicate a serious internal challenge to the conception of competitiveness with which I have associated the Services Directive? Moreover, does it not also indicate that such a challenge was successfully mounted? This might seem like a credible objection. But it is based, I think, on a frequent misperception – in the form of a mischaracterization of the opposition to the Services Directive. For such opposition was never couched in terms of an alternative understanding of competitiveness. Opposition there most certainly was, but it was cast principally in terms of the costs (and the likely asymmetries in the distribution of the costs) of adjustment to the envisaged process of service liberalization. It was, in short, the social costs, not the economic advantages of service liberalization that were contested (see, for instance, ETUC, 2005; Social Platform, 2005; and for further analysis, Brouard and Tiberj, 2006). Nowhere in the debate were the anticipated efficiency and employment gains arising from service liberalization challenged; nowhere was the conception of competitiveness on which these in turn were predicated scrutinized and inter-rogated.[9] Thus, as I have sought to demonstrate, the rationale for both the original and revised versions of the directorate were predicated on a common set of assumptions about the character of service markets and the process of competition to which they give rise. It is the validity of that characterization and those assumptions that I have challenged in this article. The revision of the Services Directive might well have served to lessen its immediate impact. But there is only so much solace that one can draw from an acknowledgement that the directive's deleterious effects will now be released more slowly.

Conclusion

What stops us from recognizing the likelihood of such effects is not the dangerous obsession with competitiveness to which Krugman drew our atten-tion in 1994, but a new and possibly yet more virulent obsession – that with cost competitiveness. Our policy-makers, it seems, have long since ceased to view the competition between nations and, indeed, regions, as analogous to that between corporations. But sadly, they seem to have yet to realize the dangers of viewing the dynamics of competition in all markets for goods and services as analogous to that for cheap consumer goods. Until such time as they do, what they themselves present and seek to defend as the European social model is seriously in jeopardy as cost competitiveness threatens to become not just a dangerous obsession, but an obsessive compulsive disorder.

References

Allen, D. and Smith, M. (2001) 'External Policy Developments'. *JCMS*, Vol. 39, No. 1, pp. 97–114.

Anderson, C. (2006) 'Bye, Bye Bolkestein: New Europe Betrayed'. *The Brussels Journal*, 2 February, available at: «http://www.brusselsjournal.com».

Brouard, S. and Tiberj, V. (2006) 'The French Referendum: The Not So Simple Act of Saying No'. *PS*, Vol. 39, No. 2, pp. 261–8.

Commission (2006) *Global Europe: Competing in the World* COM(2006), 4 October.

DG Trade (2006) 'Press Release: Trade and Competitiveness'. Brussels: DG Trade, 4 October 2006, available at «http://eceuropa.eu/trade/issues/sectoral/competitiveness/pr041006_en.htm).

ETUC (2005) *ETUC Position Paper: The Proposal for a Directive on Services in the Internal Market*. Brussels: ETUC, January.

[9] The ETUC's position paper, for instance, states that it 'has examined the proposal for a directive and recognizes the major growth potential in terms of employment' arising from services liberalization. Indeed, it goes on to refer to the potential for the creation of growth and jobs as 'substantial and attainable', before expressing concerns about some of the anticipated social costs of the original proposal (2005, pp. 1 and 3).

European Parliament and Council (2006) 'Directive 2006/123/EC of 12 December 2006 on Services in the Internal Market'. OJ L 376, 27.12.2006, pp. 36–68.

Gros, D. (2005) *Perspectives on the Lisbon Strategy: How to Increase the Competitiveness of the European Economy*. Studies and Analyses, No. 308 (Warsaw: Centre for Social and Economic Research).

Jabko, N. (2006) *Playing the Market: A Political Strategy for Uniting Europe, 1985–2005* (Ithaca, NY: Cornell University Press).

Kerremans, B. (2005) 'Managing the Agenda: The EU's Rationale for a New Round of Trade Negotiations'. In Overhaus, M., Maull, H.W. and Harnisch, S. (eds) *European Trade Policy and the Doha Development Agenda*, available at: «http://www.deutsche-aussenpolitik.de».

Krugman, P. (1994) 'Competitiveness: A Dangerous Obsession'. *Foreign Affairs*, March/April, pp. 28–44, as reprinted in Krugman, P. (1996) *Pop Internationalism* (Cambridge, MA: MIT Press).

Mandelson, P. (2005) 'Strengthening the Lisbon Strategy: The Contribution of External Trade to Growth and Competitiveness in Europe', speech at the High Level Summit on the Lisbon Agenda, Stockholm, Sweden, 15 February.

Mandelson, P. (2006a) 'Ambition and Realism: Europe's Approach to the Doha Round'. Speech, European Commission Representation, Helsinki, 25 April.

Mandelson, P. (2006b) 'Providing Leadership in the Doha Round'. *Hindustan Times Leadership Summit*, 18 November.

Mandelson, P. (2006c) 'Global Europe', speaking points, 4 October.

Meunier, S. (2005) *Trading Voices: The European Union in International Commercial Negotiations* (Princeton, NJ: Princeton University Press).

Meunier, S. and Nicolaïdis, K. (2006) 'The European Union as a Conflicted Trade Power'. *Journal of European Public Policy*, Vol. 13, No. 6, pp. 906–25.

Nicolaïdis, K. and Schmidt, S.K. (forthcoming) 'Mutual Recognition on Trial: The Long Road to Services Liberalization.' *Journal of European Public Policy*.

Nietzsche, F. ((1997) 'Epigrams and Arrows'. In *Twilight of the Idols*, Polt, R. trans. (Indianapolis, IN: Hackett, first published 1889).

Schmidt, V.A. (forthcoming) 'Trapped By Their Ideas: French Elites' Discourses of European Integration and Globalization.' *Journal of European Public Policy*.

Social Platform (2005) 'Keep Services Social: Urgent Action Needed on the Services Directive', Social Platform Common Position Paper, Brussels, February.

Taggart, P. (2006) 'Keynote Article: Questions of Europe – The Domestic Politics of the 2005 French and Dutch Referendums and their Challenge for the Study of European Integration', *JCMS Annual Review of the European Union in 2005*, pp. 7–15.

Watson, M. and Hay, C. (2003) 'The Discourse of Globalization and the Logic of No Alternative: Rendering the Contingent Necessary in the Political Economy of New Labour'. *Policy and Politics*, Vol. 31, No. 2, pp. 289–306.

Young, A. (2007) 'Negotiating With Diminished Expectations: The EU and the Doha Development Round'. In Lee, D. and Wilkinson, R. (eds) *The WTO After Hong Kong: Progress In and Prospects For the Doha Development Agenda* (London: Routledge).

Review Article: The Politics of Legal Integration*

LISA CONANT
University of Denver

Introduction

Legal integration is commonly credited as one of the most important forces promoting the development of the European Union (EU) and its institutions. The Court of Justice of the European Communities (ECJ) and the legal system it constructed are also often heralded as the most state-like features of the EU within debates about the character of the EU as a particularly advanced international institution, a unique form of supranational governance, or an emerging federal state. Scholarly interest in the politics of legal integration originated with the puzzle that a supranational court had transcended state sovereignty. Parallel to broader debates on integration between intergovernmentalists and neofunctionalists, an international relations debate between rational choice institutionalists and neofunctionalists ensued as scholars adapted theories of international organization to frame explanations of legal integration (Burley and Mattli, 1993; Garrett, 1992). This literature conceptualizes the EU as an international institution and examines the relative power of supranational and national institutions. Meanwhile interest in EU judicial politics coincided with a newfound interest in the role of courts around the world and political scientists began to study legal integration in the light of domestic public law literatures (Conant, 2002; Kelemen, 2003, 2006; Kelemen and Sibbitt, 2004). An increasing number of scholars have adopted

* Sections of this article, in revised form, are reprinted by permission of Sage Publications Ltd from Conant, L. 'Judicial Politics'. *Handbook of European Union Politics* (Conant, 2007). The author thanks Mark Pollack, Uli Sedelmeier and Alasdair Young for their comments.

a comparative approach, developing arguments that are relevant to national courts and the ECJ as they explore how the EU legal system privileges and disadvantages various societal actors. I will argue that the EU legal system shares a closer institutional affinity with domestic, rather than international, legal systems. As a result, future scholarship could more fruitfully explore the dynamics of legal integration by taking theoretical inspiration from the nuanced studies of judicial politics in domestic settings.

The article proceeds in three sections. Section I discusses the state of interdisciplinarity among legal scholars and political scientists and provides an overview of accounts that address the puzzles of international relations theory. Section II summarizes the findings of subsequent scholarship and extends the analysis into the domain of comparative politics. Section III and the conclusion discuss an emerging literature that situates legal integration within a domesticated context, which generates questions that reach beyond the classic concerns of integration theory.

I. Law, Social Science and Legal Integration

Legal and social science scholarship both contribute to understandings of EU law and politics but discussions typically proceed within disciplinary boundaries. Because the aspirations and methodologies of law and social science diverge, much of the literature from either field is remote to the concerns of the other field. For instance, legal scholarship intends to train and inspire practising lawyers and judges. As a result, its content tends to be factually descriptive and/or normatively prescriptive: it instructs us in what the current status of the law is and provides justifications for why the law should develop in a particular direction in the future. Nuanced explorations of the details of individual cases and trends in fields of case law are common. This scholarship is important to inform social scientists of ongoing developments, but few try to participate in a dialogue with legal scholars.

Social scientists focus their attention on explaining why case law developed in one direction or another, how various actors are using case law to serve political ends and what impact case law has on policy outcomes. Efforts to marshal systematic evidence about a range of cases and relate legal evidence to other types of economic, political or social indicators are more typical here. Attempts to aggregate data on litigation can seem fruitless to legal scholars when they reject the categories that social scientists create. By contrast, political scientists may consider the evidence presented in legal scholarship to be anecdotal and find arguments about the evolution of law to be conflated with normative philosophy about the way an author wishes case law to develop rather than an empirically grounded account of the current state of law (Alter *et al.*, 2002; Joerges, 1996).

A minority of scholars regularly cross the disciplinary divide to publish in both law and social science venues or incorporate both legal and social science scholarship in their research. Some of these scholars begin in one field but communicate to both fields, adapting their mode of inquiry to suit the other discipline (Burley and Mattli, 1993; Weiler, 1994; Stone Sweet, 2004). Scholars most likely to engage the attention of both disciplines tend to focus on institutionalist analysis of law and courts (Alter, 2001; Shapiro and Stone Sweet, 2002), socio-legal dynamics (Harlow and Rawlings, 1992; Chalmers, 2000; and see the discussion below about whether the EU's legal system is analogous to a domestic system) or normative analysis (Joerges and Dehousse, 2002; Shaw, 1998). One clear instance of cross-fertilization includes the awakening of interest in legal integration among political scientists, whose attention to developments in the 1980s led them to explore the implications of an existing legal scholarship on legal integration.

Legal Integration and the End of Sovereignty

Legal scholars identified how ECJ decisions limited state sovereignty and forged a new supranational legal order. Most importantly, the doctrine of direct effect transformed European treaties and legislation from traditional international laws that governed inter-state relations into a set of higher order legal norms that bind private and public actors alike and the doctrine of supremacy subordinated national to European law. Observing that states originally rejected these principles, legal scholars attribute the ultimate acceptance of a directly effective and supreme European legal order to factors such as functional necessity, unanimously adopted legislation, respect for judicial independence, confidence in the legitimacy of legal processes and deference to the national courts that enforce many ECJ judgements (Everling, 1984; Hartley, 1986; Stein, 1981; Weiler, 1982, 1991).

The striking claims of this literature sparked interest in legal integration among political scientists. The spectre of a supranational court eliciting the obedience of states was puzzling from the perspective of traditional international relations theories. Geoffrey Garrett developed a rational choice institutionalist explanation of the ECJ's role, where the Court's mandate derives from its collective utility in enforcing pre-established bargains related to trade liberalization and efficiently filling gaps in the 'incomplete contract' of European law. Garrett initially claimed that the ECJ encourages compliance by aligning its decisions with the preferences of the most powerful states (Garrett, 1992, 1995). Garrett and his collaborators later refined their position, arguing that a tension between legal consistency and politically acceptable rulings generates strategic interactions that preserve the appearance of judicial autonomy while simultaneously respecting state interests. Finally, the ECJ tolerates periodic non-compliance to ward off efforts to reverse its case law or limit its jurisdiction (Garrett *et al.*, 1998). Consistent with realist approaches to international relations, states submit to nothing that threatens their interests.

Garrett ultimately abandoned this dichotomy between supranational and national institutions and developed a model to explain interactions within the evolving rules established by the treaties. Here, the ECJ enjoyed substantial autonomy to promote integration in the era prior to the Single European Act (SEA) because states needed to agree unanimously to all reforms. Although qualified majority voting simplified efforts to overturn unwelcome ECJ decisions legislatively, the shift towards a genuinely bicameral legislature with the expanding powers of the European Parliament (EP) should mean a return to substantial gridlock and greater autonomy for the ECJ (Tsebelis and Garrett, 2001). Relying entirely on a logic of institutional rules that could be applied within domestic contexts, the most recent rational choice institutionalism has left the international relations framework behind and situated the EU within comparative politics.

Garrett's early dismissal of judicial autonomy inspired a challenge by neofunctionalists who contended that legal integration eroded the dominance of states. Adapted from Ernst Haas' pioneering work, the neofunctionalist legal dynamic involves a technocratic network of experts that conspires with societal forces that have an incentive to promote regional co-operation. Anne-Marie Slaughter and Walter Mattli argue that the ECJ appeals to shared professional norms and self-interests to co-opt national judiciaries and constrain national governments. In this account, convincing legal argumentation legitimates ECJ rulings in the eyes of legal professionals and the mechanism for dialogue between national judges and the ECJ creates or expands opportunities to exercise judicial review. When national courts resolve disputes involving EU law, they may send 'references' to the ECJ that inquire about the meaning of EU provisions. The ECJ replies with a 'preliminary ruling', which the national court subsequently applies. Because EU law applies directly and is supreme to national law, national courts can use preliminary rulings to 'overturn' incompatible national law. Meanwhile, national governments accept ECJ decisions because legal justifications 'mask' the implications of rulings and 'shield' the ECJ from attack (Mattli and Slaughter, 1995; Burley and Mattli, 1993).

Neofunctionalists eventually acknowledged the intrusion of politics, accepting that courts cannot stray too far from majority political preferences if they wish to avoid efforts to restrict their jurisdiction. By arguing that judges avoid such political attacks, Mattli and Slaughter (1998) situated the logic of legal integration within a comparative framework. This early literature remained largely theoretical and descriptive, with next to no systematic empirical testing of competing accounts, but it inspired new research agendas. Subsequent waves of scholarship test competing claims against empirical evidence and specify theoretical expectations.

II. Testing the Theories

Much of the literature exploring legal integration is framed to speak to the international relations debate about the relative power of EU and national institutions. A literature specifying the nature of interactions between law, politics and society in the EU has focused on quantitative and qualitative analysis of ECJ case law, the participation of national courts in the EU legal system and the institutional incentives that generate variable degrees of autonomy.

Responsiveness to EU Law

Alec Stone Sweet and Thomas Brunell (1998) advanced neofunctionalism by specifying variations in societal demand for legal integration and testing the relationship between intra-EU trade, national court references to the ECJ and density of EU legislation. In this account, societal interactions generate conflicts over the rules governing exchange relations. EU judges and legislators resolve disputes by creating legal norms to govern transactions. By decreasing contracting costs, the new rules encourage more exchange, which ultimately leads to more conflicts that reactivate the initial cycle. To test their hypothesis, Stone Sweet and Brunell created a data set of all cases referred to the ECJ from 1961 to the mid-1990s.[1] Relating this data to trade flows, they find strongly positive linear relationships between the level of trade between Member States and the number of references their courts send to the ECJ and intra-EU trade flows, the production of EU secondary legislation and rising references. Since they did not eliminate references that have nothing to do with trade, however, the model includes spurious correlation. Clifford Carrubba and Lacey Murrah (2005) repeat this error in a regression analysis that tests this hypothesis against alternative explanations. Social scientists might avoid such flaws through more careful attention to the content of the law that they analyse. Another study that correlated sources of societal

[1] Available at: «http://www.iue.it/RSCAS/Research/Tools/ReferencesECLaw/Index.shtml».

demand for EU law, including the volume of trade and the size of EU migrant worker populations, to references related to those subjects found weaker and less conclusive relationships (Golub, 1996a).

Scholars have begun to examine legal data systematically in order to test the competing claims in the literature concerning the extent to which societal actors can successfully deploy the EU legal system against national governments, the ECJ's rulings aim to placate Member States or promote EU institutions and states comply with EU law. Stone Sweet and Brunell (1998) tracked the outcomes of ECJ preliminary rulings in 91 cases on social policy in order to determine the propensity of the ECJ to rule for or against Member States. They found that litigants disproportionately attacked rules that represented the lowest common denominator positions in Council legislation and that the ECJ ruled against Member States in 53 per cent of its decisions and aligned its judgement with the position advocated by the European Commission in 88 per cent of cases (Stone Sweet and Brunell, 1998, p. 76). Interpreting this finding to confirm ECJ autonomy and allegiance with societal interests, Stone Sweet and Brunell support the neofunctionalist position.

Rachel Cichowski (1998) examined 36 environmental disputes that originated in references to the ECJ from 1976 to 1996 and found that litigants disproportionately attacked Member States who either opposed EU environmental co-operation (France), took the most cavalier attitude towards implementation (Italy), or upheld strict standards that generate obstacles to trade (Netherlands). Parallel to the social policy study, the ECJ did not hesitate to confront Member States, declaring national violations of EU law in 47 per cent of cases and siding with the position of the Commission 97 per cent of the time. The ECJ was less likely to reject how governments transposed directives, however, finding national practices to be incompatible with EU law in only 18 per cent of these cases. Finally, when faced with a conflict between environmental protection and free trade, the ECJ favoured free trade norms in 66 per cent of cases (Cichowski, 1998, pp. 396–7). Cichowski's study therefore supports a neofunctionalist reading of interactions between societal interests, EU institutions and Member States, but its nuances also suggest a Court that defers to national efforts to comply with EU rules and favours business interests.

Bernadette Kilroy (1999) completed the largest study of ECJ case law to date on the relationship between ECJ decisions and Member State preferences. Her original data set includes 293 randomly selected ECJ judgements on the free movement of goods and social provisions from 1958 to 1994. This data set is the first to include not only the preliminary rulings that derive from national court references, but also 'direct actions', which are cases litigated exclusively at the ECJ and/or Court of First Instance.[2] After coding observations and ECJ decisions, Kilroy used an ordered probit analysis to estimate the likely effect of the independent variable, such as an observation concerning a national measure, on the dependent variable: the ECJ decision to declare a violation of EU law or not. Parallel to the findings of neofunctionalists, Kilroy found that the ECJ declared a violation of EU law in 55 per cent of cases, upheld national law in 36 per cent of cases and took an intermediate position in the remainder of judgements. Furthermore, Kilroy did not find any evidence to support Garrett's hypothesis that the ECJ is most likely to rule in favour of the preferences of larger states.

Kilroy's findings do suggest, however, that the expression of support for a national rule by any state – other than Italy – increases the likelihood that the ECJ will not declare a violation (Kilroy, 1999, p. 400). Kilroy argues that her findings support the hypothesis that the ECJ rules to avoid non-compliance with its rulings, because the expression of a position by a simple majority, a blocking minority, or even a smaller coalition of states has a statistically significant effect on the probability of a particular type of ECJ ruling. She found that the probability of the ECJ upholding a national rule was only 23 per cent when no state makes an observation, but increased to 73 to 96 per cent when a simple majority of states articulates support for a national rule and 56 per cent in the case of support from a blocking minority (Kilroy, 1999, pp. 405–6). This evidence supports the hypothesis on which rational choice institutionalists and neofunctionalists largely converged: the ECJ is unlikely to rule against majority preferences.

Further tests yield conflicting results. Daniel Kelemen (2001) examined all ECJ cases adjudicating disputes about trade and environment norms until 1997 and found evidence to support the 'convergence' hypothesis that courts are strategic actors seeking to maintain their legitimacy by avoiding rulings that will be rejected. Situating his study in the context of the positive political theory of courts pioneered by scholars of United States (US) courts, Kelemen compares the EU case to the General Agreement on Tariffs and Trade/World Trade Organization (WTO) dispute resolution panels in a qualitative analysis. Kelemen found that ECJ decisions accommodate political demands when pressures to uphold national measures are high and legal reasons to invalidate are weak. In cases where political and legal incentives were low or mixed, however, ECJ decisions were mixed as well, but Kelemen concludes, in

---

[2] Although Member States, EU institutions and private parties directly affected by an EU act can pursue a direct action, the vast majority of direct actions are initiated by the Commission in infringement proceedings concerning alleged violations of EU law by Member States, private firms appealing penalties that the Commission has imposed for infractions of EU competition law and EU staff contesting employment or benefit policies.

contrast to Cichowski (1998), that the ECJ has not routinely ruled against national environmental standards in disputes alleging trade barriers (Kelemen, 2001).

In contrast to the conclusions of Kilroy and Kelemen, recent analyses of ECJ case law support neofunctionalism. Margaret McCown (2003) advances the hypothesis that judicial precedents influence how litigants subsequently premise, structure and sequence their arguments in legal proceedings, with the result that gradual changes in litigants' positions lead to the incremental acceptance of once unwelcome ECJ rules. Tracking the response of the Council of Ministers to 25 legal challenges by the EP, McCown concludes that intergovernmental actors do not attack ECJ decisions directly, but defensively argue in favour of narrow readings of past precedents. Over time, this results in a process of dispute resolution that is increasingly based on the acceptance of previous case law (McCown, 2003).

While framing her inquiry according to the intergovernmental/ supranational dichotomy, McCown (2003) draws comparisons between the impact of precedents and the operation of institutions that are relevant to debates in comparative politics. In another study, Cichowski (2004) examined all 88 ECJ preliminary rulings related to social provisions from 1971 to 1993 and found that 56 per cent of judgements declared a national provision to be in violation of EU law. Once again, the ECJ did not shy from confronting more powerful Member States, declaring violations against the four largest states in 57 per cent of cases. Similar to other studies, the Commission's observations were the most likely (91 per cent) to predict the ECJ's decision. Finally, Cichowski uses the number of states submitting observations as an indicator of the significance of a dispute. Although she does not provide information about how many observations it takes to get assigned a low or high magnitude ranking, Cichowski (2004, pp. 495–500) claims that the ECJ declared national practices to be in violation of EU law in 100 per cent of cases with the highest magnitude ranking, in contrast to declaring violations in only 52 per cent of cases with the lowest magnitude ranking. Cichowski concludes that legal integration operates to diminish Member State control and empower individuals.

Discrepancies in these findings, however, limit the number of definitive conclusions this literature produces. Although all of the analyses involve similar schemes to code cases and examine some combination of the same policy areas, methodological differences and case selection generate contradictory findings. First, Kilroy's regression analysis (probit) of direct actions and preliminary rulings yields a fundamentally different result than Cichowski's descriptive statistics on preliminary rulings in that Kilroy finds that the expression of support for a national rule by any state except Italy decreases the chance that the ECJ declares a violation of EU law (Kilroy, 1999, p. 400), while Cichowski (2004, pp. 499–500) draws attention to the fact that the ECJ declared violations in all cases in which many states made observations. By counting observations, but not coding who sided with whom, however, Cichowski is unable to track the influence that observations might have had on the ECJ. For instance, states may intervene in a case in order to express their disapproval of another state's national law and their agreement with the Commission. If the ECJ then declared a violation, it would be siding with one or more Member States against another. Moreover, neofunctionalists limit their analyses to preliminary rulings as cases that arise from society. The omission of direct actions – which constitute almost half of all ECJ cases – from the analysis makes neofunctionalist claims about ECJ autonomy and collusion with societal forces against states suspect as most direct actions involve either a direct clash between Member States and the Commission in infringement proceedings or parties from society challenging EU, not Member State, actions.

Second, Kelemen's (2001) qualitative analysis of direct actions and preliminary rulings leads him to conclude that the ECJ responds affirmatively to political pressure and does not systematically favour free trade over environmental protection, while Cichowski's (1998) more quantitative coding of preliminary rulings leads her to conclude that the ECJ acts autonomously of Member States and privileges free trade norms.

Consensus emerged on two findings, however: the ECJ does not appear to favour larger over smaller states and is most likely to agree with the legal analysis of the Commission. The first finding suggests that the ECJ operates quite neutrally. The second finding is parallel to the similarly high success rate of the US Solicitor General in federal litigation, which is indicative of the advantages gained by repeat players (Galanter, 1974) who possess specialized information and control over prosecution in the case of infringement proceedings. The remaining disagreement about the responsiveness of the ECJ to state interests might be fruitfully read outside the international relations frame, as an indication that the ECJ is a typical court that periodically must consider political factors in its deliberations.

Meanwhile, studies of compliance do not find pervasive disobedience. A recent volume edited by Michael Zürn and Christian Joerges (2005) comparing the EU with Germany and the WTO found that EU compliance rates surpassed those of the domestic and global cases. In a quantitative study of compliance at all stages of EU infringement proceedings, Tanja Börzel (2001) finds that any appearance of growing non-compliance is a statistical artifact that can be explained in terms of changes in enforcement strategy and a growing number of laws to be complied with and Member States that need to comply. Patterns of non-compliance also fail to confirm any of the theoretical explanations of legal integration. The disparate rankings of the three most 'powerful' states defy the traditional expectations of rational choice institutionalism: the UK ranks as a relatively compliant state, Germany is average and France is one of four states with a consistent pattern of non-compliance (Börzel, 2001; Huelshoff *et al.*, 2005). By contrast, neofunctionalism cannot account for variations in compliance since the theory predicts only successful legal integration.

The Role of National Courts in the EU Legal System

A second focus of empirical inquiry in legal integration includes the role that national courts play. Many accounts address the puzzle of an effective supranational legal system, but their explanations tend to be grounded in political dynamics that travel well to domestic settings. The majority of scholarship on national courts focuses on their role in sending references to the ECJ for preliminary rulings. Karen Alter (1996, 2001) advanced neofunctionalist analyses by identifying national courts' interests in referring questions to the ECJ, but her explanation of judicial competition also contributes to comparative understandings of judicial politics. Observing that national supreme courts sit at the apex of national legal hierarchies and therefore face demotion given the supremacy of EU law, Alter problematized the earlier neofunctionalist assumption that references empower all national judges. National supreme courts could traditionally reverse unwelcome decisions by lower court judges, but a reference by a lower court to the ECJ for a preliminary ruling circumvents national review processes. The EU legal system offered the opportunity to exercise judicial review to all judges, but Alter demonstrates that lower court judges faced the strongest incentive to send references. Using qualitative case studies of French and German courts, Alter (1996, 2001) demonstrates that the stream of references from lower courts led higher courts to begin to send their own references in an effort to influence the ECJ because nothing could stop the tide of lower court references and supreme courts shied from overt defiance. Both Alter (2001) and Weiler (1994) attribute habitual compliance to the fact that national courts enforce over half of all ECJ rulings through this decentralized reference procedure.

In-depth qualitative research on case studies has generally yielded more compelling findings than efforts to explain aggregate national trends in references. As mentioned in the previous section, efforts to correlate trade with all references include a large percentage of spurious correlation. Carrubba and Murrah's (2005) effort to correlate references with indicators such as public support for integration, the presence of a monist or dualist legal tradition,[3] judicial review and the public's political awareness is problematic given that only some of these variables can be aggregated at the national level. For instance, variations across specialized court systems within Member States, such as the discrepancy between a high rate of referral from the French judiciary courts and a low rate from administrative courts (Alter, 2001), defy efforts to make sense out of referral rates as they both relate to a 'monist' tradition, which should theoretically facilitate the reception of international law in France. Furthermore, constitutional tribunals monopolize judicial review in most Member States, but these courts are much less likely to send references than other courts. More attention to the institutional nuances that legal scholars identify could correct such methodological shortcomings.

Research on British judges' responses to the opportunity for empowerment also produces mixed results. Although references for preliminary rulings from courts in the United Kingdom (UK) approximated those of France during the first decade and a half of each state's membership, UK references subsequently grew more slowly and remain disproportionately low in comparison to the UK's population size and intra-EU trade activity (Conant, 2001, p. 106; Golub, 1996a; Stone Sweet and Brunell, 1998; Weiler and Dehousse, 1992). Damian Chalmers' (2000) study of all reported UK national court judgements on EU law from 1973 to 1998 suggests that British judges have not embraced opportunities for judicial empowerment. After analysing the content of all judgements, Chalmers demonstrates that UK courts typically apply EU provisions without directly addressing the status of incompatible national provisions and judges entertained the question of whether national legislation might need to be suspended in only *two* cases.

Despite trends of increasing interaction between national courts and the EU legal system, a growing body of research demonstrates that national judges contest EU legal developments. Doctrinal analyses have demonstrated that many national courts did not readily accept the ECJ's rulings on direct effect and supremacy (Slaughter *et al.*, 1998) and some constitutional courts that accepted the EU legal system nonetheless justified supremacy according to their own terms in order to reassert domestic constitutional norms (Alter, 1996, p. 479; Boom, 1995; Conant, 2002, p. 93; Ruggiero, 2002). In a study of British environmental disputes, Jonathan Golub (1996b) demonstrates that judges interpreted EU law independently, refraining from sending references, when they wanted to shield domestic practices from unwelcome ECJ rulings.

Such strategic action by national courts is confirmed in a broader study as well. Stacy Nyikos (2000) examined national court references, ECJ responses

---

[3] In monist systems international law can take effect without any need for national implementing measures whereas dualist systems formally require the domestic transposition of international provisions.

to those references and national court implementation of preliminary rulings to explore how *all* judges try to increase their autonomy. She finds that national courts include opinions with their questions in an effort to influence the ECJ; the ECJ redefines issues in cases by adding or suppressing questions; and national courts typically comply with ECJ decisions but also evade unwelcome decisions by re-referring issues or reinterpreting the facts of cases. Nyikos's research challenges the notion of a clear European judicial hierarchy and normalizes legal integration by comparing strategies of issue definition to practices of the US Supreme Court.

More generally, existing research on national practices indicates independent and variable approaches to legal interpretation. Data that I compiled from a broad range of sources on national court rulings related to EU law show that the overwhelming majority of all national court decisions on EU law are independent decisions that do not involve references to the ECJ (Conant, 2002, pp. 81–2). Subsequent analyses of French, German and UK case law, drawn from the legal data bases Jurifrance (now Legifrance), Juris and Lexis, show that national courts in all three states are more likely to interpret treaty provisions independently than to cite ECJ case law. All court systems except the French 'judiciary' courts were also more likely to cite regulations and directives than to cite ECJ case law (Conant, 2002, pp. 82–3). An analysis of the Commission's survey on the application of EU law indicates that national courts vary in the extent to which they look to ECJ preliminary rulings as sources of precedent to guide their decisions (Conant, 2002, pp. 66–8). Further, comparison of national court and ECJ rulings related to nationality discrimination in public sector employment and social benefits demonstrates that national courts do not necessarily refer cases that involve uncertainty about the meaning of EU law or follow ECJ principles in areas where case law exists (Conant, 2002, pp. 173–4, 209–10).

Chalmers's (2000) comprehensive study of EU legal claims in UK courts shows that efforts to invoke EU law are more successful when EU law extends state powers to control behaviour or reinforce private legal relationships and less successful when EU law prevents the state's control over immigration, application of criminal sanctions, or protection of private property rights. As a result, it has been easier to enforce EU sex equality provisions, which consolidate employment contracts and more difficult to enforce free movement of persons rights, which liberalize immigration rules, or EU environmental and competition laws, which often disrupt private contracts.

National courts are crucial to enforcing EU law, but much more research on independent judicial review of EU law is necessary. References for preliminary rulings represent a tiny fraction of national court interpretation of

EU law. Researching national case law systematically and comparatively poses challenges because databases possess variable analytical search capabilities, include different fractions of the reported judgements in a country, operate in the national languages of the countries whose case law they index and are not available for all Member States, which leaves archival research based on much more labour-intensive searching the only option. Despite these hurdles, scholars should try to look beyond an exclusive focus on ECJ decisions and references in order to explore how the majority of EU law is actually adjudicated, avoiding the blind spots associated with a disproportionate focus on a central high court and its 'constitutional' judgements, a problem Shapiro laments in the US public law literature (Gillman, 2004).

Institutional Design and Principal-Agent Analyses

A third stream of scholarship explores institutional designs that privilege various organizational actors. While Garrett's (1992) rational choice institutionalism portrayed the ECJ as an agent of Member State principals, with a relative emphasis on the ways in which principals constrain their agent, a number of scholars have deployed principal-agent analysis to highlight agency slippage that facilitates judicial autonomy. Alter (1998) demonstrates that Member State principals intended the system of preliminary rulings to be a mechanism to *challenge* EU law, but they were unable to reverse the ECJ's conversion of this system into a means of *enforcing* EU law because the unanimity rules that govern treaty revision and many forms of secondary legislation preserve ECJ choices that benefit at least a single Member State. By enticing national courts to send references to the ECJ and apply EU law on their own, the ECJ became a principal that established its own agents of enforcement.

In a further theoretical refinement, Jonas Tallberg (2000) brings in the 'supervisor' role from institutional economics to argue that the Member States *collectively* act as a principal who adopts beneficial common policies, the Commission and ECJ jointly act as supervisors who monitor compliance and the Member States *individually* act as agents who must implement common policies. Because two principal-agent relationships become subject to shirking, the range of strategies to maintain autonomy increases for both the ECJ and Member States. Tallberg's analysis of efforts to reverse the ECJ's declaration of state liability confirms the difficulty of using treaty revision to reverse unwelcome ECJ rulings, but his research on national responses to this doctrine show that inaction has kept this remedy largely ineffective. Parallel to Kilroy's analysis, therefore, gaps in Member State implementation can check the ECJ.

Mark Pollack (2003) explicitly extends principal-agent analysis of legal integration beyond the international relations debate by comparing the constraints and opportunities of the ECJ to those faced by its national counterparts. His comparison reveals that the ECJ enjoys relatively more discretion. Furthermore, Member States have strategically reacted to the ECJ by limiting and specifying new delegations of power. In another study with implications for comparative politics, Dorothee Heisenberg and Amy Richmond (2002) analyse the institutional design of the ECJ and European Central Bank, arguing that the more open-ended mandate of the ECJ, while politically easier to achieve, provided the Court with an opportunity to expand its competence incrementally. This institutional design facilitated judicial empowerment, but has also left the ECJ more vulnerable to accusations that it illegitimately exceeds its mandate.

III. The EU's Legal Order: Analogous to a Domestic System?

This scholarship on institutional design, combined with empirical research on national court activity, casts doubt on the utility of efforts to determine whether it is the ECJ or Member States that reign supreme. In this section, I review the growing literature that abandons the national/supranational dichotomy and links legal integration to comparative politics through explicit comparisons with domestic contexts. Specifically, scholars have begun to ask new questions that are marginal to integration theory and derive instead from the more general judicial politics literature as they explore the factors that condition access to justice, influence the impact of law and affect the EU's democratic legitimacy.

Access to Justice

The EU's legal system has been a pioneer in granting private actors access to an 'international' court, thereby extending protections available to individuals within domestic systems to the European level. Private parties have responded by litigating before the ECJ at a rate that dwarfs all other international courts, with the exception of the European Court of Human Rights (ECHR) (Alter, 2006; Cichowski, 2006). In addition to aggregate accounts, explorations of access to justice reveal the importance of actors' practical capacity to litigate and the availability of organizational support for legal mobilization. First, relatively conservative rules on standing in EU disputes, such as a lack of class actions and public interest group standing, reduce opportunities for litigation that are often available in domestic settings (Alter, 2000; Conant, 2002; Kelemen and Sibbitt, 2004). Second, studies of the sectoral concentration of references (Chalmers, 2000; Conant, 2001; Harlow and Rawlings, 1992) and citations to ECJ case law (Conant, 2002) demonstrate that commercial enterprises, societal interest organizations and public enforcement agencies are most likely to gain access to courts to enforce EU legal norms because they are most likely to possess the knowledge and financing necessary for litigation. Close examination of the disproportionate concentration of UK references on EU gender equality provisions reveals the efforts of a public enforcement agency – the Equal Opportunities Commission – and organized labour (Alter and Vargas, 2000; Harlow and Rawlings, 1992). Moreover, disproportionately high rates of UK social security references are backed by Social Security Tribunals designed to minimize the costs of bringing disputes and Citizens' Advice Bureaux that provide a unique form of legal aid (Conant, 2001). By contrast, Deborah Mabbett (2005) argues that the variety of institutional structures intended to promote the interests of the disabled, including only a few organizations designed to enforce rights, will impede the development of a European jurisprudence on disability rights. Finally, although very disadvantaged actors, including foreign welfare recipients, have managed to gain access to the ECJ (Conant, 2004, 2006), the dominant trend is still one in which powerful interests exploit litigation opportunities most successfully (Conant, 2002; Costa, 2003; Börzel, 2006).

Apart from questions of resources and standing, attitudes and practices related to litigation condition the extent to which actors seek EU legal redress. States with higher levels of domestic litigation, such as Germany, also have higher rates of EU litigation (Conant, 2001). Further, nearly 90 per cent of interest groups operating in the EU prefer to avoid litigation as a political strategy (Kelemen, 2003). Groups that enjoy access to domestic agencies are particularly unlikely to commit to legal strategies that place them in an adversarial relationship with officials (Mabbett, 2005).

Impact of Law on Policy

Research based on case studies in a number of different policy areas demonstrates that innovative ECJ decisions do not exert any automatic impact on outcomes outside the courtroom. The typical dynamic is one in which Member States comply with the specific requirements of a judgement as it relates to parties to the litigation and subsequently ignore the ramifications that the interpretation may have for the universe of similarly situated parties. Active legal and political mobilization is usually necessary to override this tendency for 'contained compliance' (Conant, 2002). For example, in their research on the famous *Cassis de Dijon* case, Karen Alter and Sophie Meunier (1994) find that the ECJ interpretation developing the mutual recognition approach to harmonization did not create direct policy effects. The judicial mechanism to implement mutual recognition influenced only 115 products prior to the SEA. Yet Alter and Meunier argue that the ECJ case triggered the Commission to advocate the replacement of harmonization with mutual recognition, which then triggered the mobilization of groups with contending interests. The political struggle ultimately culminated in the compromise to apply mutual recognition on top of a base of minimally harmonized standards.

In case studies examining the ECJ's application of competition rules to telecommunications, electricity and air transport and efforts to prohibit nationality discrimination in access to public sector employment and social benefits, my research demonstrates that innovative ECJ interpretation remains relevant to litigants alone until a broader mobilization of support for judicial principles develops (Conant, 2002, 2003, 2004). Building on US public law and organizations scholarship, I specify the patterns of legal and political mobilization that are most likely to contribute to policy changes and deduce the likelihood for various forms of mobilization according to the magnitude and distribution of consequences associated with ECJ interpretation. Intense interest in high-magnitude costs and benefits that are concentrated is likely to inspire collective political and legal mobilization by organized actors that may largely ratify (telecommunications) or delay and dilute (electricity and air transport) judicial choices, while intense interest in high-magnitude costs and benefits that are diffused is likely to inspire individual legal mobilization that is unlikely to affect outcomes beyond the courtroom (most of the social benefits litigation) unless institutional support emerges to sustain legal pressures for reforms (public sector employment). In these accounts, actors most advantaged in political arenas retain important advantages over the disadvantaged because the ability to organize collective action, track official developments and raise funds are valuable in political and legal arenas. Tanja Börzel's (2006) case study examining the enforcement of EU environmental law in Germany and Spain reveals the same empowerment of the already powerful within EU legal arenas.

A debate has emerged about the extent to which legally inspired policy reform reflects an Americanization of European politics. Daniel Kelemen (2003) draws on Robert Kagan's (2001) studies of regulatory federalism in the US to argue that EU-driven economic liberalization and the fragmented European regulatory process encourage adversarial legalism in the EU, which is characterized by detailed and prescriptive rules, transparency and disclosure requirements, formal and adversarial dispute resolution, costly legal contestation, frequent judicial intervention in administration and frequent litigation by public authorities and private parties. In a series of case studies, Kelemen demonstrates that adversarial legalism is beginning to manifest itself in a variety of policy areas (Kelemen and Sibbitt, 2004; Kelemen, 2006). Meanwhile, Kagan (2006) remains sceptical that the EU is moving towards the adversarial legalism that he argues is distinctive of US regulatory politics. Acknowledging a growing trend towards legalization in the EU, Kagan attributes rising litigation rates to forces associated with modernization and argues that entrenched institutional factors in national legal cultures will prevent the adoption of the exceptional features of US adversarial legalism.

The Rule of Law and Democratic Legitimacy

A literature that evaluates the democratic legitimacy of EU judicial politics is developing links to comparative assessments of democracy. Using Eurobarometer surveys, Gregory Caldeira and James Gibson (1995) test hypotheses about diffuse and specific sources of support for courts from the US politics literature to evaluate the ECJ's legitimacy. As a relatively obscure institution, they argue that the ECJ is unlikely to build support by satisfying 'constituent demands', but the Court may find its decisions affecting its legitimacy as it comes under future scrutiny. Without much information on the ECJ, ordinary citizens form their views based on the ECJ's connection to the EU. Gibson and Caldeira (1998) find that the EP has little legitimacy to transfer to the ECJ and that national high courts, while enjoying greater legitimacy, are not necessarily able to transfer it to EU institutions. Finally, because the ECJ does not yet enjoy widespread support, it has few resources to elicit compliance in controversial cases.

Anke Grosskopf (2001) develops this analysis further, comparing public support for established courts including the US Supreme Court and West German Federal Constitutional Court with newly emerging courts, including the Federal Constitutional Court in East Germany and the ECJ in East and West Germany. In contrast to Gibson and Caldeira, Grosskopf demonstrates that constitutional courts inhabit an 'interconnected support universe' that facilitates the transfer of legitimacy from national courts to the ECJ. She concludes by arguing that the ECJ faces more legitimacy challenges as a result of being fairly new, rather than being supranational.

Another study of democratic legitimacy focuses on the extent to which the ECJ upholds the rule of law. Clifford Carrubba (2003) designs a formal model that, assuming there is some legitimacy cost for a non-compliant government, assesses the likelihood that the ECJ can guarantee that no EU body acts above the law. He draws on the finding that mass publics remain largely unaware of the ECJ to conclude that the Court is not yet in a good position to hold Member States legally accountable. By contrast, empirical research indicates that legal compliance in the EU is comparatively high, but this does not yet translate into democratic legitimacy (Zürn and Joerges, 2005).

Conclusion

All courts that resolve constitutional and administrative litigation rule against governments who control the mechanisms of coercion and enforcement (Conant, 2002; Fisher, 1961). Yet force is only relevant to a small fraction of legal relationships, typically reflecting a crisis rather than the norm (Bickel, 1962). The high volume of the ECJ's case load (Alter, 2006), along with habitual compliance (Conant, 2002; Zürn and Joerges, 2005), suggest that the ECJ is a legitimate court that can be compared more fruitfully to domestic courts than international institutions. While the international relations debate offered some compelling explanations of how this situation emerged, nuanced studies of domestic judicial politics should inspire more of the future scholarship on legal integration.

Observers of domestic contexts emphasize how individuals and organizational actors contest the balance of power within existing institutional arrangements and the ensuing political outcomes (e.g. Fisher, 1988; Bickel, 1962). The development of the EU as a political system layered above states is distinctive, but there is little reason to believe that its institutional dynamics defy those of all other democratic polities. Explanations of the emergence of a viable political system need not declare the permanent supremacy of any single layer of governance. Instead, these explanations may explore how legal and political outcomes evolve over time in ways that reflect the interactions of various institutional venues and different constellations of interest and power. Rather than asking which level of governance imposes the last word, it may be more interesting to explore how the 'last word' is a moving target evolving from the disputes of actors who face distinctive opportunities and constraints in promoting their goals. Research on the largely uncharted territory of national judicial review of EU law could uncover important insights here and contribute to a more complete understanding of legal integration. More collaboration among legal scholars and social scientists could be particularly helpful in pursuing legally informed and empirically grounded comparative analyses of the national application of EU law. Further case studies can situate courts in a broader political context, with judges as one actor among others contributing to outcomes. Showing how judicial influence varies depending on differences in the configuration of interests and institutions, I follow Shapiro in arguing that this type of research is most likely to advance our understanding of legal integration (Gillman, 2004).

References

Alter, K. (1996) 'The European Court's Political Power'. *West European Politics*, Vol. 19, No. 3, pp. 458–87.

Alter, K. (1998) 'Who are the "Masters of the Treaty"?' *International Organization*, Vol. 52, No. 1, pp. 121–47.

Alter, K. (2000) 'The European Union's Legal System and Domestic Policy'. *International Organization*, Vol. 54, No. 3, pp. 489–518.

Alter, K. (2001) *Establishing the Supremacy of European Law* (New York: Oxford University Press).

Alter, K. (2006) 'Private Litigants and the New International Courts'. *Comparative Political Studies*, Vol. 39, No. 1, pp. 22–49.

Alter, K. and Meunier-Aitsahalia, S. (1994) 'Judicial Politics in the European Community'. *Comparative Political Studies*, Vol. 26, No. 4, pp. 535–61.

Alter, K. and Vargas, J. (2000) 'Explaining Variation in the Use of European Litigation Strategies'. *Comparative Political Studies*, Vol. 3, No. 4, pp. 452–82.

Alter, K., Dehousse, R. and Vanberg, G. (2002) 'Law, Political Science and EU Legal Studies'. *European Union Politics*, Vol. 3, No. 1, pp. 113–36.

Bickel, A. [1962] (1986) *The Least Dangerous Branch*. Reprint (New Haven, CT: Yale University Press).

Boom, S. (1995) 'The European Union after the Maastricht Decision'. *American Journal of Comparative Law*, Vol. 43, No. 2, pp. 177–226.

Börzel, T. (2001) 'Non-compliance in the European Union'. *Journal of European Public Policy*, Vol. 8, No. 5, pp. 803–24.

Börzel, T. (2006) 'Participation through Law Enforcement'. *Comparative Political Studies*, Vol. 39, No. 1, pp. 128–52.

Burley, A. and Mattli, W. (1993) 'Europe before the Court'. *International Organization*, Vol. 47, No. 1, pp. 41–76.

Caldeira, G. and Gibson, J. (1995) 'The Legitimacy of the Court of Justice in the European Union'. *American Political Science Review*, Vol. 89, No. 1, pp. 356–76.

Carrubba, C. (2003) 'The European Court of Justice, Democracy and Enlargement'. *European Union Politics*, Vol. 4, No. 1, pp. 75–100.

Carrubba, C. and Murrah, L. (2005) 'Legal Integration and Use of the Preliminary Ruling Process in the European Union'. *International Organization*, Vol. 59, No. 2, pp. 399–418.

Chalmers, D. (2000) 'The Much Ado about Judicial Politics in the United Kingdom'. Harvard Jean Monnet Working Paper 1/100.

Cichowski, R. (1998) 'Integrating the Environment'. *Journal of European Public Policy*, Vol. 5, No. 3, pp. 387–405.

Cichowski, R. (2004) 'Women's Rights, the European Court and Supranational Constitutionalism'. *Law & Society Review*, Vol. 38, No. 3, pp. 489–512.

Cichowski, R. (2006) 'Courts, Rights and Democratic Participation'. *Comparative Political Studies*, Vol. 39, No. 1, pp. 50–75.

Conant. L. (2001) 'Europeanization and the Courts'. In Green Cowles, M., Caporaso, J. and Risse, T. (eds) *Transforming Europe* (Ithaca, NY: Cornell University Press), pp. 97–115.

Conant, L. (2002) *Justice Contained* (Ithaca, NY: Cornell University Press).

Conant. L. (2003) 'Europe's No Fly Zone?'. In Börzel, T. and Cichowski, R. (eds) *The State of the European Union*, Vol. 6 (New York: Oxford University Press), pp. 235–54.

Conant, L. (2004) 'Contested Boundaries'. In Migdal, J. (ed.) *Boundaries and Belonging* (New York: Cambridge University Press), pp. 284–317.

Conant, L. (2006) 'Individuals, Courts and the Development of European Social Rights'. *Comparative Political Studies*, Vol. 39, No. 1, pp. 76–100.

Conant, L. (2007) 'Judicial Politics'. In Jørgensen, K., Pollack, M. and Rosamond, B. (eds) *Handbook of European Union Politics* (London: Sage), pp. 213–29.

Costa, O. (2003) 'The European Court of Justice and Democratic Control in the European Union'. *Journal of European Public Policy*, Vol. 10, No. 5, pp. 740–61.

Everling, U. (1984) 'The Member States of the European Community before their Court of Justice'. *European Law Review*, Vol. 9, pp. 215–41.

Fisher, L. (1988) *Constitutional Dialogues* (Princeton, NJ: Princeton University Press).

Fisher, R. (1961) 'Bringing Law to Bear on Governments'. *Harvard Law Review*, Vol. 74, No. 6, pp. 1130–40.

Galanter, M. (1974) 'Why the "Haves" Come Out Ahead'. *Law & Society Review*, Vol. 9, No. 1, pp. 95–160.

Garrett, G. (1992) 'International Co-operation and Institutional Choice'. *International Organization*, Vol. 46, No. 2, pp. 533–60.

Garrett, G. (1995) 'The Politics of Legal Integration in the European Union'. *International Organization*, Vol. 49, No. 1, pp. 171–81.

Garrett, G., Kelemen, R. and Schulz, H. (1998) 'The European Court of Justice, National Governments and Legal Integration in the European Union'. *International Organization*, Vol. 52, No. 1, pp. 149–76.

Gibson, J. and Caldeira, G. (1998) 'Changes in the Legitimacy of the European Court of Justice'. *British Journal of Political Science*, Vol. 28, No. 1, pp. 63–91.

Gillman, H. (2004) 'Martin Shapiro and the Movement from "Old" to "New" Institutionalist Studies in Public Law Scholarship'. *Annual Review of Political Science*, Vol. 7, pp. 363–82.

Golub, J. (1996a) 'Modeling Judicial Dialogue in the European Community'. Working Paper, RSC 96/58 (Florence, IT: European University Institute).

Golub, J. (1996b) 'The Politics of Judicial Discretion'. *West European Politics*, Vol. 19, No. 2, pp. 360–85.

Grosskopf, A. (2001) 'A Supernational Case'. *Dissertation Abstracts International, A: The Humanities and Social Sciences*, 61 (9), 3750-A. (Available from UMI, Ann Arbor, MI. Order No. DA9985047.)

Harlow, C. and Rawlings, R. (1992) *Pressure Through Law* (New York: Routledge).

Hartley, T. (1986) 'Federalism, Courts and Legal Systems'. *American Journal of Comparative Law*, Vol. 34, No. 2, pp. 229–47.

Heisenberg, D. and Richmond, A. (2002) 'Supranational Institution-Building in the European Union'. *Journal of European Public Policy*, Vol. 9, No. 2, pp. 201–18.

Huelshoff, M., Sperling, J. and Hess, M. (2005) 'Is Germany a "Good European?" ' *German Politics*, Vol. 14, No. 3, pp. 354–70.

Joerges, C. (1996) 'Taking the Law Seriously'. *European Law Journal*, Vol. 2, pp. 105–35.

Joerges, C. and Dehousse, R. (eds) (2002) *Good Governance in Europe's Integrated Market* (New York: Oxford University Press).

Kagan, R. (2001) *Adversarial Legalism* (Cambridge, MA: Harvard University Press).

Kagan, R. (2006) 'American and European Ways of Law'. Paper presented at the Annual Meeting of the American Political Science Association, Philadelphia, 31 August to 3 September.

Kelemen, R.D. (2001) 'The Limits of Judicial Power'. *Comparative Political Studies*, Vol. 34, No. 6, pp. 622–50.

Kelemen, R.D. (2003) 'The EU Rights Revolution'. In Börzel, T. and Cichowski, R. (eds) *The State of the European Union*, Vol. 6 (New York: Oxford University Press), pp. 221–34.

Kelemen, R.D. (2006) 'Suing for Europe'. *Comparative Political Studies*, Vol. 39, No. 1, pp. 101–27.

Kelemen, R.D. and Sibbitt, E. (2004) 'The Globalization of American Law'. *International Organization*, Vol. 58, No. 1, pp. 103–36.

Kilroy, B. (1999) 'Integration through the Law'. PhD Dissertation. University of California, Los Angeles. (Available from UMI, Ann Arbor, MI. Order No. AAT 9940492.)

Mabbett, D. (2005) 'The Development of a Rights-based Social Policy in the European Union'. *Journal of Common Market Studies*, Vol. 43, No. 1, pp. 97–120.

Mattli, W. and Slaughter, A. (1995) 'Law and Politics in the European Union'. *International Organization*, Vol. 49, No. 1, pp. 183–90.

Mattli, W. and Slaughter, A. (1998) 'Revisiting the European Court of Justice'. *International Organization*, Vol. 52, No. 1, pp. 177–209.

McCown, M. (2003) 'The European Parliament before the Bench'. *Journal of European Public Policy*, Vol. 10, No. 6, pp. 974–95.

Nyikos, S. (2000) 'The European Court of Justice and National Courts'. *Dissertation Abstracts International, A: The Humanities and Social Sciences*, 61 (6), 2459-A. (Available from UMI, Ann Arbor, MI. Order No. DA9975557.)

Pollack, M. (2003) *The Engines of European Integration* (New York: Oxford University Press).

Ruggiero, C. (2002) 'The European Court of Justice and the German Constitutional Court'. *Studies in Law, Politics and Society*, Vol. 24, No. 1, pp. 51–80.

Shapiro, M. and Stone Sweet, A. (2002) *On Law, Politics and Judicialization* (New York: Oxford University Press).

Shaw, J. (1998) 'The Interpretation of European Union Citizenship'. *Modern Law Review*, Vol. 61, No. 3, pp. 293–317.

Slaughter, A., Stone Sweet, A. and Weiler, J. (eds) (1998) *The European Court and the National Courts – Doctrine and Jurisprudence* (Oxford: Hart Publishing).

Stein, E. (1981) 'Lawyers, Judges and the Making of a Transnational Constitution'. *American Journal of International Law*, Vol. 75, No. 1, pp. 1–27.

Stone Sweet, A. (2004) *The Judicial Construction of Europe* (New York: Oxford University Press).

Stone Sweet, A. and Brunell, T. (1998) 'Constructing a Supranational Constitution'. *American Political Science Review*, Vol. 92, No. 1, pp. 63–81.

Tallberg, J. (2000) 'Supranational Influence in EU Enforcement'. *Journal of European Public Policy*, Vol. 7, No. 1, pp. 104–21.

Tsebelis, G. and Garrett, G. (2001) 'The Institutional Foundations of Intergovernmentalism and Supranationalism in the European Union'. *International Organization*, Vol. 55, No. 2, pp. 357–90.

Weiler, J. (1982) 'Community Member States and European Integration'. *Journal of Common Market Studies*, Vol. 20, No. 1, pp. 39–56.

Weiler, J. (1991) 'The Transformation of Europe'. *Yale Law Journal*, Vol. 100, No. 8, pp. 2403–83.

Weiler, J. (1994) 'A Quiet Revolution'. *Comparative Political Studies*, Vol. 26, No. 4, pp. 510–34.

Weiler, J. and Dehousse, R. (1992) '*Primus Inter Pares*. The European Court and the National Courts'. Unpublished manuscript. (Florence: European University Institute).

Zürn, M. and Joerges, C. (eds) (2005) *Law and Governance in Postnational Europe* (Cambridge: Cambridge University Press).

JCMS 2007 Volume 45 Annual Review pp. 67–87

Governance and Institutional Developments: Coping Without the Constitutional Treaty

DESMOND DINAN
George Mason University

Introduction

If all had gone well, the Constitutional Treaty would have entered into force on 1 November 2006. In the event, the negative outcomes of the Dutch and French referendums in spring 2005 consigned the Constitutional Treaty to limbo. Even if the Dutch and French referendums had turned out differently, the Constitutional Treaty might have been blown off course by a negative referendum result in another Member State, such as the United Kingdom. Alternatively, implementation would possibly have been held up by an unfavourable ruling in the German Constitutional Court.

Whatever might have been, the Constitutional Treaty remained unimplemented by the end of the year. Public opinion throughout the European Union (EU) was supremely unconcerned about this situation. By contrast, many politicians and officials directly involved in EU affairs continued to advocate implementation of the Constitutional Treaty and grew increasingly frustrated with the status quo. Understandably, perhaps, they blamed the Dutch and French results on the vagaries of domestic politics and the actions of a few highly-motivated malcontents. While claiming to be aware of the extent of public unease throughout the EU, European elites seemed incapable of putting the Constitutional Treaty aside and, instead, using the formidable array of legal instruments and political opportunities already at their disposal to enhance institutional efficiency and improve policy output.

Prospects for reviving an altered version of the Constitutional Treaty gradually picked up as the year progressed. The Austrian presidency had the unwelcome task of wrapping up the period of reflection, proclaimed by the European Council in June 2005, and reporting back to the European Council in June 2006 (see Pollack and Puntscher-Riekmann, this volume). There, EU leaders adopted a 'twin track' approach: on the one hand, exploiting existing institutional openings to deliver a 'Europe of results'; on the other, exploring opportunities over the next year for rescuing as much as possible of the Constitutional Treaty. Hopes for a successful second track – a revival of the Constitutional Treaty under a less controversial name, plus a few other modifications – rose toward the end of 2006, thanks to German Chancellor Angela Merkel's devotion to the issue and promise to make it a centrepiece of her country's Council presidency in the first half of 2007. Uncertainly about the outcome of the spring 2007 French presidential election nevertheless clouded the matter, with Nicolas Sarkozy, the centre-right candidate, expressing interest only in a mini-treaty dealing with institutional reform and Ségolène Royal, the socialist candidate, being non-committal.

Indeed, the debate about the Constitutional Treaty in 2006, especially looking forward to 2007 and 2008, demonstrated the importance of the much-maligned rotating Council presidency and the impact on EU developments of changes of national governments, especially in the big Member States. Everything seemed to hinge on the still relatively new German government and the soon-to-be new French president; and on the German presidency in early 2007 and the French presidency in late 2008. Even so, it was clear by the end of 2006 that pressing ahead with ratification of an unchanged Constitutional Treaty was simply not an option. At best, the treaty's hard-fought institutional provisions might be salvaged as part of an inter-governmental agreement on a document that would be less ambitious in name and scope than its ill-fated predecessor.

At the same time, the successful functioning of the EU throughout 2006 under the terms of the existing treaties suggested that the fate of the EU was not necessarily bound up with that of the Constitutional Treaty. Following the rancour of the ratification crisis and the bitter budgetary dispute in 2005, relations between national leaders were relatively harmonious in 2006. Thankfully, the European Council lacked the personal fireworks that had characterized its meetings during the previous year. The Council and the European Parliament (EP) closed a number of long-standing, divisive and important legislative dossiers and the Commission, Council and EP easily reached an Inter-Institutional Agreement on the Financial Perspectives for 2007–13.

The relationship between institutional reform and enlargement loomed large towards the end of 2006, in the run up to Bulgaria's and Romania's accession to the EU in January 2007. Regardless of exaggerated fears of possible institutional sclerosis once the two countries joined, enlargement to 27 countries would trigger the Nice Treaty's provision for a reduction in the Commission's size to fewer than the number of Member States before the EU enlarged again. National leaders deferred discussion of the issue, while acknowledging at their summit in December 2006 the general link between enlargement and institutional reform, a link as old as the EU itself. Faced with public disquiet over enlargement and problems with Turkey's candidacy (see Lavenex and Schimmelfennig, this volume), the European Council found a formula to keep Turkey's accession negotiations alive while making EU expansion beyond 27 Member States conditional on major institutional reform. This implied some form of resolution to the constitutional impasse.

Even taking into account the prospect of further enlargement, it was evident by the end of 2006 that the EU could function satisfactorily without the Constitutional Treaty. Procedural reform, unrelated to the Constitutional Treaty but impelled in part by the ratification setback, was noteworthy in the areas of Council decision-making, better regulation and comitology. Looking at the bigger picture, the Commission continued to take a back seat to both the Council and the EP, which remained institutionally assertive notwithstanding a noticeable tendency for MEPs to divide along national lines more than political groups on sensitive policy issues. Overall, the EU was coping much better than expected under the existing treaty arrangements which, though clumsy and heavily criticized, were far from unworkable.

I. Reflection and Response

Fifteen of the then 25 Member States had ratified the Constitutional Treaty by the end of 2006 (see Table 1). A few die-hard supporters of the Constitutional Treaty, such as Valéry Giscard d'Estaing, chairman of the Convention that had drafted the document and Guy Verhofstadt, Prime Minister of Belgium, wanted to press ahead regardless. They hoped to be able to invoke Declaration 30 of the Constitutional Treaty, which stipulated that if, two years after the signing ceremony, four-fifths of the Member States had ratified but one or more of the others had 'encountered difficulties' with the process, the European Council could address the issue. Presumably, the leaders of national governments whose countries had ratified would pressure the others to bring their countries into line, although it was not clear how that

DESMOND DINAN

Table 1: Ratification of the Constitutional Treaty as of December 2006

Member State	Status
Austria	Ratified in parliament May 2005
Belgium	Ratified June 2006 following lengthy parliamentary procedures and government approval
Cyprus	Ratified in parliament June 2005
Czech Republic	No action taken
Denmark	No action taken
Estonia	Ratified in parliament May 2006
Finland	Ratified in parliament December 2006
France	Rejected in referendum May 2005
Germany	Approved in parliament May 2005; not yet signed by President
Greece	Ratified in parliament April 2005
Hungary	Ratified in parliament December 2004
Ireland	No action taken
Italy	Ratified in parliament January–April 2005
Latvia	Ratified in parliament June 2005
Lithuania	Ratified in parliament November 2004
Luxembourg	Approved in referendum July 2005; Ratified in parliament October 2005
Malta	Ratified in parliament July 2006
Netherlands	Rejected in referendum June 2005
Poland	No action taken
Portugal	No action taken
Slovakia	Ratification delayed by Constitutional Court July 2005
Slovenia	Ratified in parliament February 2005
Spain	Approved in referendum February 2005; Ratified in parliament April–May 2005
Sweden	No action taken
United Kingdom	No action taken

Source: Author's own data.

would happen. In the event, the vast majority of national leaders were uninterested in calling a special meeting of the European Council, even had the requisite number of Member States (20) ratified the Constitutional Treaty before the end of 2006.

According to Giscard, it was undemocratic to allow France and the Netherlands to derail the Constitutional Treaty, given that a majority of Member States had subsequently ratified it. Moreover, 'It is not France that has said no. It is 55 per cent of the French people; 45 per cent of the French people said yes.' Why not resubmit the same document to a second referendum? After all, Giscard pointed out, 'People have the right to change their opinion. The people might consider [that] they made a mistake' (*Financial Times*, 23 May 2006). Giscard acknowledged that the

Constitutional Treaty was unlikely ever to be approved in a referendum in Britain. His proposed solution was a special arrangement for Britain within the EU, analogous to its position outside the euro area. Prime Minister Jean-Claude Juncker of Luxembourg, a fierce critic of British Prime Minister Tony Blair, went so far as to claim that 'It is absolutely possible that the EU will move forward without the British if they reject the constitution' (*Die Welt*, 15 June 2006).

Given the role of the European Council in concluding the Constitutional Treaty and responding to the ratification crisis, it is hardly surprising that the issue preoccupied many of the EU's national leaders. Verhofstadt and Juncker, both ardent Euro-federalists, constituted the 'full-steam ahead' faction in the constitutional debate. The on-going impasse prompted Juncker and Verhofstadt to revive the idea of forming a core group of like-minded Member States dedicated to deeper integration. French President Jacques Chirac reiterated his oft-expressed preference for what he called a 'pioneer group' of countries committed to deeper integration, which would differ institutionally but not much in membership and policy scope from Verhofstand's and Juncker's conception of a core Europe. Romano Prodi, the former Commission President and successor in mid-2006 to Silvio Berlusconi as Prime Minister of Italy, called as well for an *avant-garde* to press ahead in areas such as internal security, foreign policy and defence, should the Constitutional Treaty languish indefinitely. The impracticability of such proposals and the negative reaction to them from most of the newer Member States, as well as from Germany, meant that they succeeded only in raising the temperature of the constitutional debate without contributing constructively to it.

In contrast to Juncker and Verhofstadt, a few national leaders wanted the issue simply to go away. Despite his personal enthusiasm for European integration, Blair must have been relieved not to have to champion a document that had little appeal in his country and that would certainly be rejected in a referendum. Gordon Brown, who by the end of 2006 looked likely to succeed Blair by Summer 2007, was not known as a fan of the EU and seemed unlikely to want to foist the Constitutional Treaty onto a strongly Eurosceptical UK.

Ireland's Bertie Ahern was in a different position. As chairman of the European Council in the first half of 2004, he had resuscitated the intergovernmental conference and helped craft the final compromise on the Constitutional Treaty. Ahern exuded pride of authorship when he spoke at a plenary session of the EP, in November 2006, on the challenge ahead. The Irish Prime Minister asserted that the Constitutional Treaty was essential for the EU and hoped that it would eventually be implemented. In that case, wondered Martin Schulz, leader of the Socialist Group (PES) in the EP, why had Ahern not begun the ratification process in Ireland? The answer, of course, was that Ahern was still bruised by Ireland's initial rejection of the Nice Treaty in the 2001 referendum and did not want to fight another ratification battle until it was absolutely necessary to do so.

A number of other national leaders would have been happy to see the Constitutional Treaty fade away. Mirek Topolanek, who became Prime Minister of the Czech Republic in September 2006, was an avowed Eurosceptic. He famously used a scatological term to describe the Constitutional Treaty and was utterly uninterested in the ratification process. Prime Minister Jarosław Kaczyński and President Lech Kaczyński of Poland were equally indifferent to the Constitutional Treaty, as was Robert Fico, who became Prime Minister of Slovakia in July 2006. Indeed, the extent of the hostility towards the Constitutional Treaty of these and other right-wing politicians in some of the new Member States generated considerable concern throughout the EU, not because of their right to criticize the document but because of their apparent disdain for well-established European norms and procedures.

Dutch Foreign Minister Bernard Bot was undoubtedly correct when he said, early in 2006, that the existing version of the Constitutional Treaty was 'dead' (*Agence Europe*, 12 January 2006). There was no way that it could be put, unchanged, to a second referendum in France or the Netherlands. Nor was there much support for tearing up the Constitutional Treaty and starting another intergovernmental conference all over again. As Luxembourg's Foreign Minister observed, 'The idea of simply scrapping the constitutional project or renegotiating it from scratch is absurd, for no other viable compromise will ever emerge from the debates that we have heard over the last two years' (Asselborn, 2006, p. 22).

The most obvious, cosmetic change would be to name the Constitutional Treaty something else. For Finland's Foreign Minister, changing the name would be a 'minor point', as 'everyone agrees it was a mistake to call it a constitution' (*Financial Times*, 29 May 2006, p. 4). Germany's Foreign Minister pointed out that his country's constitution was called a Basic Law; perhaps the EU's constitution could be called a Fundamental Treaty. Stephen Wall, a senior adviser to Tony Blair during the intergovernmental conference on the Constitutional Treaty, was more forthright: 'It never was a constitution and I kick myself [. . .] for not realizing that [such] hubris would be [its] undoing' (Wall, 2006).

Other changes to the Constitutional Treaty mooted during the period of reflection were more significant and compelling. At a press conference in January 2006, long before he became a candidate in the French presidential election, Sarkozy advocated keeping the key institutional reforms in the existing document, notably the EU foreign minister, permanent European Council president and extension of qualified majority voting (he repeated these ideas in a speech in Brussels in September 2006). Sarkozy was confident that those reforms, repackaged in a mini-treaty, need not be put to a referendum in France and would easily be approved by the national parliament. Support strengthened throughout the year for replacing the Constitutional Treaty with a shorter document consisting mostly of a declaration of the EU's values and objectives, as well as institutional arrangements.

The Austrian presidency had no illusions about the difficulty of reaching a consensus on the constitutional question in the first half of 2006, but was responsible for reporting to the European Council in June, by which time the period of reflection would have run its year-long course (see also Pollak and Puntscher Riekmann, this volume). By that time the Austrians should have been able to draw on the results of national debates on the Constitutional Treaty, envisioned as part of the period of reflection. However, these were few and far between. Most Member States preferred to let the matter drop. The Dutch government launched only a web-based national consultation; the French government shied away from a national debate of any kind. For their part, the Austrians organized the 'Sound of Europe', a celebration of European integration held in Salzburg in January 2006, on the 250th anniversary of Mozart's birth. The event attracted plenty of media attention but hardly resonated among ordinary Austrians, let alone other Europeans.

More tangibly, Austrian Prime Minister Wolfgang Schüssel recognized the importance for the EU of addressing citizens' concerns and delivering practical results. He wanted the EU to provide more open and effective decision-making within the existing treaty framework and to focus on delivering concrete policy results. Thinking along the same lines, the French government submitted a memorandum to the Austrian Presidency in April 2006 pointing out how the existing treaties could be used more effectively to move ahead in areas such as justice and home affairs, foreign and security policy and economic governance (*Agence Europe*, 27 April 2006; see also Pollak and Puntscher Riekmann in this issue).

The Austrian presidency could draw as well on a number of initiatives undertaken by the Commission and the EP during the period of reflection. 'Plan D' (Democracy, Dialogue, Debate) was the Commission's flagship programme. Launched in late 2005 in response to the Dutch and French rejections, Plan D sought to promote a favourable image of the EU and connect European citizens with the Commission in Brussels. Led by Commission Vice-President Margot Wallström, Plan D included frequent visits by Commissioners to the Member States, especially outside the national capitals, 'open houses' at Commission offices in the national capitals and a 'grand consultation' that brought together 200 citizens from the 25 Member States in Brussels in October. In May 2006, the Commission issued 'Plan D and the Period of Reflection', a predictably upbeat assessment of the initiative. In fact, there was little evidence that Plan D had any appreciable effect on public opinion generally, let alone on attitudes toward the Constitutional Treaty. Apart from Plan D, but related to the constitutional impasse, the Commission attempted to revamp its overall communications strategy. In February 2006, also under Wallström's direction, the Commission issued the White Paper on European Communication Policy, to which the other institutions and interested parties responded throughout the year (Commission, 2006a).

The Commission considered its overall contribution to the period of reflection during a retreat in late April. Its appraisal was realistic: nobody argued that the Constitutional Treaty could come into effect without changes. Once again, Commission President José Manuel Barroso explained that he did not want the EU to get bogged down in a political quagmire over ratification, preferring to focus on concrete action rather than empty declarations. Afraid that institutional issues were too divisive for the Member States, Barroso emphasized the importance of maximizing the existing treaties and demonstrating the EU's effectiveness while trying to salvage parts of the Constitutional Treaty. Accordingly, the Commission approved a list of initiatives in various policy areas that would demonstrate a 'positive agenda' and a 'Europe of results'. These ranged from policing and fine-tuning the single market to strengthening internal security (*European Report*, 3 May 2006).

The Commission released its programme on 10 May (Commission, 2006b). The day before, at a forum in Brussels for national parliamentarians and MEPs, Barroso announced that the Commission would start sending all new legislative proposals and consultation documents directly to national parliaments as well as to the EP. Because the Constitutional Treaty included a provision to that effect, some critics accused Barroso of 'cherry picking' and thereby weakening the integrity of the Constitutional Treaty as a whole. Barroso was unapologetic. Why not take an initiative that, according to those who had drafted the Constitutional Treaty, would strengthen the EU's legitimacy? The Commission would not be obliged to abide by the national parliaments' responses, only to take them into consideration, in light of the subsidiarity principle, as it weighed the next legislative step.

In contrast to what it saw as the Commission's indifference to the Constitutional Treaty, the EP pressed for continued ratification by the Member States. Of course, opinion within the EP was as varied as it was throughout the

EU, but the institution's leadership strongly supported the Constitutional Treaty, which was reflected in the EP's resolution on the period of reflection (European Parliament, 2005). If changes were needed in order to make the Constitutional Treaty palatable to French, Dutch and other voters, the EP wanted them kept to a minimum. Moreover, the EP recommended a timetable for revising the Constitutional Treaty that would culminate in an EU-wide ratification effort before – or possibly coinciding with – the next direct elections, in 2009. Clearly, the EP feared that continuing uncertainty about the Constitutional Treaty would further erode public support for the EU and contribute to yet another decline in voter turnout.

Apart from adopting reports and passing resolutions on the Constitutional Treaty, the EP organized a number of events to generate public and political support for it. These included Parliamentary Forums at the EP's headquarters in Brussels, where MEPs solicited the views of various constituencies, such as the social partners (in March) and civil society (in May). The EP held Citizens' Forums, open to the general public, in several Member States throughout 2006. The EP also asked national leaders known for their whole-hearted support of the Constitutional Treaty to rally MEPs during plenary sessions (Verhofstadt did so in May; Ahern in November).

Finally and perhaps most noteworthy, the EP organized, along with the Austrian and Finnish Council Presidencies and their respective national parliaments, Inter-Parliamentary Forums, in May and December (respectively), to bring together MEPs and national parliamentarians from all the Member States as well as the candidate countries. Some national leaders and the Commission President attended as well. Despite their willingness to participate in such events, some national parliaments nevertheless resented what they saw as the EP's condescending attitude towards them. Thus, the presidents of the Austrian, Finnish and German parliaments wrote to EP President Josep Borrell in January 2006 to complain that a recent EP report on the period of reflection treated national parliaments as 'an appendix' of the EP.[1] The leaders of these and other national parliaments were quick to point out that their institutions had already adopted strategies for dealing with the ratification crisis and did not have to act in harness with the EP.

The prominence of national parliaments during the period of reflection and, before that, in the Convention on the Future of Europe, as well as the provisions of the Constitutional Treaty dealing with national parliaments, demonstrated the growing importance of these bodies within the EU system

---

[1] The letter is available on the web site of Paavo Lipponen, Speaker of the Finnish parliament, at: «http://www.paavolipponen.org/cgi-bin/ajankohtaista.php?key=142».

of governance. However, the rising profile of national parliaments demonstrated as well the extent to which they differed from each other in constitutional importance, internal organization and political influence. Far from being a homogeneous group, national parliaments are individual institutions with varying levels of interest in, and aptitude for, policy-shaping at the European level.

The EP hoped that its various initiatives in the first part of 2006 would influence the European Council's review of the period of reflection at the June summit. By that time, it was widely accepted that the period of reflection would be extended for at least a year. At the summit, EU leaders conceded that the period of reflection had not amounted to much, describing it merely as 'overall [having] been useful'. The European Council welcomed the various national and institutional initiatives, such as the Austrian presidency's Sound of Europe and the Commission's Plan D and concluded, rather hopefully, that the period of reflection had so far shown that 'citizens remain committed to the European project' (Council, 2006).

More realistically, the European Council mentioned twice in its summit conclusions the importance of demonstrating to citizens the 'added value' of EU policies and programmes. Hence the European Council's adoption of a functional track as one of the twin approaches to moving the Constitutional Treaty forward. This track included a number of measures that seemed unlikely to have much appeal for ordinary Europeans – more transparency in Council decision-making, better application of the principles of subsidiarity and proportionality, reform of the comitology procedure and better law-making and regulation. In addition, the European Council welcomed the Commission's decision to submit new proposals and consultation papers to national parliaments, but, reflecting some national governments' indifference to the idea, asked only that the Commission 'duly consider' the parliaments' comments.

As for the other track ('Pursuing Reform'), the European Council agreed that the German presidency would report back by June 2007 with an assessment of Member State positions and possible ways forward. The European Council's examination of that report would form the basis 'for further decisions on how to continue the reform process', with a view to wrapping the whole thing up by the second half of 2008, when France would be in the Council presidency. In addition, the European Council called for the adoption by EU leaders, meeting in Berlin in March 2007, on the 50th anniversary of the signing of the Rome Treaty, of a political declaration 'setting out Europe's values and ambitions and confirming their shared commitment to deliver them'. Clearly, the Berlin Declaration was intended to add momentum to the treaty reform process, although the European Council's restrained rhetoric indicated the national leaders' acceptance that, at best, a less imposing document than the Constitutional Treaty would eventually be ratified and implemented.

The conclusions of the June summit let the incoming Finnish Presidency off the hook with regard to the Constitutional Treaty. Nevertheless, the Finns held bilateral consultations with other Member States and proudly ratified the Constitutional Treaty in their parliament just before their presidency came to an end. EU leaders barely discussed the Constitutional Treaty at the December European Council. By that time hopes were so high that the incoming German presidency would find a way out of the constitutional impasse that Germany's foreign minister deliberately played down expectations. For her part, Chancellor Merkel made several statements in late 2006 about Germany's determination to find a satisfactory solution, in close co-operation with the succeeding Portuguese and Slovenian presidencies.

Another significant development as 2006 drew to a close was the call by Spain and Luxembourg, the two countries that had ratified the Constitutional Treaty by referendum, for a meeting in January 2007 of the so-called 'friends of the constitution' – leaders of the countries that had so far ratified it. The others would be invited to attend a meeting with the friends of the constitution the following month. It was unclear what purpose the proposed special summits would serve. On the contrary, it was apparent that they could be counterproductive by strengthening opposition to the Constitutional Treaty in the face of an apparent effort to strong-arm those Member States that had yet to ratify, or had rejected the Constitutional Treaty outright. President Chirac's and Chancellor Merkel's coolness towards the idea suggested that the meetings might not happen and that the German presidency alone would orchestrate efforts in the months ahead to resolve the constitutional dilemma.

II. Institutional Developments and Inter-Institutional Relations

The question of the Commission's size and composition returned to the fore in late 2006 in the run up to Bulgaria's and Romania's accessions. The Nice Treaty called for a reduction in the Commission's size to fewer than the number of Member States before the EU enlarged beyond 27 countries. The Constitutional Treaty provided a formula for doing so – two-thirds the number of Member States, with an equal rotation among them in the nomination of Commissioners – a formula that could be adopted without having to wait for implementation of the Constitutional Treaty itself. The Finnish presidency began exploratory talks on what could have been a straightforward issue, but soon retreated, preferring to concentrate on more immediate and more tractable problems.

In the meantime, Barroso struggled to find suitable portfolios for the new Commissioners from Bulgaria and Romania. He came up with consumer protection (for the Bulgarian Commissioner) and multi-lingualism (for the Romanian Commissioner), which he carved out of existing portfolios. The thinness of the multilingualism portfolio highlighted the difficulty of finding meaningful responsibilities for 27 Commissioners and reminded everyone concerned of the wisdom of reducing the Commission's size, something easier said than politically done.

Barroso was unhappy with the first Commissioner-designate nominated by the Romanian government, someone tainted by allegations of corruption and links with the Communist-era secret police. Apart from personally disliking the individual, the last thing that Barroso wanted was a row with the EP over the candidate's credentials. Fortunately, the Romanian government withdrew its first choice and nominated instead an uncontroversial replacement. The EP was pleased with this development, preferring not to confront Barroso during the investiture hearings for the two new Commissioners-designate. Having rejected two of Barroso's original team in November 2004, the EP was content to let things go this time around. Indeed, the EP chose to vote in December 2006 only on the suitability of the two nominees, not on the entire college, basing its actions on Bulgaria's and Romania's accession treaties rather than on the Nice Treaty, which provides for the EP to approve the college as a whole. Accordingly, the EP's role in vetting the two Commissioners-designate was purely consultative. Nevertheless, in keeping with the institution's assertiveness, especially in the area of appointments and oversight, President Borrell declared in October 2006 that 'Our opinion will be decisive, even though legally our role is merely advisory' (European Policy Centre, 2006a). The relevant parliamentary committees easily approved the Commissioners-designate in November, with the EP as a whole endorsing them wholeheartedly in the December plenary session.

Perhaps because it wanted to avoid inviting what it would have seen as excessive EP scrutiny, the Commission decided during a retreat in September 2006 not to use the occasion of the appointment of the two new Commissioners to overhaul the college as a whole. Coming two years into the Barroso Commission's five-year term, amid complaints about the poor performance of some Commissioners, the arrival of two new members might have been a good time to reshuffle a number of portfolios. Barroso decided not to do so, perhaps in part because he did not want to antagonize those Member States whose commissioners would have lost out in the reshuffle. After all, Barroso wanted to stay on good terms with national leaders in the hope of being reappointed for a second term as Commission President.

The pending arrival of two additional Commissioners was grist to the mill of commentators who claimed that the Commission was already too large and unwieldy. Like the EU itself, the Commission nevertheless managed to function quite well with 25 members and presumably would do so with 27 members. The Commission's relative effectiveness was due in part to the clustering of Commissioners who worked on different aspects of key policy issues. For instance, a new group, under Commissioner Franco Frattini, met for the first time in September 2006 to deal with immigration. Complaints about the Commission's internal affairs centred on low staff morale as well as on organizational weakness, which an influx of officials from Romania and Bulgaria, at all levels, would do nothing to quell.

Nor was morale helped by an extraordinary public attack launched by Commissioner Günter Verheugen against senior officials. In an interview in a leading German newspaper, Verheugen blamed staff inertia and recalcitrance for the slow pace of the Commission's high-profile initiative to simplify and reduce Community regulation, an initiative that Verheugen directed.[2] Salacious reports soon afterwards of Verheugen's romantic involvement with his recently-promoted *chef de cabinet* fuelled speculation of staff retaliation and livened up the usually staid media coverage of Brussels. Verheugen survived both his officials' wrath and the media's frenzy, but his effectiveness as a senior Commissioner – both a vice-president and a hold-over from the previous Commission – was undoubtedly impaired.

Apart from that colourful episode, Verheugen's position was noteworthy because, like his colleagues from the other big Member States which had, under the terms of the Nice Treaty, lost one of their Commissioners, he was now his country's sole representative on the Commission. Moreover, he was a social democrat from a country whose government – albeit a grand coalition – was led throughout 2006 by a conservative. Eagerness to appeal to the more business-friendly preferences of Merkel and her Christian Democratic Union colleagues may have accounted for Verheugen's tilt to the right, which seemed appropriate in any case given that he held the industry and enterprise portfolio.

Regardless of Verheugen's plight, the Commission's apparent loss of political influence in 2006 was consistent with a long-term trend. It was due

---

[2] Verheugen's comments and the response of the Commission officials' union to them are contained in an open letter from the unions to the college of the Commission, 24 October 2006, available at: «http://www.unionsyndicale.org/public/t_061119_07.pdf».

more to the behaviour of national governments and the forcefulness of the EP than to the inherent weakness of the Commission itself.

The Commission also suffered from aggressive EP oversight. The 2005 framework agreement on relations between the two institutions arguably has tilted the balance firmly in the EP's favour. The greater frequency of inter-institutional meetings and of Commissioners' visits to EP committees and plenary sessions has given MEPs ample opportunity to assert their authority and, often, to berate the Commission. The arrangement whereby the Commission presents to the EP its annual policy strategy early each year and follows up later with its legislative and work programme, became in 2006 an exercise in Commission-bashing, at least on the part of many MEPs from groups other than the Group of the European People's Party and European Democrats (EPP-ED). Commissioner Wallström, with responsibility for communications and inter-institutional relations, was tireless in promoting harmonious dealings with the EP and defence of the Commission's prerogatives, but even she became irritated with the EP's attacks on her proposed communication policy.

A statement by Hans-Gert Pöttering, leader of the EPP-ED, describing the EP as 'the European institution which has the greatest European ambition [. . .] The Parliament today is very powerful and influential and at the same time a very responsible body', was typical of the EP's self-confidence (*European Report*, 17 July 2006). The EP is indeed an important institution, although its level of responsibility is difficult to judge. Certainly the EP acquitted itself well on the legislative front, having managed in 2006 to broker agreements on the services directive and the chemicals regulation, two complicated, high-profile and politically delicate matters.

Yet the EP's conduct of its own affairs seemed at variance with its image of itself and the high standards that it demanded of the other institutions. One of the most jarring issues, as so often in the past, was the way in which the two largest political groups, the EPP-ED and the PES, divvied up the spoils of office between them. The most striking example in 2006 was the preparation for a change of EP president. Under the terms of a 'technical agreement' reached between the two groups in July 2004, which divided the presidency of the 2004–09 term between them, a member of the EPP-ED was due to replace Borrell in January 2007. This arrangement engendered considerable resentment in the other groups and even among some members of the EPP-ED and the PES, who felt that the presidency should always be contested in an open election, not decided behind closed doors and then approved by a majority from the two largest groups. In defence of the agreement, Borrell explained that 'the president of the EP is not a government leader, he does not have a political programme. This agreement is not a coalition but a practical solution' (European Policy Centre, 2006a).

Everyone assumed that Pöttering would succeed Borrell, but Pöttering took nothing for granted, only declaring his candidacy at the last moment. Pöttering's determination not to risk reaching the highest office in the EP may help to explain his reluctance to rock the boat in any respect in 2006. That cleared the field for Schulz, the PES leader, to make the running within the EP and in relation to the other institutions. Schulz was merciless in his criticism of the Commission in general and Barroso in particular, repeatedly castigating the Commission President for his apparent willingness to let the Constitutional Treaty languish. Attacking Barroso, the centre-right President of a predominantly centre-right Commission, was a way for Schulz to distinguish himself and his group in the EP. When asked about his aggressiveness towards Barroso, Schulz replied that the Commission President 'should be fighting for these institutional reforms [in the Constitutional Treaty] like no other. It's in his own interest, but instead he gives up. That for me is an excellent reason to be hard on him' (*European Report*, 12 June 2006).

Borrell proposed modest reforms of the EP early in 2006, including the possibility of fewer and better own-initiative reports; better co-operation between committees; more time for committee meetings; and the possibility of an additional monthly plenary session in Brussels. Borrell circulated a questionnaire on the subject to political group leaders in June, but the heads of the two main groups, including Borrell's own PES, were unenthusiastic. Schulz was uncharacteristically coy about EP reform, considering how loudly he championed reform in the Commission and the Council. Pöttering's reticence may have been due to his desire to launch – and take the credit for – a reform effort once he became EP President in January 2007. Only Graham Watson, leader of the Liberals, responded positively. Not surprisingly for a British MEP, he was especially eager to improve the quality of debates. Nevertheless the EP's debating rules remained unchanged by the end of the year, as did most other EP procedures.

The question of the EP's permanent location, a bone of contention since the origins of the European Economic Community, resurfaced in 2006 thanks to a petition calling for the EP's seat to be situated permanently and exclusively in Brussels and thanks also to a scandal that came to light over excessive payments made by the EP to the City of Strasbourg for the use of buildings there. The Campaign for Parliamentary Reform (CPR), consisting largely of MEPs worried about the negative image of their institution, launched the petition in May, via the internet. They modelled it on an article in the Constitutional Treaty establishing a 'European Citizens'

Initiative', which would allow citizens to request the Commission to act on a matter that came within its purview, as long as the request was based on a petition signed by at least one million people 'from a significant number of Member States'. Thus, the CPR cleverly exploited interest in the Constitutional Treaty to highlight popular discontent, as well as discontent within the EP, over the institution's monthly trek between Brussels and Strasbourg.

The petition garnered its one millionth signature in September, although it was impossible to verify the identity of the signatories, most of whom gave an address in the Scandinavian Member States. Earlier, the Conference of Presidents of the Political Groups, the EP's most senior leadership body, asked Borrell to raise the issue of the EP's location in his customary remarks to the European Council, at the opening session of its next meeting, in June. Eager to avoid a predictable outburst by President Chirac, an implacable defender of the EP's presence in Strasbourg, the Austrian presidency prevailed upon Borrell not to press the point.

Undaunted, the CPR submitted the petition to the Commission, which was powerless to act upon it. MEP Cecilia Malmström, a leader of the CPR, left the EP to become Swedish foreign minister in September 2006. Given her involvement in the issue, it seemed possible that the Swedish government would raise it at the December meeting of the European Council, but nothing of the sort happened. Even those governments opposed to Strasbourg were unwilling to confront Chirac on a question that could be decided only by unanimity in the European Council. Moreover, a number of Member States other than France were happy with the status quo. Nevertheless the intensity of the anti-Strasbourg operation underscored a peculiarity of the EU's institutional arrangement that is a source of public ridicule and dissatisfaction. The logic of moving the EP entirely to Brussels is compelling, but the politics remain daunting.

Chirac offered an olive branch to the EP when he remarked in October 2006 that 'the [EP's] role [. . .] is tending to increase, as a result of the quality of its work [. . .] the [EP] is without a doubt becoming increasingly important, in the best sense of the term' (Chirac, 2006). Chirac may have had in mind some of the EP's legislative achievements, notably the compromise between the political groups on the services directive. Yet neither he nor many of the other national leaders were willing to concede much ground to the EP on the constitutional question. In particular, they resisted the EP's efforts towards the end of the year to become directly involved in drafting the declaration to be issued in Berlin in March 2007. Even within the scope of the existing treaties, most national governments were unwilling to give additional authority to the Commission, such as in the area of energy policy, a subject much discussed throughout the year. This was further evidence of the trend in the EU towards greater national direction and less supranational control over key policy areas.

III. Procedural Reforms

Notwithstanding the plight of the Constitutional Treaty in 2006 – indeed, in part because of it – the EU introduced a number of important technical reforms, notably concerning the quantity and quality of regulation, the openness of legislative decision-making and the rules for implementing laws under the notoriously arcane comitology procedure. Following the 2003 Inter-institutional Agreement on Better Law-making, efforts to reduce and improve regulation remained high on the EU's agenda, with the European Council reiterating its importance in June 2006. The purpose of the initiative was to make EU regulation more user-friendly and reduce the administrative costs associated with implementation, especially for small and medium-sized enterprises.

Prompted by the European Council, the Commission produced an assessment in November 2006 of progress to date on the better regulation initiative, focusing on simplification, repeals and withdrawals of existing legislation and impact assessments for new legislation. The Commission devoted an entire section of its 2007 Legislative and Work Programme, presented to the EP in October 2006, to better regulation. Many MEPs criticized the Commission for withdrawing proposals unilaterally; others agreed that, as part of its exclusive right to initiate legislation, the Commission was entitled to withdraw legislation as well, at least up to a certain stage in the decision-making process. A vocal group of left-wing MEPs protested that the better regulation initiative was a gift to influential industry lobbies, which have always complained about over-regulation in the EU. Responding to pressure from national governments, Barroso set up an Impact Assessment Board under his personal direction, to encourage greater use of assessments of the likely environmental, economic and social impacts of intended legislation.

The Constitutional Treaty included changes to the comitology procedure. With the Constitutional Treaty on hold, the EP pressed for an amendment to the current arrangements, which were based on Council Decision 1999/468/ EC. The EP deeply resented this Decision and had long demanded a role in the implementation of directives and regulations commensurate with its position as a co-legislator. Discussions between the Council, Commission and EP on comitology reform proceeded swiftly in early 2006, so much so that the three parties concluded an Inter-institutional Agreement in June, paving the way for Council Decision 2006/612/EC in July. The reform may have improved the EP's position and certainly demonstrated the EP's ability to negotiate successfully with the Council, but it made an already convoluted system even more complicated and, possibly, more opaque. Nor did the EP get everything that it wanted, having agreed to give up the so-called sunset clause, a provision of the existing regime whereby the EP could insist upon attaching to new legislation a time limit on the granting of implementing powers to the Commission. As the sunset clause gave the EP considerable leverage over the Council, its loss could outweigh some of the undoubted benefits for the Parliament of the new arrangements.[3]

Finally, at the other end of the legislative lifecycle, the constitutional impasse convinced national governments of the urgency of improving openness in Council decision-making. France, traditionally opposed to the idea, relented in early 2006, although Britain, traditionally in favour of it, baulked in the run-up to the June summit, arguing that opening Council meetings to public view would merely drive deal-makers into back rooms, away from the cameras. Britain yielded at the summit, where national leaders agreed on measures to make the work of the Council more transparent. Henceforth, Council deliberations under the co-decision procedure would mostly be open to the public, through video-streaming on the internet. Moreover, a record of all votes by Council members, together with explanation of those votes, would be published. The incoming Finnish Presidency implemented the European Council's decision with alacrity, thereby heralding a development with potentially important implications for EU governance.

Conclusion

In a speech to the Finnish Parliament shortly before the beginning of the country's presidency, Prime Minister Matti Vanhanen remarked that, compared to when it last held the presidency, in 1999, the EU was now more inter-governmental in nature. In addition, he identified two key problems: weak legitimacy and ineffective decision-making (Vanhanen, 2006). The trend towards greater inter-governmentalism was certainly perceptible throughout 2006, particularly in the rise of economic nationalism and continuing complaints by some national governments about unpopular competition policy decisions by the Commission or unpopular rulings by the European Court of Justice. The Commission, the EU's archetypal

[3] For an assessment of the new Decision and of the negotiations that led up to it, see Christiansen and Vaccari (2006).

supranational institution, remained politically weak. At the same time, the EP, another supranational institution, was as influential as ever, although the susceptibility of its members to divide along national lines on key legislative issues, such as the chemicals regulation, was notable.

Enlargement to 25 Member States, with two more joining in January 2007, undoubtedly changed the features and persona of the EU. The commensurate increase in the Commission's size and in the membership of the Council and the European Council further undermined the collegiality and cosiness of these bodies. Decision-making became more complex, but not necessarily less effective, contrary to what the Finnish Prime Minister claimed. Already a large and heterogeneous body, the EP coped best with the impact of enlargement. There, the leaders of the main political groups ensured that co-decision worked. Nor was Council decision-making evidently impaired by the use of the Nice formula for qualified majority voting.

One of the most obvious consequences of enlargement has been the near-constant churning in the composition of the Council and the European Council as a result of frequent changes in government in an EU of 27 Member States. Change is inevitable and is often a good thing. For instance, Angela Merkel's arrival in the European Council brought a breath of fresh air to a body long impaired by personality clashes between some of its most prominent members. But frequent and sometimes unpredictable change can weaken institutional coherence and continuity. Thus, the election of Eurosceptic governments, notably in some of the new Member States (see Henderson and Sitter, this volume), threatened to undermine the effectiveness of the Council and, especially, the European Council. Nevertheless, despite these and other institutional challenges and prevailing concern about the viability of the Constitutional Treaty, it is both remarkable and reassuring that, in the words of Luxembourg's Foreign Minister, the EU 'continues to manage its day-to-day business successfully on the basis of the provisions outlined in the Nice Treaty' (Asselborn, 2006, p. 20).

Further Reading

The short pieces by the European Policy Centre (2006b, 2006c, 2006d, 2006e) provide lively and incisive accounts, from a leading European think tank, of the four EU summits held during the year from a leading European think tank.

Heisenberg (2006) assesses Angela Merkel's approach toward the EU, based largely on the new Chancellor's position on the EU budget and on the Stability and Growth Pact.

Schmidt (2006) takes a novel look at the democratic deficit, arguing that it is situated not so much at the EU as at the national level, where the institutional presence and policies of the EU have altered the traditional workings of national democracies.

Héritier (2007) provides a fresh perspective on EU governance and institutional developments by looking beyond formal Intergovernmental Conferences to explore long-term institutional change, ranging from legislative procedures to the investiture of the European Commission.

References

Agence Europe (2006) 12 January and 27 April.

Asselborn, J. (2006) 'An Unwarranted Pessimism: Rethinking the European Integration Debate'. *Harvard International Review*, Vol. 28, No. 3, pp. 20–4.

Chirac, J. (2006) 'Conférence de presse de Jacques Chirac, Président de la République à l'occasion de la réunion informelle des chefs d'État et de gouvernement de l'Union européenne'. Lahti, Finland, 20 October, available at: «http://www.elysee.fr/elysee/elysee.fr/francais/interventions/conferences_et_points_de_presse/2006/octobre/conference_de_presse_donnee_a_l_occasion_de_la_reunion_informelle_des_chefs_d_etat_et_de_gouvernement_de_l_union_europeenne.63781.html».

Christiansen, T. and Vaccari, B. (2006) 'The 2006 Reform of Comitology: Problem Solved or Dispute Postponed?' *Eipascope* 2006/3, pp. 9–17.

Commission of the European Communities (2006a) 'White Paper on European Communication Policy'. COM (2006) 35 final, 1 February.

Commission of the European Communities (2006b) 'Communication from the Commission to the European Council, "A Citizens' Agenda": Delivering Results for Europe'. COM (2006) 211 final, 10 May.

Council of the European Union (2006) 'Presidency Conclusions, Brussels'. European Council, 15–16 June.

Die Welt (2006) 15 June.

European Parliament (2005) 'Committee on Constitutional Affairs, Report on the period of reflection: the structure, subjects and context for an assessment of the debate on the European Union', final, A6-0414/2005, 16 December, available at: «http://www.europarl.europa.eu/sides/getDoc.do?pubRef=-//EP//NONSGML+REPORT+A6-2005-0414+0+DOC+PDF+V0//EN».

European Policy Centre (2006a) 'Borrell Assesses his Presidency in a Positive Light'. 8 March, available at: «www.epc.eu/en/ae.asp?TYP=ABOUT&LV=224&see=n&PG=AE/EN/direct_inpbo&AI=41».

European Policy Centre (2006b) 'Energizing Debate Keeps the EU Show on the Road' (March 2006), available at: «http://www.epc.eu/en/pub.asp?TYP=ER&LV=294&see=y&t=15&PG=ER/EN/detail&l=&AI=581».

European Policy Centre (2006c) 'On the Slow Road to Recovery, Destination Unknown' (June 2006), available at: «http://www.epc.eu/en/pub.asp?TYP=ER&LV=294&see=y&t=15&PG=ER/EN/detail&l=&AI=608».

European Policy Centre (2006d) 'Great Expectations' (October 2006), available at: «http://www.epc.eu/en/pub.asp?TYP=ER&LV=294&see=y&t=15&PG=ER/EN/detail&l=&AI=646».

European Policy Centre (2006e) 'Wishful Thinking?' (December 2006), available at: «http://www.epc.eu/en/pub.asp?TYP=ER&LV=294&see=y&t=15&PG=ER/EN/detail&l=&AI=667».

European Report (2006) 3 May, 12 June and 17 July.

Financial Times (2006) 23 May.

Heisenberg, D. (2006) 'Merkel's EU Policy: "Kohl's Mädchen" or Interest-driven Politics?' *German Politics & Society*, Spring, Vol. 24, No. 1, pp. 108–18.

Héritier, A. (2007) *Explaining Institutional Change in Europe* (Oxford: Oxford University Press).

Schmidt, V.A. (2006) *Democracy in Europe: The EU and National Polities* (Oxford: Oxford University Press).

Vanhanen, M. (2006) Address to Parliament on Finland's EU Presidency, 21 June, available at: «http://www.eu2006.fi/news_and_documents/speeches/».

Wall, S. (2006) 'Reform in Europe Can Wait a Bit Longer'. *Financial Times*, 14 June, p. 17.

JCMS 2007 Volume 45 Annual Review pp. 89–106

Internal Policies: Reinforcing the New Lisbon Message of Competitiveness and Innovation

DAVID HOWARTH
University of Edinburgh

Introduction

The reinvigorated Lisbon strategy was one of the central priorities of the Austrian and Finnish EU Council presidencies of 2006. Beyond a rhetorical commitment, two major pieces of legislation under the Lisbon strategy – the Services directive and the REACH (registration, evaluation and authorization of chemicals) regulation – were agreed during the year. The priorities of the Austrian and Finnish presidencies also reflected the post-Kok Report revised goals of the Lisbon strategy, giving primacy to competitiveness and job creation over social and environmental protection. The two presidencies' most substantial internal policy accomplishments thus concerned competitiveness, in the sense of liberalization and lowering the regulatory burden.

This article examines the main internal policy developments in 2006 in terms of the renewed focus of the Lisbon strategy. It begins by providing a brief overview of the Lisbon strategy before developing its arguments: the aims of the Austrian and Finnish presidencies incorporated the revised goals for the Lisbon strategy after the Kok Report and the substantive achievements of the two Council presidencies also reflect these goals. This article then examines legislative and policy developments during the year in this context, focusing in particular upon the Services directive and REACH as the two most important internal legislative developments of 2006 – and arguably the decade.

I. The Evolving Lisbon Strategy

In its November 2004 mid-term report to assess the Lisbon strategy, the high-level group chaired by Wim Kok underscored the need to lend the strategy clear meaning, noting that, at mid-term, it was 'about everything and thus about nothing' (Kok *et al.*, 2004, p. 16). The two categories of the strategy – competitiveness policies and welfare policies, both subject to the open method of co-ordination (OMC) – suggested different and potentially conflicting priorities. Competitiveness policies focus on the information society, research and development, enterprise, the internal market and the macro economy. Welfare policies include education, employment, modernizing pension systems, addressing social exclusion and the renewed European social model. There were also environmental goals and the umbrella concept of sustainable development.

The initial language of the Lisbon strategy also reflected the inherent ambiguities of the 'competitiveness' concept (see Hay, this volume). The strategy posited that increased dynamism of European industry and enhanced social and environmental protection were interrelated components of future competitiveness. Industrial competitiveness could be driven by environmentally friendly innovation and enhanced social provision, in addition to intensified investment in research and development and liberalization of markets. The terminology of Lisbon thus promised environmentally sustainable development, economic growth, competitiveness, regionally-balanced growth and sustainable welfare systems.

These various aims also produced a contested discourse, in which a wide range of actors, including business groups, trade unions and environmental interest associations, sought to invoke Lisbon to advance their own preferences (Smith, 2006, forthcoming). It is not surprising that many informed observers have been sceptical of both the goals of the Lisbon strategy and the efficacy of the OMC to achieve many of them (see Verdun, 2006). Ultimately, the OMC has been a convenient formula that has enabled Member State governments to place competitiveness and social cohesion issues high on the EU agenda, while protecting national policy-making autonomy in these areas.

II. The Arguments

The reinvigorated Lisbon strategy was one of the central priorities of the Austrian and Finnish EU Council presidencies of 2006. In addition to considerable rhetorical emphasis on the strategy, the two presidencies also focused on advancing specific pieces of legislation that were presented as contributing to Lisbon's goals. The two most important pieces of legislation in this regard, the Services directive and the REACH regulation, were approaching the end of their legislative cycle after considerable intergovern-mental and inter-institutional debate and bargaining. The deft handling of the respective presidencies, however, helped to break deadlocks between the European Parliament (EP) and the Council of Ministers and overcome dis-agreements among the Member States to enable the adoption of these two pieces of legislation, which otherwise might well have been delayed to 2008.

The aims of the Austrian and Finnish presidencies reflected the revised goals for the Lisbon strategy after the Kok Report. The Kok Report did not settle the ambiguities of Lisbon. It acknowledged, for example, that environ-mental technologies can boost competitiveness and create first-mover advan-tages for European industry. Yet the report decisively gave primacy to competitiveness and job creation over social and environmental protection. Thus since 2004, a dominant framing of Lisbon has emerged in which competitiveness is defined by the minimization of the regulatory burden on industry. While debates continue in Europe over the best means to enhance competitiveness, Lisbon has become infused with meaning because a domi-nant conception of competitiveness has become embedded in EU institutions and notably the European Commission (Smith, 2006, forthcoming; and see Hay, this volume). For van Apeldoorn (2006) and others, this shift demon-strates the increasing dominance of neo-liberalism in European socio-economic governance. In its statement of strategic objectives for 2005–09, the Commission emphasized the critical role of impact assessment as an integral component of its quest for 'better regulation', a 'reduced regulatory burden on business, and a reinvigorated Lisbon Agenda' (see also Commission, 2007, p. 17). Moreover, while the Commission has responded to pressures from indus-try with a sustained focus on developing methods for quantifying administra-tive burdens, the Commission has not granted comparable attention to measuring environmental, social and health benefits. The rhetorical focus placed upon competitiveness also reflects the ideological and political circum-stances of the governments in power in the two Council presidencies. The Austrian centre-right coalition government led by Chancellor Schüssel empha-sized competitiveness, although the message was tempered somewhat by national elections in the second half of 2006. The Finnish centrist coalition government placed competitiveness and innovation unequivocally at the heart of its presidency's ambitions. The substantive accomplishments of the Austrian and Finnish presidencies were directed primarily at liberalization and lowering the regulatory burden. Legislative achievements in the fields of environmental and social policy at the EU-level were minimal, despite the continued rhetorical emphasis placed upon environmental and social protection. This legislative achievement likewise parallels the revised emphasis of the European Commission.

III. The 2006 Push for 'Competitiveness' and 'Innovation'

Competitiveness (with innovation) was one of the main priorities of both the Austrian and Finnish Council presidencies and the central topic of the Lahti European Council in October. The Finns named it as their top and overarching priority.[1] The two Council presidencies claimed they would focus on competitiveness across the various Council formations. The Austrian presidency also rhetorically focused upon competitiveness specifically in terms of the needs of small and medium-size enterprises (SMEs). Both presidencies closely linked competitiveness with the theme of innovation.

This theme was developed in the Aho Report, 'Creating an Innovative Europe', published in January 2006. At the request of the Hampton Court European Council of October 2005 the European Commission had asked a group of four high-level experts, chaired by the former Finnish Prime Minister Esko Aho, to propose ways in which Europe's research and innovation performance might be enhanced. The Report encourages Member State governments to take urgent action on research and innovation 'before it is too late' and calls for a Pact for Research and Innovation, which political, business and social leaders should endorse to demonstrate their commitment to creating an 'Innovative Europe'. The Aho Report (2006) also calls for a new policy direction to tackle productivity and social challenges and to redress the large gap between political rhetoric about the knowledge society and actual public spending. It proposes a four-pronged strategy: (1) create innovation-friendly markets by removing remaining obstacles to the single European market; (2) strengthen research and innovation by directing more financial and human resources towards the creation of an Innovative Europe; (3) increase structural mobility, encompassing not just the movement of people but also of organizations, infrastructure and resources; and (4) foster a culture that celebrates innovation.

Given that 'competitiveness' and 'innovation' are the major goals of the Lisbon Agenda, arguably other presidencies would have emphasized them. Nonetheless, it might be argued that Finland was in a particularly strong position to lead in this area. Finland has achieved high levels of technology-led growth over the past decade and the Finnish state has played an active role in pushing innovation as a means of creating sustainable growth and fostering competitiveness (Cordis, *Euroabstracts* 27 July 2006). According to the 2005

---

[1] 'For Finland, this [competitiveness] is a national as well as a Presidency mission. In both cases, it comes right at the top of the agenda' (Vanhanen, 2006).

and 2006 Innovation Scoreboards – the European Commission's method for evaluating and comparing innovation performance in the Member States – Finland is a 'star performer on innovation', matched only by Sweden. It sits in first place for innovation demand and innovation governance and Finnish firms are 'strongly skewed' towards creative innovation: some 32 per cent were identified as either strategic or intermittent innovators. The World Economic Forum's (WEF) Global Competitiveness Report ranked Finland as the second most competitive economy in the world in both 2005 and 2006 (World Economic Forum, 2005, 2006). Finland's success in this area was also recognized in the selection of former Prime Minister Aho to lead the group of 'wise-men'.

Armed with the Aho Report, the Austrian and Finnish presidencies placed particular emphasis on encouraging a supportive framework for research and development that encourages innovation and strengthens the knowledge-based economy and skills. Innovation was linked closely to enterprise. Efforts were made to prepare and complete prior to the end of 2006 the final steps to launch the Framework Programme for Competitiveness and Innovation (CIP), which is to run from 2007 to 2013. Adopted by the EP and the Council on 24 October, the CIP is intended to stimulate greater investment in innovation, particularly among SMEs, and is closely linked to other policy areas (energy, information technology, research and the environment).

The Austrian and Finnish governments also launched and furthered other Lisbon-related policy activity during 2006, such as the Research and Innovation action plan and new aspects of SME policy for growth and jobs. The Finns announced the extension of the Living Labs initiative which – based on a successful Finnish policy – aims to stimulate the institutional, structural and financial changes necessary for innovation-based growth and Europe's global competitiveness. The development of a broad-based innovation policy was one of the main themes for the Finnish presidency.

In line with the consensus reached at the October Informal Meeting of Heads of State or Government in Lahti, the December European Council confirmed the need for a strategic approach to create an innovation friendly environment in Europe. During the Finnish presidency, the Competitiveness Council set the strategic priorities for innovation actions at the EU level. Progress in implementing these priorities is to be examined as part of the follow-up to the Lisbon strategy.

IV. The Services Directive

Achieving an agreement on the Service directive – commonly referred to as the Bolkestein directive after the then internal market Commissioner who was its leading proponent – was presented by the Austrian presidency as one of its concrete priorities and a vital element of the Lisbon strategy's objectives of increasing competitiveness in the internal market, stimulating economic growth and creating jobs. Yet, the Services directive also became the focus of divisions between economic liberals and those prioritizing the preservation of western European social models (see also Hay, this volume). Thus, different interpretations of the Services directive effectively demonstrated competing visions of the competitiveness goal of the Lisbon strategy. The resulting directive demonstrates that the Kok Report's insistence upon the elimination of existing barriers to the operation of the internal market was heeded, but only in part. Significant qualifications to the liberalizing thrust of the directive were incorporated.

The free movement of services in the EU internal market is a long-established goal, implied in the market-creating provisions of the Treaty of Rome. Yet, despite the immense importance of services to the economy, accounting for over two-thirds of EU gross domestic product, numerous regulatory barriers remained – effectively demonstrating the limited nature of the internal market. The Services directive was initiated by the Commission in early 2004 and the Kok Report called for its quick adoption by the end of 2005. The Commission's draft directive sought to eliminate effectively the numerous obstacles faced by service providers by allowing companies and individuals to operate across the EU based on their home country rules – the 'country of origin' principle. However, western European trade unions opposed this principle on the grounds that it risked contributing to a 'race to the bottom' in social and labour market policies. The 'Polish plumber' became the symbol of the threat that an influx of workers from central and eastern European Member States would pose to wages and an erosion of social and labour standards in the wealthier Member States. The 'country of origin' principle thus met the entrenched opposition from certain Member State governments, notably the centre-right government in France. The Bolkestein directive – which opponents dubbed the 'Frankenstein directive' – contributed to French and Dutch voters rejecting the Constitutional Treaty in 2005 (see Eurostat, 2005; Hainsworth, 2006; Ivaldi, 2006; Taggart, 2006).

In addition to concerns about the corrosive impact upon social and labour market policies in the wealthier Member States, there were also concerns about the workability of Article 16 of the Commission's draft which enshrined the 'country of origin' principle. Not only did it go significantly beyond the rights granted by the European Court of Justice and Court of First Instance, it also created potentially serious implementation problems given the immense difficulty of enforcing 'country of origin' legislation in other Member States.

On 16 February, a large majority of the members of the EP – 394 votes to 215, with 33 abstentions – agreed a substantially modified version of the draft directive based on a compromise hashed out between the EP's two largest political groups. Many of those opposed were from the new central and eastern European Member States. The EP's version involved 211 amendments, many of which worked to weaken the liberalizing thrust of the Commission's draft directive. The more controversial elements of the Commission's version were eliminated. The 'country of origin' principle was replaced by that of the 'freedom to provide services', according to which Member States of destination must respect the right of service providers established in other Member States to operate freely. Any restrictions on this freedom must be non-discriminatory, proportional and justified on grounds of public policy, public safety, public health or environmental protection. The EP also exempted several sectors from the directive altogether: healthcare, audiovisual companies, temporary work agencies, taxis and other transport operators, as well as casinos and other gambling venues.

Despite these exemptions, the legislation promises to promote greater competition in the internal market. Several dozen concrete obstacles to the free movement of services were banned outright, notably requiring service providers to have an office and be registered in those Member States in which they operate. Thus businesses in most sectors were given the right to open a subsidiary in other Member States without going through lengthy, complex and often discriminatory authorization procedures.

Facing national elections, the Austrian government holding the Council presidency advocated a directive that both opened service markets – this tying strongly into its competitiveness and SMEs-focused themes – but preserved national social and regulatory standards. The mixed message reflected the extent that liberalization of the market in services was particularly sensitive in those states on the 'front-line' with the new central and eastern European Member States. Thus at the start of the Austrian presidency, Chancellor Schüssel said he wanted to involve 'social partners' – employers and trade union leaders – in seeking a 'balanced' outcome in the services debate (*Financial Times*, 10 January 2006).

For their part, the central and eastern European Member States were strongly in favour of the Commission's original draft directive, with Poland leading the opposition to 'watering it down'. Piotr Wozniak, Poland's economy minister, said he wanted to toughen the Commission's draft services directive to create more cross-border competition (*Financial Times*, 14 March 2006). As many as 15 countries – including most new EU Member States in central and eastern Europe, Finland and the UK – were unhappy with the EP's amended directive. UNICE, the European employers' confederation, was also strongly in favour of the original draft and also opposed the EP's amendments.

Yet entrenched opposition to the original draft in certain key Member States persuaded the Commission to backtrack on its previously liberalizing emphasis and to accept all the key EP amendments. Charlie McCreevy, the internal market commissioner distanced himself from his more controversial predecessor, Bolkestein, who had pursued a more aggressive liberalizing agenda. McCreevy argued that a more radical attempt to create a free market in services was 'never ever going to become a piece of legislation' (*Financial Times*, 4 April 2006). The Commission, however, indicated that it would seek to prepare specific legislation for those sectors that had been excluded from the directive by the EP, including healthcare. Martin Bartenstein, the Austrian economics minister, welcomed McCreevy's position, saying 'we need pragmatic solutions rather than presenting proposals which never come to an end' (*Financial Times*, 4 April 2006).

In April, the Commission sought to demonstrate its responsiveness to the concerns of central and eastern European Member State governments by presenting new legal guidance on an existing piece of EU legislation designed to guarantee that employees, such as construction workers, can work abroad on fixed duration contracts. The Commission committed itself to reinforcing its monitoring of national bureaucratic hurdles to temporary foreign workers and threatened legal action in the case of specific breaches of EU legislation. In particular, the Commission sought to challenge long notification periods and excessive documentation required by some governments.

On 29 May, the EU Member States reached a political agreement on the Services directive, one of the most bitterly divisive pieces of recent European legislation. The Council accepted the Commission's revised directive – based on the EP's demands – but made some additional minor and slightly liberalizing amendments. It added the requirement that national governments must scrutinize large sections of their domestic legislation to see whether it imposes unfair requirements on foreign service providers wishing to enter their markets and any such requirements must be justified. Furthermore, it agreed to empower the Commission to provide 'orientations' to Member States to ensure they meet the criteria in the directive. The compromise was achieved after a final push by central and eastern European governments to improve access for their workers and service companies to the wealthier Member States.

Although only cosmetic changes were adopted, all Member States voted in favour of the directive, with the exception of Lithuania, which abstained in protest to the significant watering down of the Commission's proposal. Minutes before the final agreement France gave way on one final request by Italy, accepting that bailiffs and solicitors at appeal courts should not be subject to national restrictions (*Financial Times*, 30 May). Member States have three years to put the directive into practice, following its approval in a second reading in the EP on 15 November.

V. REACH

On 18 December, the EP and the Council signed the REACH regulation (Regulation EC 1907/2006) after almost a decade of drafting and three years of legislative work and intensive inter-institutional and intergovernmental debate. This major piece of legislation will replace an outdated 40-year-old regulation. It will impose a regulatory burden on companies that requires them to register some 30,000 chemical substances with a new agency. It will be necessary for companies to prove that the substances that they produce and use pose no threat to the environment and to human health.

The regulation was the subject of considerable lobbying by representatives of industrial interests (notably Cefic, the body that represents Europe's chemical industry) and environmentalist groups and their respective supporters. Industry was concerned that the regulation would impose expensive testing on companies, which would raise costs and drive production and jobs abroad. Of particular concern to business was the requirement in the Commission's original draft directive that companies must substitute hazardous chemicals with safer alternatives. The EU's trading partners also expressed concern that the regulation – which would apply to all imports – would hurt their exporting industries unless they adopted EU regulatory standards. Some went so far as to argue that REACH in its original form would be incompatible with the EU's obligations under World Trade Organization rules.

During the course of the debate the positions of the Council, Commission and EP shifted progressively towards that of industry. The Council's position shifted notably with the change of government in Germany in 2005 and the departure of the Green Party from the governing coalition. The German government subsequently adopted a strongly pro-industry position on REACH.

In November 2005, the EP agreed to decrease the regulatory burden on companies, especially small and medium-size businesses, by amending the regulation to exempt more than two-thirds of chemical substances produced in lower volumes from the full testing and registration requirements. This meant that up to 20,000 of the substances covered by REACH would require additional testing only if they either are already known to pose a risk or are circulated widely. Even when chemicals are produced in higher volumes companies can seek waivers from the full burden of regulation.

On 10 October 2006, the EP approved an amended REACH regulation, which still required the substitution of up to 2,000 dangerous chemicals, a provision that the Council opposed, preferring that companies should only be required to show that their hazardous chemicals could be 'adequately controlled'. Through the end of November, there remained the possibility that the directive might be derailed with the EP in favour of substitution and the Council in favour of control guarantees. In the conciliation committee (the final stage of the EU legislative process), however, the EP's representatives agreed to substantially watered-down provisions on substitution. These will require companies only to identify whether safer alternatives exist to the most dangerous substances that they use and to prepare a 'substitution plan'. Environmental groups and their MEP supporters criticized the agreement as a 'sell-out' to the chemical industry. In the meantime, UNICE expressed concern that the rules on substitution could result in 'too much bureaucracy' (*Financial Times*, 1 December 2006). The final version of the regulation thus departs considerably from the Commission's original draft. Yet, reflecting its shift towards a more business-friendly approach, the Commission also voiced its support for a revised draft.

Smith (2006, forthcoming) argues that the agreed REACH regulation reflects the post-Kok-Report conceptualization of Lisbon, which emphasizes easing the regulatory burden as a key to competitiveness. He argues that this conceptualization gained footing through those EU institutions that had an important role in shaping the directive: the Competitiveness Council, the Commission's Directorate General-Enterprise and the EP's committees on Internal Market and Consumer Affairs and on Industry, Research and Energy. When institutional actors and organized concentrated interests, such as the national chemicals sector industry federations, frame debates over environmental issues in terms of competitiveness, environmentalists and their supporters are in a position of relative weakness and are unable to pose an effective alternative frame. 'Competitiveness framing' typically acknowledges the importance of environmental protection, but subsumes the environment frame by positing that a robust business environment is a pre-condition for investments in production processes that can improve environmental quality (Smith, 2006, forthcoming).

VI. The 'Better Regulation' Drive

The Commission ambitions with regard to regulation are, ostensibly, all-embracing:

The aim is to ensure that the regulatory environment for Europe's businesses and citizens delivers on European objectives such as the creation of a fair and competitive marketplace, the welfare of its citizens and the effective protection of public health and the environment, while at the same time cutting the administrative costs which hamper productivity and job creation. (Commission, 2007, pp. 17–18)

These aims were the guiding principles that officially drove the Commission's strategic review of EU regulation in 2006, the results of which were presented on 14 November. Yet the overriding focus of substantive efforts to improve regulation was to decrease the regulatory burden on companies.

Two working papers accompanied the review: a first progress report on the strategy for the simplification of the regulatory environment (Commission, 2006b) and a paper on measuring administrative costs and reducing administrative burdens in the EU (Commission, 2006c). The Commission claims that impact assessment is its main tool for producing better legislation. This involves identifying and anticipating the potential economic, social and environmental implications of new legislative proposals. In March 2006, a common methodology for measuring the administrative costs of new legislation was agreed and incorporated into the Commission's guidelines on impact assessments. In addition, in November, the Commission set up an Impact Assessments Committee composed of senior officials working independently of the competent directorates general and answerable to the President of the Commission. The EP and the Council have also produced their own impact assessments of their substantial amendments to Commission proposals, resulting in several dozen proposed amendments being withdrawn. The Commission announced in its work programme for 2007 the withdrawal of 10 additional legislative proposals. Consultation on improved regulation continued with the wider public as well as Member State governments, notably within the new high-level group of national experts on regulation. The programme to modernize and simplify existing EU legislation – launched in October 2005 – continued in 2006 with some 50 simplification proposals presented. Forty-seven simplification initiatives were announced for 2007.

VII. Other Competitiveness-Oriented Achievements and Non-Achievements

In terms of completing the internal market, the Services directive was supplemented by surprisingly little legislation in 2006. Demonstrating the limited progress, the Finnish presidency's official statement of its results (Finnish Government, 2006) emphasized the achievement of a political agreement on the Directive on Pre-packaging, which aims, through liberalizing package sizes, to encourage free movement and guarantee customers a wide freedom of choice between different package sizes. There was progress made preparing the Directive on the Portability of Supplementary Pensions, and in the field of electronic communication, including discussions of the Commission's new (12 July) proposal for regulating 'roaming' charges on mobile telephone calls within the EU. Existing Community legislation on pharmaceuticals was complemented with the finalization and adoption of a regulation on paediatric medicines. Groundwork was also laid for the adoption of legislative initiatives relating to medical devices and advanced therapies. According to the Finnish Council President (2006): 'these initiatives support the competitiveness of the European pharmaceutical industry and patient safety'.

In addition, the Seventh Framework Programme (FP7) of the European Community and Euratom for research, technological development and demonstration activities (2007–13) was finalized on 18 December. Launched at the beginning of 2007, FP7 is the biggest EU funding programme to date (approximately €55 billion). The Commission presents it as a crucial tool in realizing the Lisbon Strategy's growth and competitiveness pillars. Under FP7's fourth specific programme, 'Capacities', key aspects of European research and innovation will be supported including: research infrastructures; research for the benefit of SMEs; regional research-driven clusters; unlocking the full research potential in the EU's 'convergence' regions; science in society issues; and international co-operation activities.

Different national tax regimes in the EU create a significant obstacle for free movement and impose costs on companies that operate in different Member States. The costs are particularly burdensome for SMEs. The Commission estimates that these compliance costs can be as high as 30 per cent of tax paid for small businesses, compared with only 1.9 per cent for large corporations (*Financial Times*, 10 January 2006). Only 3 per cent of SMEs operate across EU borders. Harmonization of corporate tax policies has thus been actively supported by the pan-European small business association (the UEAPME). In early January 2006, as part of the launch of the Austrian presidency's efforts on behalf of SMEs, the Commission announced plans to simplify the tax regime for companies with fewer than 250 employees and less than €50 million annual turnover, allowing them to apply home state corporate tax rates and rules to calculate profits. However, the scheme, to run for a five-year trial, is to be voluntary and depends on Member States agreeing to respect each other's tax systems. A formula for dividing business tax revenues between the Member States according to their shares of the total payroll and/or turnover must be agreed in subsequent bilateral or multilateral treaties. The Commission compares the scheme to the arrangements between

US states or Canadian provinces and a bilateral German–Dutch trial for companies. The voluntary nature of the scheme, however, has created scepticism as to the likelihood of widespread bilateral and multilateral agreements. Member States with higher corporate tax rates, such as France, are unlikely to agree to a scheme allowing foreign companies from Member States, such as the UK and Ireland, with significantly lower rates to operate according to their own national tax rules and rates.

In the area of social policy, only one piece of legislation – concerning health and safety at work – that might increase the social policy burden on companies was adopted and none was proposed in 2006. Fourteen years after the Commission first proposed action, the EP and the Council finally adopted, on 5 April, the directive on the minimum health and safety requirements regarding the exposure of workers to risks arising from physical agents (artificial optical radiation) (Directive 2006/25/EC). The directive imposes a number of obligations on employers, including risk assessment, reduction of exposure, health surveillance and information and training for workers exposed to risks from artificial optical radiation at work. The number of affected companies is limited. The EP and the Council also adopted the Community programme for employment and social solidarity ('Progress'), which is intended to support financially the implementation of EU objectives in the fields of employment and social affairs. It takes the form of a single, streamlined financial instrument divided into five sections: employment, social protection and inclusion, working conditions, anti-discrimination and diversity and gender equality.

In the realm of employment policy there was one new funding initiative. On 20 December, the EP and the Council agreed to establish the European Globalization Adjustment Fund. The fund has a symbolic importance as its aim is to provide additional support for workers made redundant because of major structural changes in world trade patterns. The fund is designed to complement the efforts of Member State governments through financing specifically tailored support services designed to help individuals facing immediate and serious social difficulties because of economic change.

With regard to the Working Time Directive, agreement continued to prove elusive. The Austrian and Finnish presidencies failed to achieve a compromise between those Member States (led by the UK) that seek to maintain opt-outs from the maximum 48 hour working week mandated by the directive and those (led by France) that seek to close loopholes. Several Member State governments have not amended national legislation to correspond with the rulings of the European Court of Justice applying the Working Time Directive because adherence to the decision would cause strains in the provision of medical care and introduce significant budgetary effects.

In the realm of environmental policy, several pieces of legislation were agreed, although most are only limited modifications of pre-existing legislation. None can be described as a major departure from existing practice or a major leap forward in the protection of the environment. With regard to water protection, on 15 February, the EP and the Council signed Directive 2006/7/EC concerning the management of bathing water quality and Directive 2006/11/EC on pollution caused by certain dangerous substances discharged into the aquatic environment. The former updates the legislation in force with a view to reducing health risks to bathers by focusing on the most pressing health risks, in particular intestinal enterococci and *Escherichia coli*. The latter directive codifies and replaces, but does not make any substantive changes to a pre-existing directive. The Council and EP also reached agreement on the Ground Water Directive (17 October), which seeks to improve protection for groundwater by establishing evaluation criteria and setting maximum limits for pollutants while balancing the prerogatives of Community and national authorities in the light of the subsidiarity principle.

On 15 March, the EP and the Council signed Directive 2006/21/EC on the management of waste from extractive industries to ensure the protection of the environment and human health. On 14 June, the EP and the Council signed Regulation (EC) No. 1013/2006 on shipments of waste which aims to strengthen, simplify and clarify the control procedures of a pre-existing regulation currently applicable to shipments of waste. On 6 September the EP and the Council adopted Directive 2006/66/EC on batteries and accumulators and waste batteries and accumulators. Replacing an existing directive, the new legislation is aimed at minimizing the adverse effects of batteries and accumulators on the environment while laying down a number of requirements designed to ensure the correct operation of the internal market in that respect. On 21 November, there was agreement on the 'Inspire' Directive establishing an infrastructure for spatial information. Inspire is intended to act as a key geographical and environmental information and control instrument in accordance with the Sixth Action Programme for the Environment. The EU's target of halting the loss of biodiversity by 2010 was an important element of the Austrian and Finnish presidencies' rhetoric on environmental protection and, in December, the Council adopted conclusions on biodiversity on the basis of a Commission communication and action plan from earlier in the year.

The two Council presidencies' rhetoric also placed considerable focus on the co-ordination of EU environmental policy in the context of international obligations and negotiations. Thus, on 8 February, the Commission presented the fourth 'national communication' from the European Community under the United Nations Framework Convention on Climate Change. In addition, two pieces of legislation were adopted on 17 May to address green house gas emissions: Regulation (EC) 842/2006 on certain fluorinated greenhouse gases and Directive 2006/40/EC relating to emissions from air conditioning systems in motor vehicles.

Conclusion

The implementation of the revised version of the Lisbon strategy can thus be seen to have had some success in 2006. The Services directive will remove numerous regulatory burdens on companies seeking to engage in cross-border activities in the EU Internal Market and thus enhance competition. The REACH directive reflected a regulation-lite approach to the chemical sector that significantly watered down the original proposals. Several policies, from research to transport were also shaped by a strong competitiveness focus. The limited legislative developments in environmental and social policy fields effectively demonstrated the renewed focus of the Lisbon strategy. The rhetoric of the Austrian and, in particular, the Finnish Council presidencies further highlighted the shift in focus. The debate that followed the publication of the Kok Report thus seems to have resulted in a transformation of the conceptualization of the Lisbon strategy towards 'competitiveness'. As this frame becomes more deeply embedded as the compass for EU policy making, Member States and EU institutions may find it increasingly difficult to assert agendas that cut against this grain. For van Apeldoorn (2006) the emphasis placed upon competitiveness represents the menacing transcendence of the neo-liberal project and the down-grading of previously emphasized elements of the neo-mercantilist and the social-democratic projects that have had an important position in transnational European socio-economic governance.

Nonetheless, it is crucial to qualify the significance of 'competitiveness' as a driver of EU-level policy. The outcome of the debate over the Services directive demonstrates the potency of alternative goals for Member State governments. In a range of areas from copyright to corporate tax to financial services, Member State governments have placed other objectives above that of competitiveness qua liberalization, which effectively explains the very weakness of initiatives in these areas in 2006. Other objectives have also prompted Member State governments to adopt a slew of high-profile protectionist actions in 2006, including several intervening to block takeovers of national firms by other EU-based firms. Moreover, major obstacles remain to the operation of a true internal market that the liberalizing Commission and supportive Member States governments will fail to overcome for some time. In terms of real policy output, 'competitiveness' will thus continue to be counter-acted by other ideational influences and political obstructionism.

Key Readings

Mundschenk *et al.* (2006) is an edited volume by economists focusing on the competitive and growth goals of the Lisbon Strategy. Chapters explore the determinants of growth, cohesion strategies and the role of institutions, education, R&D and technological progress in economic performance.

Pisani-Ferry and Sapir (2006), prepared in response to a request from the Austrian presidency and presented to EU finance ministers, make recommendations for better realizing the Lisbon objectives.

Verdun (2006) provides a brief, critical and multidisciplinary overview of progress in achieving the goals of the Lisbon strategy.

References

Aho Report (2006) 'Creating an Innovative Europe: report of the Independent Expert Group on R&D and Innovation appointed following the Hampton Court Summit', Summary, January. Available at «http://ec.europa.eu/invest-inresearch/pdf/2006_aho_group_report_en/pdf». Accessed on 15 January 2007.

Commission of the European Communities (2005) 'The Specific Programme "Capacities" implementing the 7th Framework Programme (2007–2013) of the European Community for Research, Technological Development and Demonstration Activities'. Proposal for a Council Decision, 443, 2005/0188/CNS.

Commission of the European Communities (2006b) 'First Progress Report on the Strategy for the Simplification of the Regulatory Environment'. Working paper 691. Available at: «http://ec.europa.eu/enterprise/regulation/better_regulation/docs/docs_admin_b/en_690.pdf». Accessed on 30 January 2007.

Commission of the European Communities (2006c) 'Measuring Administrative Costs and Reducing Administrative Burdens in the European Union'. Working paper 691. Available at: «http://ec.europa.eu/enterprise/regulation/better_regulation/docs/docs_admin_b/en_691.pdf».

Commission of the European Communities (2006d) 'A Strategic Review of Better Regulation in the European Union'. Communication from the Commission, 689 final, 14 November.

Commission of the European Communities (2006e) 'Fourth National Communication from the European Community under the UN Framework Convention on Climate Change (UNFCCC) (required under Article 12 of the United Nations Framework Convention on Climate Change)'. Communication from the Commission 40.

Commission of the European Communities (2007) *General Report on the Activities of the European Union* (Luxembourg: OOPEC).

Cordis *Euroabstracts* 27/07/06, 'Innovation under Finland's EU Presidency'. Available at: «http://cordis.europa.eu/aoi/article.cfm?article=1687&lang=EN», accessed on 2 February 2007.

European Parliament and the Council of the European Communities (2006) 'Establishing a Community Programme for Employment and Social Solidarity – Progress'. Decision No. 1672/2006/EC of 24 October.

Eurostat (2005) 'The European Constitution: Post-referendum Survey in France'. Flash Eurobarometer EB171.

Financial Times (2006) 10 January, 14 March, 4 April, 30 May, 1 December.

Finnish government (2006) 'Finland's Presidency of the EU – results, 22 December 2006' (Unofficial translation – subject to change), available at: «http://www.eu2006.fi/en_GB/», accessed on 30 January.

Hainsworth, P. (2006) 'France Says No: The 29 May 2005 Referendum on the European Constitution'. *Parliamentary Affairs*, Vol. 59, No. 1, pp. 98–117.

Ivaldi, G. (2006) 'Beyond France's 2005 Referendum on the European Constitutional Treaty: Second-Order Model, Anti-Establishment Attitudes and the End of the Alternative European Utopia'. *West European Politics*, Vol. 29, No. 1, pp. 47–69.

Kok, W. (ed.) (2004) 'Facing the Challenge: The Lisbon Strategy for Growth and Employment'. Report from the High Level Group chaired by Wim Kok, November (Luxembourg: Office for Official Publications of the European Communities); see «http://ec.europa.eu/growthandjobs/group/index_en.htm».

Mundschenk, S., Stierle, M., Stierle-von Schutz, U. and Traistaru-Siedschlag, I. (eds) (2006) *Competitiveness and Growth in Europe: Lessons and Policy Implications for the Lisbon Strategy* (London: Edward Elgar).

Pisani-Ferry, J. and Sapir, A. (2006) 'Last Exit to Lisbon', Bruegel Policy Brief, March, available at: «www.bruegel.org/Public/PolicyContributions.php?ID=428». Accessed on 10 January 2007.

Smith, M.P. (2006) 'Lisbon Lives: Institutional Embedding of the Competitiveness Objective'. *EUSA Review*, Fall 2006, pp. 9–11.

Smith, M.P. (forthcoming 2008) 'All Access Points Are Not Created Equal: Explaining the Fate of Diffuse Interests in the EU'. *British Journal of Politics and International Relations*.

Taggart, P. (2006) 'Keynote Article: Questions of Europe – The Domestic Politics of the 2005 French and Dutch Referendums and their Challenge for the Study of European Integration'. *JCMS Annual Review* 2005, pp. 7–25.

Van Apeldoorn, B. (2006) 'The Lisbon Agenda and the Legitimacy Crisis of European Socio-Economic Governance: the Future of "Embedded Neo-Liberalism" '. Paper presented at the 4th convention of the Central and East European International Studies Association (CEEISA), University of Tartu, Estonia, 25–27 June 2006. Available at: «http://www.ceeisaconf.ut.ee/orb.aw/class=file/action=preview/id=166433/apeldoorn.doc». Accessed on 10 January 2007.

Vanhanen, M. (2006) Address to the European Parliament, 21 June. Available at: «http://www.eu2006.fi/news_and_documents/speeches/press/en_GB/1150877429794/?u4.highlight=». Accessed on 20 February 2007.

Verdun, A. (ed.) (2006) 'Taking Stock of the Lisbon Agenda: Is Lisbon Flawed, Necessary, Window-Dressing, or All of the Above?' EUSA Review Forum. *EUSA Review*, Vol. 19, No. 4, pp. 1–11.
World Economic Forum (2005/2006) «http://www.weforum.org/», accessed 10 January 2007.

Justice and Home Affairs

JÖRG MONAR
Université Robert Schuman de Strasbourg

Introduction

Throughout 2006 much of the EU's attention in the justice and home affairs (JHA) domain was focused on refugee and migration issues, especially because of a series of emergency situations in the Mediterranean and the Canary Islands. In response the EU expanded its external action to reduce migratory flows, particularly from African countries and reinforced its co-operation on external border protection, which gave the young FRONTEX border agency a rapidly increasing role and helped to secure substantial funding for the new External Borders Fund. In the sphere of judicial co-operation progress was made with the application of the principle of mutual recognition to both civil and criminal law matters, although other important instruments – such as the European Evidence Warrant – remained stalled. The balance sheet in the field of anti-terrorism was rather chequered, with implementation again appearing as a major problem. The European Court of Justice's (ECJ) annulment of the passenger name recognition (PNR) agreement with the US provided an interesting *intermezzo*. The decision-making and implementation problems, especially in the 'third pillar' JHA areas, prompted a substantial initiative and debate regarding the use of the Treaties' *'passerelle'* clauses, but in the end the Member States failed – at least provisionally – to agree to this form of communitarization through the back door.

Journal compilation © 2007 Blackwell Publishing Ltd, 9600 Garsington Road, Oxford OX4 2DQ, UK and 350 Main Street, Malden, MA 02148, USA

I. Developments in Individual Policy Areas

Refugee Policy

If the EU needed any reminder that its wider neighbourhood can be the source of major flows of 'real' refugees, the war in Lebanon provided a strong one, as an estimated 40,000 refugees from the conflict zone arrived by sea and air in Cyprus in July. The overwhelmed Cypriot authorities asked for a rapid evacuation of the substantial number of EU nationals, which the Commission and Member States' embassies co-ordinated in rather chaotic circumstances. The EU's 'Civil Protection Mechanism' – primarily intended to help in cases of natural disasters – was activated and several Member States sent civil protection teams to Cyprus to help the authorities cope with the situation, with the Commission's 'Monitoring and Information Centre' (MIC) serving as an assessment and co-ordination centre. An emergency aid package was also adopted to help the refugees remaining in Lebanon.

While EU action provided some relief, initial decision-making was slow; the provision of help by the other Member States varied widely and in many cases was far from rapid. The most prominent refugee policy solidarity instrument – the European Refugee Fund – again proved to be of little use due to its cumbersome procedures under which projects first need to be designed and approved before they can result in any action. In addition, the Council did not declare a situation of 'mass influx', which, under the terms of the 2001 Temporary Protection Directive, would have required the Member States to show their solidarity by each declaring how many of the refugees they would be willing to accept.

While the Lebanese refugee crisis amply demonstrated the need for further progress in EU capabilities, controversies continued to overshadow one of the most important instruments adopted so far, the December 2005 Procedures Directive (see Monar, 2006). The outrage caused in the European Parliament (EP) by the Council's final rejection of all of its proposed amendments to the Directive contributed much to the EP's application in March to the ECJ for an annulment of the Directive. As there was no legal ground on which the Parliament could attack the many substantive points of the Directive with which it disagreed, the application for annulment focused on procedural issues, namely a presumed violation of the EP's right to co-decision as regards the adoption of the common lists of 'safe countries of origin' and 'European safe third countries', which the Council had reserved to itself.[1] Crucial both for assessing the admissibility of certain asylum applications and for sending refugees back to the respective countries, these lists continued to

---

[1] Case C-133/06, *Official Journal* C 108 of 6 May 2006.

be much contested by the United Nations High Commissioner for Refugees (UNHCR) and non-governmental organizations that defend refugee rights. The Commission and the Member States themselves actually had considerable difficulties agreeing on a common list of 'safe countries of origin'. Towards the end of 2005 a list of ten African countries emerged, but major disagreements persisted, in particular, over the inclusion of Benin and Botswana (where the death penalty is applied and homosexuality is a crime) in the list and in April 2006 Commissioner Frattini dropped Niger from the list because of the continued practice of genital mutilation (*Agence Europe*, 2006). There were tensions over the list even within the Commission and during the second half of the year its adoption was put on the backburner, also in part because of the Parliament's pending Court case.

With such protracted haggling over legislative measures and their implementation, it seemed an almost logical step that on 20 February the Commission proposed strengthening 'practical co-operation', including sharing best practice in asylum procedures; adopting common guidelines on country of origin information; streamlining of procedures to make EU financial instruments more rapidly available in emergency situations; funding training measures; and beginning work on a European Support Office for all forms of co-operation in the asylum domain (Commission, 2006a). The Commission's proposals were broadly endorsed by the Council on 27 April in its 'Conclusions on strengthened practical co-operation in the field of asylum' (Council, 2006h). The Council also acknowledged the importance of strengthened practical co-operation for convergence of decision-making on asylum cases and a better pooling of resources and expertise, but was lukewarm in its support for the proposed asylum office, as many Member States remained doubtful about its added value.

During 2006 the EU also moved closer to implementing its first 'Regional Protection Programmes' (RPPs) aimed at enhancing the refugee protection capacity of countries of origin and transit through a variety of EU assistance instruments designed and implemented in co-operation with the respective countries and the UNHCR. The RPPs were all that (for the moment) had been left of the idea launched by the UK in 2003 and taken up in a different form by Germany in 2004 to establish regional protection zones in third countries where EU asylum applications could be processed outside of the EU territory. With the Council having decided towards the end of 2005 to target the RPPs at the EU's eastern neighbours – particularly Ukraine, Moldavia and Belarus – and the African Great Lakes Region – particularly Tanzania (Council, 2005a), the Commission took the first steps in 2006. The first projects of the RPP regarding Tanzania were approved in 2006 and are to be implemented during 2007 under the leadership of the UNHCR. They include strengthening the capacity of national authorities to protect refugees, improving security in refugee camps, promoting voluntary return of Burundian refugees, enhancing access to resettlement and registering refugees (Commission, 2006b, p. 26). This type of external action can be regarded as a 'softer' side of the EU's external refugee policy compared to the readmission agreements and the 'safe third country' and 'country of origin' concepts. Yet the objective of reducing the burden on Member States remains paramount as capacity-building in the respective third countries obviously serves the purpose of reducing refugee movements to the EU and increase the EU's opportunities for sending rejected asylum seekers back to those countries.

Immigration Policy

The unprecedented arrival of over 31,000 illegal immigrants in the Canary Islands during 2006, with many lives lost in the hazardous journey in unseaworthy boats from the African coast, highlighted again the challenges posed by unrelenting migration pressure on the EU. The problems were increased by the neighbouring African countries – especially Mauritania and Senegal – proving initially reluctant to take the migrants back. Malta and the Italy also continued to be major destinations for economic migrants, with the situation on the small Italian island of Lampedusa being at least as difficult as that in the Canary Islands, with more than 16,000 arrivals during the year. In the Mediterranean there were a significant number of deaths and also several incidents with patrol boats trying to prevent landings (Statewatch, 2006).

Because of the emergency situation in the Canary Islands, the Spanish Government asked for EU support as early as May, but it was provided rather slowly and even somewhat reluctantly. The Commission and some of the other Member States – Germany and the Netherlands particularly vocally – took the view that the surge in illegal arrivals was partly due to the 'regularization' of around 600,000 illegal immigrants in Spain during 2005, which had drastically increased the attractiveness of the country as a destination for economic migrants. In response the Spanish government argued that many of the migrants were coming from francophone African countries and were actually trying to reach France or other Member States. The Spanish government's demand for EU solidarity was strongly supported by Italy, which was not only facing similar problems but had also announced in May the regularization of a further 500,000 illegal immigrants. This contributed to the long-standing North–South tension in the EU over the issue of large-scale regularizations as potential 'pull-factors', with French justice minister Sarkozy in September even proposing a ban on such massive 'amnesties'.

programme without any prior warning. The mutual information mechanism might reduce the risk of such 'surprises' but there is nothing in it which obliges Member States to engage in prior consultations before decisions are taken, let alone to make national decisions dependent on the approval of the Council or Commission. Consequently, national autonomy in matters of asylum and immigration policy remains as extensive as before.

External Border and Visa Policy

The problems with illegal immigration by sea to the south pushed external border management issues in general high up the EU's agenda. The Council and Commission stretched the young FRONTEX border management agency to the limits of its capacity. It had to co-ordinate not only the HERA I and II operations mentioned above but also similar operations regarding illegal immigration in the central Mediterranean to support Malta (NAUTILUS) and in the eastern Mediterranean and on the Greek–Turkish land border (POSEI-DON). Responding to a request from the Council, the agency produced a comprehensive risk analysis of sea border security and illegal immigration in the Mediterranean. This was linked to a feasibility study (MEDSEA) on reinforcing monitoring and surveillance of the southern borders involving a Mediterranean Coastal Patrol Network, which would include both EU and north African countries. FRONTEX also provided support to Italian authorities during January and February to increase security at airports in conjunction with the enhanced passenger flow associated with the 2006 winter Olympic Games in Turin and co-ordinated activities involving 12 Member States to enhance border security in conjunction with the organization of the football World Cup in Germany. As a result of the sharp increase of demands on FRONTEX both its staff and budget grew more rapidly than planned in 2005; the budget increasing to €19 million for 2006 and €37 million for 2007.

   The illegal immigration pressure also created a sufficient critical mass in the Council for what could be called a strategic financial investment in external border management. After some haggling over overall resource allocations the Council and Parliament agreed in December to establish the new External Borders Fund foreseen by the 2004 to 2010 Hague Programme. With an estimated budget of €1.82 billion for 2007–13, the Borders Fund will be the by far biggest single financial instrument in the 'area of freedom, security and justice' (AFSJ) under the new Financial Perspective; an indication of the growing importance attached to external border security. The funds will be used to upgrade technical infrastructure at borders and support surveillance measures (Commission, 2006d). The new Borders Fund continues the 'solidarity' function of the former 'Schengen facility', the primary beneficiary of which had been Poland. This is relevant also because of the accession of Bulgaria and Romania in 2007 which are in need of support for the stretches of EU external land and sea borders they will become responsible for. Yet the new Fund has a more general 'solidarity' function because it is based on the principle that all Member States for which managing the EU's external borders causes costs exceeding other Member States' respective costs can receive financial support. This will inevitably mean some competition for the available funds and even before the Fund was established there was a degree of tension between the Mediterranean countries requesting a focus on sea borders and the eastern European countries requesting an emphasis on land borders (Finnish Ministry of Interior, 2006).

The Schengen border system – which remains the core of EU external border policy – was legally consolidated through the adoption on 15 March of the Regulation establishing the Schengen Borders Code (European Parliament/Council, 2006a), which entered into force on 13 October. The new Code constitutes primarily a streamlined codification of existing Schengen rules – mainly from the Schengen Manual – regarding the movement of persons across both external and internal borders, but it also further develops parts of the *acquis*, especially as regards control and surveillance measures at maritime borders, document security and the procedural rights of third-country nationals regarding checks and refusals of entry.

The Schengen countries' road towards their 'second-generation' Schengen Information System (SIS), crucial both for completing the incorporation of the new Member States and adding new law enforcement functionalities, continued to lengthen. The 'SIS II' had originally been intended to become operational by 2007, but complications during the process of awarding the necessary contracts to private companies, unresolved data protection issues and delays due to the need to adopt separate legal instruments under the 'first' and the 'third' pillars have forced Council and Commission to reschedule the entire process.

Part of the blame, however, lies with the Commission's ineffective management. In July the Commission postponed its estimate for the completion of the SIS II to the second half of 2008 at the earliest and the first half of 2009 at the latest. The delays caused a storm of protest in some of the new EU/Schengen members – especially the Czech Republic and Poland – which were not willing to wait that long for full integration into *Schengenland* and the lifting of internal border controls. The presidents of the four Visegrád countries expressed their anger in no uncertain terms at a summit meeting near Prague on 15 to 16 September, with some suggesting even hidden political motives behind the apparently technical delays (*Prague Post*, 2006). In response, the JHA Council on 4 to 5 December 2006 reached a compromise that foresees the development of an intermediate system – with the rather peculiar acronym of *SISone4all* – that will not have all the functionalities of the eventual SIS, but which will allow to integrate the new Schengen members by March 2008 at the latest (Council, 2006c). The row over the SIS II delay revealed again the sensitivity of the new Member States to the persisting Schengen controls dividing them from the 'old' EU. This sensitivity about presumed 'second class' treatment does not really reflect reality as Italy, for instance, although an EC founding member, had to wait no less than seven years after having signed up to the Schengen system before controls were lifted. Yet the year ended on a positive note for the SIS II with the Council finally adopting, on 20 December, the Regulation on the establishment, operation and use of the new system, which incorporated the various compromises negotiated on the system's new functionalities and data-exchange arrangements (European Parliament/Council, 2006b). The only remaining questions are if and when these will eventually be transformed into technical reality.

After years of negotiations, on 20 December the Parliament and Council adopted a Regulation on local border traffic at external borders (European Parliament/Council, 2006c), which provides for the possibility of issuing a 'local border traffic permit' to third-country nationals in border areas, dispensing with any visa requirement for crossings within the 'border area'. This was a major victory for the new Member States, which had long insisted on a derogation from the Schengen visa regime in order to reduce the negative impact of 'hard' external Schengen borders on trade, social or cultural exchange and regional co-operation in border regions. Unlike the three months Schengen visa, the 'border traffic permit' can be valid for between one and five years, reducing both cost and administrative hassle for the affected border residents. The 'softening' effects on the Schengen external borders will be limited, though, as the definition of 'border area' has been limited to 30 kilometres and beneficiaries will have to provide 'legitimate reasons' for obtaining such a permit; will remain subject to full Schengen security screening rules and entry and exit checks; and will have to pay a fee up to the same amount charged for a Schengen visa.

Judicial Co-operation

There were several important steps forward with regard to judicial co-operation in civil matters, particularly with regard to mutual recognition of judicial decisions, a core element of the EU's 'area of justice' concept. After protracted negotiations, the Parliament and Council adopted, on 12 December, a Regulation creating a European order for payment procedure, the aim of which is to simplify the collection of uncontested debts between Member States (European Parliament/Council, 2006d). The Regulation lays down a standard form of order to be issued by a court having jurisdiction under the rules of the 2001 'Brussels I' Regulation (EC No. 44/2001) at the request of the creditor. If the claimant's application meets the formal conditions for issuing such an order, the order is to be served on the defendant debtor. The defendant has the opportunity to oppose the claim. If s/he does so, the proceedings will continue before the court that issued the order as a normal civil or commercial litigation. If, however, the defendant does not oppose the claim, the order becomes automatically enforceable and no further *exequatur* is necessary, which in most cases will drastically reduce the time and costs involved in settling claims. The European Order for Payment will not only facilitate the settling of cross-border pecuniary claims for companies but also for citizens who may, for instance, have legitimate claims regarding accidents suffered or faulty products bought in another Member State.

Further progress was made in judicial co-operation in criminal matters with the adoption on 6 October of a Framework Decision on the application of the mutual recognition principle to confiscation orders (Council, 2006b). The Framework Decision is aimed at facilitating and accelerating the implementation of post-trial confiscation orders against proceeds from crime (money and/or other items of property) issued by one Member State in other Member States. It reduces the grounds for refusal of a confiscation order issued by abolishing the principle of double criminality for 32 forms of serious crime (including membership in a criminal organization, terrorism, trafficking in human beings, money laundering and forgery of means of payment) and by limiting the reasons for non-recognition and non-execution to a number of formal criteria. A central element of the procedure is a 'certificate', which has to accompany the confiscation order. Given that there have been quite a few problems with European Arrest Warrant forms not being completed correctly, the ten printed pages of the 'certificate' could lead to some practical problems. Yet, if the procedural requirements are met and there are no formal grounds for refusal, the competent authorities of the requested Member State(s) have to execute it 'forthwith'. In practice, however, the effectiveness of the confiscation orders could be reduced by the legal remedies granted to interested parties in the executing state, especially as these may have suspensive effect, although the substantial reasons for issuing the order cannot be challenged in the executing state. The Framework Decision of 6 October can be regarded as an overdue parallel to the European Arrest Warrant. Yet its adoption took four years from the original Danish proposal, a delay due mainly to the unanimity requirement under the 'third pillar' and national parliament reservations.

The same problems also affected the decision-making process on the European Evidence Warrant, which was destined to facilitate and accelerate the collection of evidence in other Member States for criminal proceedings. Despite more than two years of intense negotiations the Council – after protracted negotiations over, *inter alia*, the area of application and grounds for refusal – could only agree on a 'general approach' in June (Council, 2006d). This agreement was in several respects well short of the ambitions of the Commission's November 2003 proposal. The problems of decision-making on this and other 'third pillar' instruments prompted the Commission in June to propose a major reform regarding the use of the EU Treaty's *'passerelle'* provisions (see below).

The Fight Against Terrorism

After the partial reorientation of the EU's anti-terrorism approach at the end of 2005 (see Monar, 2006), the focus during the year was on implementing the new 'Strategy'. On the prevention side, the most innovative element of the 2005 reorientation, more community policing has been promoted as one way to counter radicalization and recruitment, through both training provided by the European Police College and national measures. The Commission established an expert group to provide advice on terrorist recruitment and violent radicalization patterns and in June the Council approved a 'Media Communication Strategy' to counter terrorist propaganda. On the external side, meetings for the promotion of interfaith dialogue were held and radicalization and recruitment issues have been included in capacity-building co-operation with third-countries, most notably in the case of Morocco and Algeria. On the protection side, the Commission tightened airport security measures under its implementing powers – especially as regards the size of cabin luggage and liquids which can be brought onboard – after British authorities announced in August a foiled terrorist attack on a plane at Heathrow airport and Council and Parliament agreed to expand the budget earmarked for security-related research in the 7th Research Framework Programme (2007–13), with terrorism as one of the key issues, to an unprecedented €1.4 billion. As regards the persecution of terrorist activities, progress was made with the implementation of previously agreed measures against terrorist financing, a handbook of 'best practices' in counter-terrorism for local law enforcement commanders was approved by the Police Chiefs Task Force and law enforcement co-operation with several third-countries has been expanded, including, for instance, the conclusion of an agreement between Eurojust with the US Department of Justice. On the 'response' side, i.e. preparations for the aftermath of terrorist attacks, work continued on improving emergency and crisis co-ordination mechanisms and better preparations for potential bioterrorist attacks (Council 2006e, 2006f). The formal adoption on 15 March of the Directive on the retention of telecommunication data (European Parliament/Council, 2006e), which obliges telephony and internet providers to retain for 6 to 24 months certain telecommunication data for possible law enforcement purposes, also formed part of the EU's growing anti-terrorism armoury.

Yet the overall picture of EU anti-terrorism action was far from being only positive. EU Counter-Terrorism Co-ordinator Gijs De Vries had to point again to serious deficits in both decision-making – such as the delay of the European Evidence Warrant (see above) – and implementation. As regards the latter, less than half of the Member States, for instance, had implemented in November the 2003 Framework Decision on the freezing of property and evidence although the deadline had been set for August 2005. Implementation of the 2002 Framework Decision on the European Arrest Warrant was also slow and uneven and – after six years (!) – five Member States had still not ratified and/or implemented the 2000 Convention on mutual legal assistance (Council, 2006f). Mr De Vries also criticized the fact that the network of the Financial Intelligence Units was still incomplete, that not much progress had been made on the abuse of the non-profit sector by terrorist financiers Action Taskforces, that any emergency deployment of the special intervention units of Member States regrouped in the so-called 'Atlas' network was obstructed by the Council's failure to reach unanimity on an appropriate legal framework and that the Council had failed to give an appropriate follow-up to the considerable difficulties in communication and co-ordination which a 2005 cross-border exercise regarding a simulated terrorist attack with small-pox had revealed (Council, 2006f). At the end of the year it seemed that the 2005 expansion of the anti-terrorism Strategy and Action Plan and Strategy had only made it more difficult for the EU to arrive at a better prioritization and to match better decisions with effective implementation.

The EU's international position in the fight against terrorism suffered a certain embarrassment when on 30 May the ECJ annulled the Council decision to conclude the agreement with the United States (US) on the anti-terrorism related processing and transfer of passenger name records (PNR) data (Joined Cases C-317/04 and C-318/04), forcing the EU to terminate the agreement and come to a new arrangement with the US before the deadline of 30 September set by the Court. The EP had sought this annulment in May 2004 because of both its concerns about adequate protection of personal data and its aim of asserting co-decision rights. Yet in its judgement the Court did not enter into the substance of the data protection arguments put forward by the Parliament and annulled both the Commission's data protection 'adequacy' decision and the Council's decision to conclude the agreement

Journal compilation © 2007 Blackwell Publishing Ltd

only on grounds of the chosen 'first pillar' legal base not being adequate. As a result, the Parliament's successful application for annulment turned into what could be qualified as a major 'Pyrrhic legal victory' as the Court's ruling not only made Council and Commission move to a 'third pillar' legal base for the renegotiation of the agreement – which excluded the Parliament even further – but also provided the US Government with an opportunity to force the EU to accept that the operation of the agreement would be automatically subject to subsequent changes in US legislation. Faced with the prospect of a total disintegration of the common EU approach on the PNR issue, chaos for airline passengers and huge costs for carriers in case of a non-continuation of the agreement, the Council accepted in October the US Government's letter containing the new 'interpretation' of the agreement (OJ C 259, 27.10), with the renewed outrage in the EP about this development looking rather self-inflicted. The case of the PNR agreement amply demonstrated the extent of the negative implications which the EU's complex legal architecture in the JHA domain can have on related action in external relations.

II. A New Reform Debate: The Struggle Over the Use of the *'Passerelle'* Provisions

After the setback of the Constitutional Treaty it had for a time become relatively quiet about the question of further reform of EU policy-making capabilities in the JHA domain. Yet the issue continued to loom in the background as it was clear that frustration over the slow progress in some fields – especially those still falling under the unanimity rule – was growing both in some capitals and the Commission. The political risk of this frustration leading to further fragmentation of the 'area of freedom, security and justice' continued to grow. Already on 27 May 2005 seven Member States (Austria, Belgium, Germany, Spain, France, Luxembourg and the Netherlands) had signed – entirely outside of the EU Treaty framework – the Convention of Prüm. The convention focused on stepping up co-operation in the fight against terrorism, cross-border crime and illegal immigration in respect of a number of sensitive issues such as the automated exchange of DNA and fingerprint data, the supply of data on the basis of the principle of availability and the deployment of 'air marshals' in civil aircraft (Council, 2005b). The Prüm participants continued to pursue the ratification of their Convention during the year in spite of criticisms raised against this by-passing of the EU framework and the *de facto* exclusion of the other Member States. At the same time, the so-called 'G-6' group of Member States – established in 2003 and comprising France, Germany, Italy, Poland, Spain and the UK – proceeded with its own separate co-operation on JHA issues: at a meeting near Stratford-upon-Avon on 26 October, the G-6 ministers agreed to co-operate more closely on terrorist threat identifications, the monitoring of website use by terrorist groups, sharing research on explosive, high-tech airport screening devices and the tackling of so-called 'carousel-fraud' against national VAT systems (UK Home Office, 2006).

Before this background of risks of further fragmentation and action outside of the EU framework as a result of groups of Member States seeking progress on their own, the Commission identified on 28 June in a Communication to Council and Parliament on the implementation of the Hague Programme problems of decision-making and implementation in the fields of police and judicial co-operation in criminal matters. It cited in particular the problems of agreeing on the European Evidence Warrant, on basic minimum standards for procedural rights, on condemning in the same way offences of racism and xenophobia throughout the Union and on authorizing further cross-border investigation and prosecution (Commission, 2006c). The Commission's proposal to overcome the 'numerous blockages' was encouraged by similar proposals of the French Government of 20 April (French Ministry of Foreign Affairs, 2006) and in the EP's resolution of 14 June. The Commission proposed to use Article 42 TEC to transfer matters currently falling under the 'third pillar' (Title VI TEU) to the 'first (Community) pillar' (Title IV TEC) and to use Article 67(2), second indent, TEC to bring legal migration under the EC co-decision procedure and to extend the powers of the ECJ. This use of the so-called '*passerelle*' ('bridging clause') provisions, for which Commissioner Franco Frattini campaigned with unusual vigour, got substantial backing from the incoming Finnish Presidency. In a note for the Informal JHA Ministerial Meeting in September 2006, the Finnish Presidency broadly endorsed the Commission's proposals and came out strongly in favour of a transfer of all matters under the current 'third pillar' to the 'first' as well as the adoption of all future measures under the co-decision procedure with qualified majority voting. However, being aware of the reservations of some Member States, the Presidency conceded that consideration should be given to requiring unanimity in the Council, after consultation of the EP, for particularly sensitive issues and it also pointed to the possibility of agreeing on a transitional period (of, for example, five years) for implementing the move towards co-decision. The Presidency note also backed the use of the second bridging clause regarding legal migration and the extension of the powers of the ECJ (the latter, however, with a more guarded language) (Finnish Ministry of Justice, 2006).

Yet the Commission's proposals have met with resistance right from the outset. The German Minister for Europe, Günter Gloser, rejected almost immediately the suggested use of the 'bridging clauses' as 'cherry picking' parts of the EU's Constitutional Treaty, which Germany intended to revive when taking over the EU's Presidency in 2008. There were also negative signals from Denmark, Holland, Ireland and Sweden (Euractiv, 2006). The British government, traditionally a staunch defender of national veto possibilities in the 'third pillar' fields, indicated a more flexible attitude, mainly because of concerns about the effectiveness of EU action in the fight against terrorism. Yet in a report on 'Developments in the European Union' adopted on 19 July, the Foreign Affairs Committee of the House of Commons came out sharply against the Commission's proposals, mainly because of concerns about the undermining of British veto possibilities (House of Commons, 2006). In the run-up to the Informal Ministerial Meeting in Tampere on 20 to 22 September, both the German and the Irish position against the Commission's proposals hardened in spite of strong backing by the Finnish Presidency, with the British government also shifting towards a more sceptical attitude. It also became clear, though, that both the German and the Irish Government had major concerns about giving up national veto possibilities in the sensitive field of criminal justice co-operation, especially as the proposed use of the 'bridging clauses' for the AFSJ would not give them what they had obtained 'in return' in the Constitutional Treaty for accepting such a move (*EUobserver*, 2006). In these circumstances the EU ministers of justice and of the interior were, unsurprisingly, unable to reach a consensus on the Commission's proposals at the Tampere meeting. At the JHA Council of 5 October the Finnish Presidency announced that it would seek to bring the matter on the agenda of the December European Council. But with the incoming Presidencies of both Germany and Portugal firmly committing themselves to a re-launching the Constitutional Treaty project during 2007 the 'bridging clause' option was at least temporarily put on the backburner at the European Council meeting of 14–15 December. In the end, the Finnish Presidency got only some rather vague reference to the need for the framework of the AFSJ of being 'genuinely strengthened in order to meet present challenges' and an affirmation of the 'principles acknowledged in the context of the Union's reform process' (Council 2006g, p. 6).

Although the '*passerelle*' initiative ended in provisional failure, the debate showed that most Member States were willing to back a use of the 'bridging clauses', making it likely that the initiative could be relaunched if the German and Portuguese Presidencies did not succeed in their attempts to rescue parts or all of the Constitutional Treaty. While the British House of Commons Foreign Affairs Committee was not alone in seeing there an attempt to introduce parts of the Constitutional Treaty – which it rather unceremoniously described as 'comatose and on life-support' – through the back door (House of

Commons, 2006), there can be little doubt that the proposals were primarily motivated by improving EU decision-making and implementation capacity in the JHA domain. It is an altogether different question whether the *'passerelle'* initiative was launched at the right time, given that the door towards a rescue of at least parts of the Constitutional Treaty reforms appeared not yet definitely closed. The very fact, however, that such a substantial reform initiative was taken and seriously discussed is a reflection of the continuing problems with sustaining the momentum of the construction of the 'area of freedom, security and justice' against a range of blockages and performance deficits for which the reporting period provided again ample evidence.

Key readings

For a survey and discussion of key issues of the current development of the AFSJ, see the special issue of the *Revista de Derecho de la Unión Europea* by Linde Panagia *et al.* (2006) and – with a focus on the implementation of the Hague programme – Zwaan and Goudappel (2006). Peers (2006) provides a very comprehensive, systematic and critical account of the legal issues of the AFSJ.

References

Agence Europe (2006) 29 April.

Bloomberg News (2006) 22 September.

Commission of the European Communities (2006a) 'Communication on Strengthened Practical Co-operation, New Structures, New Approaches: Improving the Quality of Decision Making in the Common European Asylum System', COM(2006)67, 17 February.

Commission of the European Communities (2006b) 'Communication on the Global Approach to Migration One Year On: Towards a Comprehensive European Migration Policy', COM(2006)735, 30 November.

Commission of the European Communities (2006c) 'Communication on Implementing the Hague Programme: The Way Forward', COM(2006)331, 28 June.

Commission of the European Communities (2006d) 'Funding Agreement to Further Develop a Comprehensive European Migration Policy', Press Release IP/06/1813, 14 December.

Council (2005a) 2686th Council Meeting, General Affairs and External Relations', Brussels, 7 November, Press Release 13621/05.

Council (2005b) 'Prüm Convention', 10900/05, Brussels, 7 July.

Council (2006a) 'Decision on the Establishment of a Mutual Information Mechanism Concerning Member States' Measures in the Areas of Asylum and Immigration', OJ L 283, 14 October.

Council (2006b) 'Council Framework Decision 2006/783/JHA on the Application of the Principle of Mutual Recognition to Confiscation Orders', OJ L 328, 24 November.

Council (2006c) 2768th Council Meeting, Justice and Home Affairs', Brussels, 4–5 December, Press Release 15801/06.

Council (2006d) 2732nd Council Meeting, Justice and Home Affairs', Luxembourg, 1–2 June, Press Release 9409/06.

Council (2006e) 'Implementation of the Action Plan to Combat Terrorism', 9589/06, Brussels, 19 May.

Council (2006f) 'Implementation of the Strategy and Action Plan to Combat Terrorism', 15266/1/06, Brussels, 24 November.

Council (2006g) Brussels European Council, 14–15 December 2006: Presidency Conclusions, 16879/06.

Council (2006h) 'Conclusions on Strengthened Practical Co-operation in the Field of Asylum', 8240/06.

Euractiv (2006) 29 June.

European Parliament/Council (2000) 'Regulation (EC) No. 44/2001 on Jurisdiction and the Recognition and Enforcement of Judgments in Civil and Commercial Matters', 22 December.

European Parliament/Council (2006a) 'Regulation (EC) No. 562/2006 Establishing a Community Code on the Rules Governing the Movement of Persons Across Borders (Schengen Borders Code)', OJ L 105, 13 April.

European Parliament/Council (2006b) 'Regulation (EC) No. 1987/2006 on the Establishment, Operation and Use of the Second Generation Schengen Information System (SIS II)', OJ L 381, 28 December.

European Parliament/Council (2006c) 'Regulation (EC) No. 1931/2006 Laying Down Rules on Local Border Traffic at the External Land Borders of the Member States and Amending the Provisions of the Schengen Convention', OJ L 405, 30 December.

European Parliament/Council (2006d) 'Regulation (EC) No. 1896/2006 Creating a European Order for Payment Procedure', OJ L 399, 30 December.

European Parliament/Council (2006e) 'Directive 2006/24/EC on the Retention of Data Generated or Processed in Connection with the Provision of Publicly Available Electronic Communications Services or of Public Communications Networks', OJ L 105, 13 April.

EUobserver (2006) 29 September.

French Ministry of Foreign Affairs (2006) Letter of French Minister for European Affairs Catherine Colonna and French Foreign Minister Philippe Douste-Blazy to Austrian Foreign Minister Ursula Plassnik of 20 April and attached 'Contribution française sur les améliorations institutionnelles à partir du cadre des traités existants', available at: «http://www.rpfrance.eu/article.php3?id_article=437#sommaire_2».

Finnish Ministry of Interior (2006) 'Financing of Management of Migration Flows', Helsinki, 7 September.

Finnish Ministry of Justice and Ministry of Interior (2006) 'Improvement of Decision-making in Justice and Home Affairs. Note for the Informal JHA Ministerial Meeting in Tampere', Helsinki, 30 August.

Frontex (2006) 'Canary Islands – Hera' Fact Sheet, 19 December 2006, available at: «http://www.frontex.europa.eu/examples_of_accomplished_operati/art5.html».

House of Commons (2006) 'House of Commons Foreign Affairs Committee: Developments in the European Union', Sixth Report of Session 2005–06, HC 768, 26 July.

Linde Panagia, E. *et al.* (2006) La Unión europea como espacio de libertad, seguridad y justicia, *Revista de Derecho de la Unión Europea* (special issue) (Madrid: UNED).

Monar, J. (2006) 'Justice and Home Affairs', *JCMS Annual Review* 2005, pp. 101–17.

Peers, S. (2006) *EU Justice and Home Affairs Law* (Oxford: Oxford University Press).

Prague Post (2006) 20 September.

Statewatch (2006) 'EU/Africa: Carnage Continues', September, available at: «http://www.statewatch.org/news/2006/sep/Immigration-analysis.pdf».

UK Home Office (2006) 'Call to Action at G6 Meeting', Press Release, 26 October, available at: «http://www.homeoffice.gov.uk/about-us/news/g6-results».

Zwaan, J. and Goudappel, F. (eds) (2006) *Freedom, Security and Justice in the European Union: Implementation of the Hague Programme* (The Hague: TMC Asser Press).

JCMS 2007 Volume 45 Annual Review pp. 125–142

Legal Developments

MICHAEL DOUGAN
Liverpool Law School, University of Liverpool

Introduction

The Community courts, during the course of 2006, delivered several judgements that attained a relatively high public profile: for example, *Parliament v. Council and Commission* on the controversial agreement between the Community and the US on the transfer of air passenger data (see Monar, this volume);[1] *Commission v. Cresson* on the appropriate penalties to be imposed on the disgraced former Commissioner whose conduct helped bring down the Santer Commission in 1999;[2] and the ruling in *Joustra* on the payment of excise duties on alcoholic beverages intended for personal consumption purchased over the internet and delivered by a transport undertaking.[3] Of course, many other rulings received less press coverage, but are significant for the development of Community law: for example, *Commission v. Spain* on the relationship between alerts issued under the Schengen Information System and the right to free movement for the family members of EU citizens;[4] *Commission v. Ireland* on the scope of a Member State's duty to respect the European Court of Justice's (ECJ) exclusive jurisdiction to resolve disputes concerning the interpretation and application of provisions of Community law;[5] *Cadman* on the degree to which the Treaty rules on equal treatment

---

[1] Cases C-317 & 318/04 *Parliament v. Council and Commission* (30 May 2006).
[2] Case C-432/04 *Commission v. Cresson* (11 July 2006).
[3] Case C-5/05 *Joustra* (23 November 2006).
[4] Case C-503/06 *Commission v. Spain* (31 January 2006).
[5] Case C-459/03 *Commission v. Ireland* (30 May 2006).

between men and women permit employers to use length of service as a
relevant criterion in determining levels of pay;[6] and *Adeneler* on the extent of
the national court's obligation to further the objectives of a Community
directive before the deadline for its implementation has expired.[7]

This chapter, however, offers a more detailed analysis of several other
rulings delivered by the Community courts that are particularly relevant for
legal developments in the European Union (EU): the exportation of welfare
benefits; rights in European Parliament elections; the status of the Charter of
Fundamental Rights; and the fight against terrorism.

I. The Exportation of Welfare Benefits and Its Impact on National Social Solidarity

One of the defining characteristics of national welfare systems has been their
territorial nature, in particular, restricting the payment of benefits to residents.
In order to facilitate the free movement of persons, Community law has made
significant incursions into that territoriality principle, especially under Regulation 1408/71 on the co-ordination of national social security systems.[8] This
measure provides for the exportation of certain welfare benefits by their
claimants across the Member States and some of those only under relatively
strict conditions.

In the mid-1990s, the Court began to interpret the Treaty's free movement
provisions so as to catch not only discriminatory provisions imposed by the
host state, but also non-discriminatory barriers to movement, including those
imposed by the home state. In particular, the Court developed the principle
that a Member State that effectively penalizes its nationals for leaving the
territory in order to exercise their free movement rights in another Member
State must justify its conduct by reference to a valid public interest objective
and the principle of proportionality.

It was not long before claimants began to explore the potential application
of this principle to challenge the territorial restrictions imposed by national
welfare states on the payment of benefits – attempting, in effect, to create a
principle of exportation beyond (and perhaps even despite) the provisions of
Regulation 1408/71. Two major judgements from 2006 demonstrate the difficult questions raised by this caselaw: *Watts*, on the obligation of national
authorities to pay for healthcare received in another Member State;[9] and *De*

---

[6] Case C-17/05 *Cadman* (3 October 2006).
[7] Case C-212/04 *Adeneler* (4 July 2006).
[8] Last consolidated text, OJ 1997 L 28, p. 1. Shortly to be replaced, for most purposes, by the new
co-ordination regime contained in Regulation 883/2004, OJ 2004 L 200, p. 1.
[9] Case C-372/04 *Watts* (16 May 2006).

Cuyper, concerning a Member State's competence to restrict unemployment benefits to claimants resident within its territory.[10]

The Ruling in Watts

The caselaw on cross-border access to healthcare is rooted in the principle that a Member State that refuses to pay for medical treatment received in another EU country, under the same conditions as it pays for healthcare domestically, is effectively penalizing its nationals for having exercised their freedom to receive services under Article 49 EC. In the process of justifying such restrictions on the Treaty's free movement provisions, the Court has created an obligation upon Member States to reimburse persons insured under the national healthcare system for the costs of treatment received abroad: under relatively generous conditions in the case of non-hospital treatment; under more stringent but carefully delimited conditions in the case of hospital treatment.

The claimant in *Watts* was a British national who was told that she would have to wait three to four months for surgery on her arthritic hips at a National Health Service (NHS) hospital (she was initially told there would be a one year wait, but this was reduced following a medical re-examination). The claimant sought permission from her local healthcare trust to have her surgery abroad, but authorization was refused on the grounds that there was no 'undue delay' in providing treatment within the NHS. Nonetheless, Watts had a hip operation in France and sought reimbursement from her local healthcare trust of the medical fees incurred.

The Court's ruling develops the caselaw on cross-border healthcare in several significant ways. First, there is the question whether Article 49 EC applies only to specific types of healthcare systems. Can it apply only to healthcare systems (such as that in the Netherlands) in which patients' sickness insurance funds contract institutions to provide patients with medical services or does it also apply to national health systems (like the NHS) where the public authorities are directly responsible for the organization and delivery of medical services? Previous caselaw was ambiguous on this point. In some rulings, the Court hinted that the application of Article 49 EC was justified by the existence of two 'commercial' transactions for the provision of services: payment by a sickness fund to its contracted institutions; and payment by the patient to a foreign institution.[11] That would catch healthcare systems like the Dutch, but not those like the British, since there is no 'commercial' relationship between the sickness fund and contracted institutions. In other cases,

---

[10] Case C-406/04 *De Cuyper* (18 July 2006).
[11] Case C-157/99 *Peerbooms* [2001] ECR I-5473.

however, the Court suggested that Article 49 EC could apply *solely* on the basis of the patient's payment for medical services provided by a foreign institution, thus applying to systems such as the NHS.[12] *Watts* confirms unequivocally that the latter interpretation is correct – which ensures that all patients can, in principle, enjoy the same opportunities to seek cross-border healthcare at their home state's expense, regardless of the manner in which the national healthcare system happens to be organized.

The second issue concerned the requirement of 'undue delay' in providing treatment to a patient within the national healthcare system, as a pre-condition for granting authorization to receive treatment abroad instead. In particular, should 'undue delay' be calculated by reference solely to the individual patient's clinical needs; or can Member States also consider the average waiting time for treatment under the local healthcare system? The Court in *Watts* recognized that the national authorities are entitled to institute a system of waiting lists in order to manage supply and set priorities on the basis of available resources. However, the Member State must ensure that the waiting time dictated by general planning objectives does not exceed the period that is medically acceptable having regard to the clinical needs of the individual patient.[13] This aspect of the judgement has attracted much criticism: balanced against the Court's well-intentioned desire to minimize the pain and suffering of individuals by liberalizing the conditions under which they might travel to another Member State for treatment is the fear that precious resources that could be invested in reducing waiting lists for all patients are being diverted in favour of paying for the treatment of those with the confidence and resources to challenge their allotted waiting time. Is such an individual right to 'queue jump' really compatible with the principle of collective solidarity which is meant to underpin the national welfare system?

That concern is reinforced by the third major issue addressed by the Court in *Watts*: the range of costs that patients are entitled to reimbursement from their home state. In particular, the Court held that Member States are not obliged to pay for any ancillary costs incurred by the patient, such as travel and accommodation (other than in the foreign hospital itself), save where such costs would be covered in the case of treatment provided within the national healthcare system.[14] There are concerns that the Court's caselaw is therefore likely to benefit a particular type of patient: those confident and articulate enough to challenge their place in the national waiting list and to travel to receive medical treatment in a foreign institution and also able to pay

---

[12] Case C-385/99 *Müller-Fauré* [2003] ECR I-4509.
[13] Cp. Case C-385/99 *Müller-Fauré* [2003] ECR I-4509. See now Article 20(2) Regulation 883/2004, OJ 2004 L 200, p. 1.
[14] On this point, see also Case C-466/04 *Herrera* (15 June 2006).

for all associated costs, including (for example) those incurred in being accompanied by relatives or friends. In other words, will the possibility of 'queue jumping' be reserved, in practice, to the middle classes?

Finally, the ruling in *Watts* sheds interesting light on the relationship between the system of cross-border healthcare established under Article 49 EC and that operating under Article 22 Regulation 1408/71 (which had already established a system of prior authorization in respect of non-emergency medical treatment). In particular, the Court seems to have completed the process of equalizing the substantive conditions applicable to each regime, under which national authorities must grant authorization to receive hospital treatment in another Member State: the definition of 'undue delay' for the purposes of Article 49 EC is to be applied also for the purposes of interpreting Article 22 Regulation 1408/71. This begs the question: what is the point of having a 'new' system of reimbursement under Article 49 EC at all, when the 'old' co-ordination system established by the Regulation could do the job just as well? In fact, the two systems remain distinct and wily patients (or rather their lawyers) will negotiate the best deal possible from their national healthcare system using a complex interplay between the Treaty and the Regulation. For example, the Regulation continues to offer distinct advantages to patients who travel from a relatively limited sickness insurance system to a relatively generous one, since it requires the home state to cover the cost of treatment as if the patient were insured in the host state (whereas Article 49 EC would tie the claimant to the levels of cover available in the home state). Conversely, the Treaty can be cited where the patient moves from a relatively munificent sickness insurance system to a more restricted one, since the patient can then rely on Article 49 EC to benefit from the full extent of cover provided by the home state. Moreover, the Treaty clearly offers more than the Regulation when it comes to extramural treatment, where Article 49 EC precludes any requirement of prior authorization being imposed by the home state as a precondition for reimbursement.

The Ruling in De Cuyper

Watts therefore shows how the Court's caselaw can complicate the relationship between Treaty provisions and applicable secondary legislation. The same forces are clearly at work, albeit in a very different context, in the *De Cuyper* case. This concerned a Belgian national in receipt of unemployment benefit. Under Belgian law, qualification for unemployment benefit depended on the claimant being resident within the national territory. De Cuyper claimed to satisfy that requirement, but it later transpired that he was actually living in France, at which point the Belgian authorities stopped paying his unemployment benefit. This appeared to be in full accordance with Regulation 1408/71, which requires the Member States to guarantee the exportation of unemployment benefits only in very limited circumstances, none of which were applicable to De Cuyper.

The ECJ, however, followed a very different style of reasoning. As an EU citizen, De Cuyper was entitled to free movement across the Member States pursuant to Article 18 EC. Even though the Belgian legislation conformed to the requirements of Regulation 1408/71, the residence requirement still had the effect of placing De Cupyer at a disadvantage simply because he had exercised his right to free movement. The onus therefore fell on Belgium to justify this restriction by reference to a legitimate public interest objective and the principle of proportionality. The Court accepted that the Belgian legislation could indeed be justified by the need for the national authorities to monitor compliance with the statutory requirements governing unemployment benefits (such as whether the claimant lived alone, or had undeclared income). A residence requirement was both appropriate and necessary to achieve that objective, since a truly effective system of monitoring required both unexpected and on the spot controls.

The significance of *De Cuyper* lies not in its final outcome, but rather in the conceptual framework laid down by the Court for assessing territorial restrictions on the payment of social security benefits. Before, Community law took for granted that national welfare systems are territorially bound and naturally entitled to restrict the payment of benefits to residents; Regulation 1408/71 merely created certain exceptions to that territoriality principle for the benefit of certain classes of migrant individuals. Now, however, Community law takes as its starting point the idea that *any* refusal by the Member State to export its own social security benefits constitutes a *prima facie* breach of the EU citizen's free movement rights which must be scrutinized to ensure it is genuinely necessary in the public interest. To that extent, *De Cuyper* signals a dramatic change in one of the conceptual foundations of the European welfare state: the exportation of benefits is no longer to be treated as some sort of privilege generously bestowed by the Community legislature upon its subjects; rather, the territoriality of the national social security systems is presumed to be a limitation on the full economic and social integration of EU citizens which requires justification.

This conceptual (r)evolution would be problematic enough if it merely pitted national territorial restrictions against the primary Treaty provisions. But the situation is rendered more complex by the fact that Regulation 1408/71 *already* exists precisely in order to negotiate a compromise between the domestic welfare states and the objective of free movement for persons. It is one thing for the Court to decide that a Member State's refusal to export benefits is a *prima facie* breach of the primary Treaty provisions, as regards those situations falling altogether outside the scope of the Regulation 1408/71.[15] It is another thing for the Court to identify and investigate barriers to free movement in those situations which are already subject to regulatory intervention by the Community legislature. The healthcare caselaw illustrates one facet of the resulting problems: two independent but interactive systems of exportation now operate in parallel to produce an increasingly complex body of legal rules.

De Cuyper illustrates how those problems can run even deeper: the Court makes clear that the relationship between the right to free movement under Article 18 EC and the co-ordination system contained in Regulation 1408/71 is not parallel but hierarchical. That is why Belgium's refusal to export its unemployment benefits had to be objectively justified, even though it was totally compatible with the co-ordination system. Future caselaw will have to explore the resultant tensions, not only between national conceptions of social solidarity and Treaty ambitions relating to EU citizenship, but also between the ECJ and the Community legislature over ultimate responsibility for the Community's emergent welfare law.

II. Rights to Vote and Stand in Elections to the European Parliament

In two major cases, the Court was asked to clarify the link between EU citizenship and the right to vote and be elected to the European Parliament (EP).

Spain v. United Kingdom raised the question whether *only* EU citizens were entitled to vote and stand in elections to the EP, or whether those rights could *also* be extended to certain third-country nationals.[16] Here, Spain argued that the UK had unlawfully extended the right to vote and be elected in EP elections to persons who are not British nationals for the purposes of Community law, in particular, certain third-country nationals – 'qualifying Commonwealth citizens' or QCCs – resident in Gibraltar. The relevant UK legislation was adopted so as to comply with the ruling of the European Court of Human Rights in *Matthews*, which had found that the fundamental rights of Gibraltarians were infringed by the lack of any right to vote in EP elections.[17] QCCs resident in the UK are also entitled to vote and stand in EP elections, but Spain's complaint was confined to the territory of Gibraltar.

---

[15] On this issue, consider also Case C-192/05 *Tas-Hagen* (26 October 2006).
[16] Case C-145/04 *Spain v. United Kingdom* (12 September 2006).
[17] Application No. 24833/94 *Matthews v. UK* (18 February 1999).

The Court noted that none of the relevant Treaty provisions (Articles 189 and 190 EC, Articles 17 and 19 EC) or the 1976 Act concerning the election of representatives of the European Parliament by direct universal suffrage expressly and precisely defines who is entitled to vote/stand in the EP elections. Moreover, none of those provisions excludes the possibility that a third-country national might be entitled to do so. It therefore fell to the Court to ascertain whether there nevertheless exists a clear link between EU citizenship and the rights to vote/stand, such as to require that those rights must always be limited to EU citizens. No such principle could be divined from the relevant legislation: for example, the reference in Articles 189 and 190 EC to the EP representing the 'peoples of the Member States' had different meanings in different countries and languages; similarly, certain other rights conferred by the Treaty upon EU citizens (such as the right to petition the EP or complain to the Ombudsman) may in fact be exercised by any resident of the Member States. Furthermore, since the number of MEPs elected in each Member State is fixed by the Treaty and elections to the EP are held in each Member State in respect of its allocation of MEPs, a given Member State's decision to extend voting rights beyond own nationals and resident EU citizens has no further effect on the choice or number of MEPs elected in other Member States.

The Court concluded that, in the current state of Community law, the definition of the persons entitled to vote/stand in the EP elections falls within the competence of each Member State 'in compliance with Community law'. The Court gave some indication of what the latter condition might mean when it continued to observe that the Treaty does not preclude a Member State from granting the right to vote/stand not only to its own nationals and resident EU citizens but also to certain persons who have 'close links' to the territory. Here, the UK could not be considered to have contravened Community law when – for reasons connected to its constitutional traditions – it chose to grant rights to vote/stand to QCCs who satisfied conditions expressing a 'specific link' with the territory in respect of which elections are held.

The ruling in *Spain v. United Kingdom* opens up many interesting points for consideration. To begin with, it contributes to the debate about whether MEPs should be considered to represent primarily the interests of their individual constituencies or Member States, rather than the collective interest of the entire EU. Factors such as the lack of a true European 'demos', the tendency of many voters to use EP elections to record protest votes against incumbent national governments and the adolescent state of the pan-European political parties, have led many commentators to favour the view that the democratic mandate of an MEP is limited to the representation of his/her own constituency. The Court's emphasis, in *Spain v. United Kingdom*, on the territorial nature of the electoral franchise to the EP might further reinforce that analysis.

This in turn raises difficult questions about the proper functioning of the EU's inter-institutional balance. For example, if and when enhanced co-operation becomes more widespread within the Community order, why should MEPs from non-participating Member States be fully entitled to vote on legislative measures affecting only the participating Member States? The territorial nature of the electoral mandate, as underlined in *Spain v. United Kingdom*, might tend to suggest that such MEPs should be treated rather like their counterparts in the Council of Ministers (where non-participating countries are entitled to take part in deliberations but not to vote).

Moreover, the principle that certain third-country nationals may be entitled to participate in the political life of the EU, through the exercise of voting rights in its popular assembly, should increase pressure on the Community institutions to take more seriously the aspiration of equalizing the economic and social rights offered to lawfully resident third-country nationals with those enjoyed by EU citizens. However, this aspect of the Court's ruling might usefully be contrasted with the relevant provisions of the Constitutional Treaty, several of which appear to be more precise about the EP's democratic franchise than the existing Treaties. For example, Article I-20 states that the EP 'shall be composed of representatives of the EU's citizens'; Article I-46 concerning the principle of representative democracy also refers repeatedly to citizens. It is therefore unclear whether the UK's electoral rules would remain compatible with EU law in the (admittedly unlikely) event that the Constitution eventually enters into force (see Dinan, this volume) – though one might rightly feel uneasy at the prospect of disenfranchizing whole classes of persons whose rights to vote/stand in the EP elections have already been sanctioned under Community law.

The issue in *Eman and Sevinger* was different: whether *all* EU citizens were entitled to vote and stand in EP elections, or whether and in what circumstances *certain* EU citizens might be denied those rights.[18] The case concerned provisions of the Netherlands Electoral Law whereby Dutch nationals resident in the Antilles or Aruba are not entitled to vote in EP elections. Dutch nationals resident in Aruba claimed that as EU citizens they should be entitled to vote at EP elections even when resident in an overseas country or territory (OCT) as referred to in Annex II to the EC Treaty.

The Court reiterated the basic principle that the definition of persons entitled to vote/stand in the EP elections falls within the competence of each Member State in compliance with Community law. In principle, the

---

[18] Case C-300/04 *Eman and Sevinger* (12 September 2006).

Netherlands had not contravened the limits on its competence by refusing a right to vote/stand to Dutch nationals residing in Aruba. First, no provision of the Treaty expressly requires that Member States hold elections to the EP in the OCTs. Second, Articles 17 and 19 EC do not confer on EU citizens an unconditional right to vote/stand in EP elections. Third, according to the standards set by the European Convention of Human Rights (ECHR), it is not an infringement of fundamental rights for states to adopt a criterion of residence in order to identify who enjoys the right to vote/stand in elections.

The Dutch rules, however, came unstuck when placed into their wider context. The Netherlands Electoral Law in fact recognized the right of all Dutch nationals resident in a third country to vote/stand in EP elections. When acting within the scope of the Treaty, Member States must respect the general principles of Community law, which, the Court recalled, include the principle of equal treatment, whereby comparable situations must not be treated differently, unless such treatment is objectively justified. Here, Dutch nationals resident in Aruba and Dutch nationals resident in a third country were in a comparable position, yet one group was entitled to vote/stand in EP elections and the other was not, and the Netherlands had failed to demonstrate that that difference in treatment was objectively justified. It was therefore incumbent upon the Dutch courts to provide the claimants with an effective form of legal redress (and of course, upon the Dutch state to amend its voting laws).

III. Legal Status of the Charter of Fundamental Rights

Although the EU does not currently possess a written bill of rights, human rights and fundamental freedoms are nevertheless protected as general principles of Community law, enforceable against both the Community institutions and the Member States when they act within the scope of the Treaty. The ECJ identifies the fundamental rights protected under Community law by reference, in particular, to the common constitutional traditions of the Member States and the provisions of the ECHR. Despite its many merits, this caselaw-based system has also attracted considerable criticism, not least in terms of legal certainty and transparency. The Charter of Fundamental Rights of the EU was drafted, at least in part, to help address such criticisms. Although 'proclaimed' by the Council, Commission and EP in December 2000, the Charter, however, formally remains a non-binding instrument that cannot be directly invoked as a ground of judicial review against Community or national action. The Constitutional Treaty purports to change this situation by incorporating the Charter (subject to certain amendments) fully into EU law. In the meantime, several Advocates General and the Court of First

Instance have referred to the Charter as a source of inspiration for the development of the general principles of Community law.[19] Having long remained silent on the issue, the ECJ finally addressed the legal status of the Charter in its *Family Reunification Directive* ruling.[20]

Directive 2003/86 was adopted under Title IV, Part Three of the EC Treaty. It determines the conditions under which third-country nationals lawfully resident in a Member State may exercise the right to family reunification. The Directive contains several provisions, however, restricting the right to family reunification as regards minors. The EP considered those restrictive provisions incompatible with fundamental rights, particularly the right to family life and the right to non-discrimination, and brought an action for their annulment pursuant to Article 230 EC. For the purposes of identifying the content of the fundamental rights against which the Directive's provisions should be assessed, the EP pointed not only to the ECHR, but also other international instruments such as the UN Convention on the Rights of the Child and (most significantly) the EU Charter of Fundamental Rights. Article 24 of the Charter makes specific reference to children's rights, including the principles that the child's best interests are paramount and that children should be able to maintain a personal relationship with both parents. The Council argued that the case should not be examined in the light of the Charter, since it does not constitute a source of Community law.

The Court's response was that, while the Charter is not a legally binding instrument, the Community legislature had acknowledged its importance in this case by stating, in the preamble to the Directive, that it observes the principles recognized not only by the ECHR but also in the Charter. Furthermore, the principal aim of the Charter, as stated in its own preamble, is to reaffirm the rights resulting, *inter alia*, from the constitutional traditions and international obligations common to the Member States. The Court later made explicit reference to certain provisions of the Charter, including Article 24 on the rights of child, when discussing whether the restrictive provisions of the Directive were compatible with fundamental rights as protected under Community law. After a lengthy analysis, the Court concluded that none of the disputed provisions could be considered unlawful and upheld the Directive's validity in its entirety.

How should one interpret the Court's ruling on the legal status of the Charter? The answer seems to be that the Court has expanded the sources of inspiration upon which it feels entitled to draw, when developing caselaw on

---

[19] E.g. AG Tizzano in Case C-173/99 *BECTU* [2001] ECR I-4881; CFI in Case T-177/01 *Jégo-Quéré* [2002] ECR II-2365.
[20] Case C-540/03 *Parliament v. Council* (27 June 2006).

the general principles of Community law: not only the common constitutional traditions of the Member States and the ECHR, but now also the Charter as proclaimed by the Community's three main political institutions at Nice. This interpretation is a legally neat solution to the question of the Charter's legal status: the Charter is not directly justiciable and is not formally a source of Community law, but it can provide a valid reference point for identifying the general principles of Community law and has thus indirectly acquired the potential for judicial enforcement. Indeed, the clear implication seems to be that, since the Charter does not seek to create any new rights, only to codify those already protected under Community law, the presence of any purported fundamental freedom within the text of the Charter can be taken as conclusive evidence that that freedom forms a binding part of the general principles of Community law.

Nevertheless, there are certain problems with this solution, however legally neat it might seem. In particular, there is a degree to which the proclamation of the Charter by the political institutions and its subsequent emancipation by the Community courts constitutes an act of self-levitation, and one that floats a little uncomfortably beside the fundamental principle that the EU is an organization of attributed powers, which enjoys only those competences conferred on it by the Member States. After all, the Court had previously established that the Community, as currently constituted, does not enjoy any general power to legislate in the field of human rights.[21] Recognition of such a power would necessitate an amendment to the Treaties themselves – an option passed over by the Member States in their capacity as Treaty-authors when they refused to confer upon the Charter the status of primary law by incorporating its text into the Treaty of Nice. Yet it would appear that the same end result has now been achieved, even in the absence of a Treaty amendment explicitly authorizing an expansion of the EU's competences in the sphere of fundamental rights.

However laudable its aims and content, the Charter remains a mere declaration by the political institutions. Of course, the Court has taken note of other political declarations (such as the Social Charter) in developing its caselaw on the general principles of Community law, but it is arguable that the Charter's background and very nature confer upon this instrument a particular constitutional significance. The ECJ's judicial endorsement in the *Family Reunification Directive* case, therefore, might give the false impression that an expression of political will can be converted into legal doctrine via a process that operates altogether outside the ordinary framework for revision of the Treaties or the adoption of secondary legislation.

[21] Opinion 2/94 [1996] ECR I-1759.

From that observation follow two others. First, the *Family Reunification Directive* ruling might risk exposing the Court to the accusation of 'cherry picking' from the stalled Constitution. Formal incorporation of the Charter into EU law was one of the main reforms incorporated into the Constitutional Treaty. As with the principle of greater transparency in the Council's legislative deliberations,[22] and enhanced participation for the EP in the supervision of the Commission's delegated powers,[23] the potential for the Charter to produce significant legal effects under Community law could be seen as an attempt partially to pre-empt those provisions of the Constitutional Treaty that seem politically worthwhile and legally salvagable.

Secondly, after the *Family Reunification Directive* case, it is possible that the existence of the Charter might relieve the ECJ of some of the burden of identifying the sources for its evolving caselaw on the general principles of Community law. Particularly in the case of controversial moral questions, a simple look at whether the purported fundamental right can be identified in the Charter might provide a short-cut to the current law, without having to conduct any more thorough analysis of the common constitutional traditions of the Member States or the jurisprudence developed under the ECHR. By way of illustration, recall the judgement in *Mangold*, in which the Court held that the principle of non-discrimination on grounds of age constitutes a general principle of Community law.[24] Several commentators have raised a sceptical eyebrow at the idea that such a proposition could be sustained by reference either to the common constitutional traditions of the Member States or the ECHR. Indeed, it is only due to the Community's equal treatment framework directive that many Member States have recently introduced legislation prohibiting discrimination on grounds of age.[25] The ECJ might have avoided the accusation that it ignored the legal facts, by simply referring to the text of Article 21(1) of the Charter: if equal treatment on grounds of age is contained in the Charter and the Charter merely codifies what exists already, then equal treatment on grounds of age must be a general principle of Community law. But that would only have made the accusation of self-levitation all the stronger.

IV. The Fight Against Terrorism and Fundamental Rights

Under a series of resolutions adopted by the United Nations Security Council (UNSC), all states were instructed to freeze the financial assets of persons and

[22] See Decision 2006/683, OJ 2006 L 285, p. 47.
[23] See Decision 2006/512, OJ 2006 L 200, p. 11.
[24] Case C-144/04 *Mangold* [2005] ECR I-9981.
[25] Jans, J. (2007) 'Annotation of *Mangold*'. *Legal Issues of Economic Integration*, Vol. 34, No. 1, pp. 53–66.

entities associated with Osama bin Laden and the Al-Qaeda network. To this end, the UNSC established a Sanctions Committee responsible for identifying and updating the list of affected persons and entities. The competent national authorities of each state are entitled to grant exemptions from the full effect of restrictive measures on humanitarian grounds (for example, to meet subsistence costs), provided that the Sanctions Committee either gives its consent or (depending on the circumstances) does not actively object to the proposed exemption.

Taking the view that implementation of the UN sanctions regime necessitated action at the Community level, the Council of Ministers adopted a series of common positions under the Second Pillar, together with implementing regulations under the First Pillar. Those measures provide for the freezing of assets across the Community territory of designated persons and entities, the list of which is updated by the Commission in the light of determinations made by the UNSC or its Sanctions Committee, subject to any exemptions on humanitarian grounds granted by the relevant Member State with the express or implied approval of the UN Sanctions Committee.

In its judgement in *Yusuf*, delivered in 2005, the Court of First Instance (CFI) ruled on the relationship between the Community's sanctions regime and fundamental rights as protected under Community law.[26] The CFI ruled that, although not a member of the UN, the Community is bound to respect the UN Charter: it must not infringe the obligations imposed on the Member States by the UN Charter; conversely, it must adopt all measures necessary to enable the Member States to fulfil those obligations. Further, the Community courts have no jurisdiction to review the lawfulness of UNSC or Sanctions Committee decisions according to the fundamental rights recognized under Community law. Moreover, in implementing the determinations of the UNSC and Sanctions Committee, as regards persons and entities associated with Osama bin Laden and the Al-Qaeda network, the Community institutions had acted under circumscribed powers and without any autonomous discretion. For the Community courts to review the lawfulness of those Community implementing measures would therefore be tantamount to calling into question, albeit indirectly, the actions of the UNSC and Sanctions Committee themselves. Nevertheless, the Community courts were entitled to determine whether decisions of the UNSC and Sanctions Committee were compatible with *jus cogens*, i.e. the body of higher rules of public international law binding on all subjects of the international legal order, including the UN, and from which no derogation is possible – though the CFI ultimately concluded

---

[26] Case T-306/01 *Yusuf* [2005] ECR II-3533.

that the UN sanctions regime did not in fact infringe any of the rights protected under *jus cogens*.

The CFI in *Yusuf* was undoubtedly faced with a very difficult and sensitive task: balancing the desire to guarantee the protection of fundamental rights, which are meant to act as an essential prerequisite for the validity and legitimacy of Community action, against the political necessity of effectively implementing a core tenet of the UN's global counter-terrorism strategy and the risks posed by openly defying the will of an organization that the EU and its Member States place at the heart of the international system of governance and law. The compromise embodied in *Yusuf* is currently being appealed before the ECJ.[27]

In the meantime, the CFI delivered two judgements during 2006 that build upon the *Yusuf* principles and throw greater legal light on the sometimes murky world of the EU's role in the 'war on terror'. The first case, *Ayadi*,[28] concerned a Tunisian national resident in Ireland whose Community bank accounts were frozen after he was designated as a person associated with Osama bin Laden by the UN Sanctions Committee. He brought an action for annulment of the Community sanctions regulation insofar as it concerned the listing of his assets, *inter alia*, on the grounds that there was an infringement of his fundamental rights as protected under Community law. Having reaffirmed the basic framework of principles established in *Yusuf*, the CFI continued to consider in greater detail the system for being removed from the list of designated persons and obtaining exemptions from the full effect of restrictive measures. All requests for removal or exemption must be presented to the Sanctions Committee by the state of nationality or residence of the named individual; individuals have no right to be heard directly and thus appear totally dependent upon the diplomatic protection afforded by the competent national authorities.

Within the operation of the system for requesting removal/exemption, however, EU Member States are bound to respect the fundamental rights protected under Community law, since this will not impede proper performance of their obligations under the UN Charter. This implies that Member States must give claimants an opportunity to present their case for review to the national authorities; the latter must take account of the difficulties claimants might encounter (for example) because they have been unable to ascertain the precise reasons or evidence for their inclusion on the sanctions list due to its confidential nature; and where justified, the Member State must promptly ensure that claimants' cases are presented fairly and impartially to

[27] Case C-415/05 *Yusuf* (pending).
[28] Case T-253/02 *Ayadi* (12 July 2006).

the Sanctions Committee. Moreover, the national courts must guarantee the possibility of an effective judicial review in respect of any failure by the Member State to fulfil the foregoing obligations, even if domestic rules would not ordinarily permit legal challenge to refusals by the national authorities to afford diplomatic protection.

The legal framework underpinning the second case, *Organisation des Modjahedines du peuple d'Iran* (OMPI),[29] differed from both *Yusuf* and *Ayadi* in a crucial respect: it concerned the UNSC resolutions instructing all states to freeze the assets of persons who commit or attempt to commit terrorist acts, but without identifying the precise persons and entities concerned, thus leaving a significant measure of discretion to the implementing authorities. Again, the Council of Ministers decided to give effect to the UNSC regime at the Community level through the adoption of Second and Third Pillar common positions and associated First Pillar regulations. The list of designated persons and entities is based on assessments made by the competent national authorities, which are then presented to the Council for adoption; the latter is obliged to review names on the list at least once every six months to ensure that there are still grounds for their inclusion. The OMPI brought an action before the CFI challenging its listing and the freezing of its assets.

This time, the CFI found that the Community institutions were not acting under powers circumscribed by the UNSC. In drawing up and maintaining the list of designated persons, the Council was exercising its own discretionary powers under the Treaty. In principle, therefore, fundamental rights as protected under Community law – including the right to a fair hearing, the duty to state reasons and the right to effective judicial protection – were fully applicable to the Community's own listing regime. Of course, the exact content of those fundamental rights had to be adapted to the particular context of anti-terrorism measures: for example, the right to a fair hearing could not require Council to hear individuals before taking the initial decision to freeze their assets, since that would remove the essential element of surprise. However, unless precluded by overriding security interests or the conduct of international relations, affected persons must be apprised of the information indicating that a decision was taken by a competent national authority; be given an opportunity to make known their views on any subsequent decision to maintain a freeze on their funds; and be informed of the reasons why the Council considered that restrictive measures should be taken in their case.

Given the broad discretion exercised by the Council in this field, judicial review by the Community courts was limited to checking that the rules

[29] Case T-228/02 *Organisation des Modjahedines du peuple d'Iran* (12 December 2006).

governing procedure and the statement of reasons had been complied with and there had been no manifest errors in assessing the facts or misuse of power. Here, the Community regime made no express provision for notifying any evidence or hearing the parties; nor had the OMPI in fact been notified of the evidence against it. Moreover, the information presented to the CFI was insufficient to enable the judges to undertake even the limited judicial scrutiny appropriate in this field. Indeed, the CFI was unable to identify with certainty exactly which assessment by which national authority provided the basis for the Council's own decision. The Council's decision to freeze the OMPI's assets was therefore annulled.

Although the CFI ruling concerned only the position of the OMPI,[30] the judgement has much more far-reaching implications. The listing system at issue in the case has, until now, been characterized by almost impenetrable secrecy – giving rise to a number of (entirely legitimate) fears. National security services could effectively operate beyond the law, or at least on the basis of possibly flawed intelligence. Member States might take drastic steps against individuals without proper scrutiny of their actions, possibly for political or diplomatic reasons. Ultimately, the EU's claim to be based on the rule of law and respect for fundamental rights would be undermined and its reputation damaged, both within and beyond its borders.

The CFI's ruling helps to redress the balance, albeit only modestly. Whilst acknowledging the sensitive nature of anti-terrorism activities and emphasizing the judiciary's limited will to second-guess decisions reached by the security services and their political masters on the available evidence, the ruling nevertheless effectively orders the Council of Ministers to introduce a new body of procedural guarantees into the listing system for the benefit of those who fall within its scope. The Council has already taken certain steps to inform affected persons and entities of the evidence against them, to be fully implemented at the next periodic review of the list, though observers will no doubt watch closely just how much information the Council is prepared to divulge and whether it will satisfy the requirements set out in *Organisation des Modjahedines du peuple d'Iran* (EUobserver.com 16 January 2007). In any case, it remains arguable that the CFI should have gone further in insisting that listing decisions be subject to more thorough substantive judicial review, albeit under conditions adapted to protect security sources and diplomatic relations, in order to ensure that the designation of a person or entity as terrorist in nature can actually be justified by the available evidence.

[30] Though OPMI remains on the list even despite the CFI's ruling.

Conclusions

It would be unwise, on the basis of this small survey of rulings, to attempt to draw out any broader lessons about the 'legal policy' of the ECJ; for every judgement which might appear 'integrationist', one could easily draw attention to another which pulls Community law in the opposite direction. What will be interesting for EU lawyers to reflect upon, however, is whether the non-ratification of the Constitutional Treaty by the French and Dutch voters might affect the ECJ's confidence in delivering more 'activist' rulings. Some commentators detected such a 'chilling effect' on the Court's caselaw, in fields like the free movement of goods, after the Danish 'no' to the Maastricht Treaty – though other commentators quite rightly pointed out that, at exactly the same time, the ECJ continued to strike out in bold new directions, in fields such as the free movement of persons.

The judgements reviewed in this article suggest that, insofar as the ECJ is influenced by the broader political environment of the Constitutional Treaty at all, that influence is similarly diverse. Whereas rulings such as *De Cuyper* or *Family Reunification* strengthen the influence of Community over national law, judgements such as *Spain v. United Kingdom* illustrate deference to the Member State's competences.

Key Reading

For further analysis of some of the issues discussed in this article, readers may find the following academic papers useful:

Arnull, A. (2006) 'Family Reunification and Fundamental Rights'. *European Law Review*, Vol. 31, No. 5, pp. 611–12.

Dougan, M. (2006) 'The Constitutional Dimension to the Caselaw on Union Citizenship'. *European Law Review*, Vol. 31, No. 5, pp. 613–41.

Drywood, E. (2007) 'Giving with One Hand, Taking with the Other: Fundamental Rights, Children and the Family Reunification Decision'. *European Law Review*, Vol. 32, No. 3, pp. 396–407.

Newdick, C. (2006) 'Citizenship, Free Movement and Health Care: Cementing Individual Rights by Corroding Social Solidarity'. *Common Market Law Review*, Vol. 43, No. 6, pp. 1645–68.

Spaventa, E. (2007) 'Fundamental What? The Difficult Relationship Between Foreign Policy and Fundamental Rights'. In Cremona, M. and de Witte, B. (eds) *EU Foreign Relations Law: Constitutional Fundamentals* (Oxford: Hart Publishing).

JCMS 2007 Volume 45 Annual Review pp. 143–162

Relations with the Wider Europe

SANDRA LAVENEX
University of Lucerne
FRANK SCHIMMELFENNIG
ETH Zurich

Summary

The accession of Bulgaria and Romania to the European Union (EU) on 1 January 2007 concluded its fifth enlargement and brought its membership to 27. Beyond the fifth enlargement, however, relations with the wider Europe were characterized by reassessment, stagnation and setbacks.

I. Enlargement

2005 was a surprisingly dynamic year for enlargement (Lavenex and Schimmelfennig, 2006). Despite the prevailing expectation of 'enlargement fatigue' and fundamental questions regarding further enlargement, actual policy proceeded very much along established paths and even provided fresh impetus for the enlargement process. In addition to Bulgaria and Romania remaining on track for accession in 2007, Croatia and Turkey started accession negotiations, Macedonia obtained candidate status, Albania made progress towards a Stabilization and Association Agreement (SAA), an important stepping stone on the way to accession negotiations, and Bosnia-Herzegovina and Serbia-Montenegro opened SAA negotiations.

The over-riding question for 2006, therefore, was whether enlargement policy would continue to move ahead despite persistent debate and dissent among the Member States and despite the candidate countries' enduring problems with meeting EU demands and requirements. In this regard 2006 proved to be a year of stagnation and setbacks. Although Bulgaria and Romania joined the EU as planned, negotiations with two key candidate countries, Serbia and Turkey, were (partially) suspended; and relations with other candidate countries stagnated. Moreover, no consensus emerged regarding extending membership promises to countries further east.

Enlargement Strategy

The EU's debate on its future enlargement strategy, revolving around the buzzword of 'absorption capacity', continued throughout 2006. As such, 'absorption capacity' is not a new issue in EU enlargement. As early as 1993 the Copenhagen European Council stated that 'the Union's capacity to absorb new members, while maintaining the momentum of European integration, is an important consideration in the general interest of both the Union and the candidate countries'. Yet this apparently technical term has never been clearly defined and its reappearance reflects a reopened political conflict among the Member States about the future course of enlargement. On the one hand, countries such as the UK, Sweden and Poland seek to keep the EU open and moving ahead with enlargement without additional requirements. Other governments, most prominently those of France and the Netherlands, however, demand that not only the EU's capacity to integrate new members be taken into account, but also public opinion. Their position reflects the failure of the referendums on the Constitutional Treaty in their countries in 2005, which they partly attribute to the rapid expansion of the EU. Thus, the meaning of the term 'absorption capacity' became contested. The more pro-enlargement actors tend to emphasize that it is not a new criterion but has been part of the 'Copenhagen criteria' all along. Others – such as Austrian Prime Minister Schüssel – seek to add cultural and financial dimensions that they claim have been neglected in the past (*EurActiv.com*, 2006).

The discussion of absorption capacity developed against the background of persistent and slightly growing public scepticism. During 2005 and 2006, the gap between supporters and opponents of enlargement has narrowed from 12 to 4 percentage points (Commission, 2006h). Whereas in the spring of 2005, 50 per cent of respondents declared themselves in favour of further enlargement and 38 per cent against, the numbers for the autumn of 2006 were 46 to 42 per cent, respectively. Support in the new Member States has continued to be higher than in the old Member States, but has decreased there as well. Finally, only 30 (Germany) to 36 per cent of the respondents (UK) in the biggest three Member States were in favour of further enlargement at the end of 2006.

© 2007 The Author(s)
Journal compilation © 2007 Blackwell Publishing Ltd

The European Parliament's (EP) 16 March resolution on the Commission's 2005 enlargement strategy paper also put special emphasis on absorption capacity and requested that the Commission submit a report by the end of the year 'setting out the principles which underpin this concept' (European Parliament, 2006a). In addition, the EP advocated a 'broader spectrum of operational possibilities', namely a 'close multilateral relationship' both for countries without membership prospects and, as an intermediate arrangement, for candidate countries as well. Thus, its centre-right majority has turned the EP from a staunch advocate of enlargement into a brake on it. Mirroring the demands of the EP, the European Council in June invited the Commission 'to provide a special report on all relevant aspects pertaining to the Union's absorption capacity', which 'should also cover the issue of present and future perception of enlargement by citizens and should take into account the need to explain the enlargement process adequately to the public within the Union' (Council, 2006).

The Commission's Enlargement Strategy for 2006–07 (Commission, 2006a) emphasizes the fundamental importance of enlargement for European integration and its positive impact on both the candidate countries and incumbent Member States, as well as the smooth integration of the most recent new Member States. The Commission proposes basing the future enlargement process on three principles. The first is 'consolidating existing commitments towards countries engaged in the process'. Conversely, the EU will be 'cautious about assuming any new commitments'. The second principle is 'applying fair and rigorous conditionality'. Thus, the pace of enlargement will continue to depend on the pace of reforms in a candidate country. At the same time, the Commission stresses that the EU needs to increase the transparency of the process and to keep the candidate countries motivated during the lengthy accession process. Greater transparency is also helpful for the third principle, 'intensifying communication with the public on enlargement', which the Commission regards primarily as a task for the Member States.

In its attempt to define absorption capacity (or 'integration capacity', as the EU now prefers to call it) better, the Commission specifies 'three main components: institutions, common policies and budget. The Union needs to ensure that its institutions continue to act effectively, that its policies meet their goals and that its budget is commensurate with its objectives and with its financial resources.' On institutions, the Commission highlights the need for a new institutional settlement 'by the time the next member is likely to be ready to join', because the Nice Treaty rules only apply to a membership up to 27. It is unclear, however, whether this implies the ratification of the Constitutional Treaty (or a substitute for it) or whether the necessary adaptations could be part of the next accession treaty (as in the past). With regard to policies and the budget, the Commission proposes including impact assessments in both its Opinions on the applicant countries and the EU's positions for the accession negotiations. In addition, administrative and judicial reforms as well as the fight against corruption will be addressed early in the accession negotiations – clearly a consequence of the experience with Bulgaria and Romania (Commission, 2006a, Annex 1; see below). The December European Council endorsed the strategy.

Three questions arise from the strategy: is there anything new? Will it make enlargement less controversial in the future? And will it slow down enlargement? On the first question, the enlargement strategy certainly does not introduce additional criteria for membership; the new elements are procedural rather than substantive. Moreover, the Commission has done everything to present the most recent enlargement as a success and its commitments to current candidate countries as definite. It has resisted the EP's call for creating institutional arrangements for 'membership lite'. The requirement of institutional reform, however, may turn out to be an obstacle given the current uncertainty about the Constitutional Treaty (see Dinan, this volume). Moreover, the explicit reluctance to enter into new commitments will make it very difficult for further countries, such as Ukraine, to join the ranks of candidate countries.

Second, although the strategy confirms the EU's commitment to enlargement, it probably will not solve the fundamental conflicts between the Member States about the desirability of enlargement in general and about Turkey's place in Europe in particular. The Member States' different preferences regarding these issues will likely translate into conflict about the precise interpretation and application of the Commission's principles. Finally, as we will argue below, the slowdown of enlargement is due more to the increasingly difficult domestic situation in the remaining candidate countries than to the details of the EU's enlargement strategy.

Bulgaria and Romania

Although Bulgaria and Romania had signed accession treaties, it was still unclear for much of 2006 whether they would be permitted to join in 2007 or only in 2008. In particular, administrative capacity, judicial reform, corruption and organized crime remained areas of major concern. A final decision had been expected in the spring of 2006. In its May 2006 progress reports, however, the Commission still listed six (against 16 in 2005) 'areas of serious concern' for Bulgarian and four (against 14 in 2005) for Romania. Rather than proposing postponing accession until 2008, however, the Commission gave both countries another chance to fulfil its demands by the final monitoring report in September. This leniency was prompted by it being clear that there would not be the necessary majority of Member States for a postponement. In addition, the EU would be able to use the safeguard clauses in the accession treaties to maintain pressure on both countries after accession.

Therefore, it did not come as a surprise that the conclusions of the Commission's final monitoring report (26 September) affirmed that both countries had made sufficient progress to be able to join in 2007. On the other hand, however, the Commission – in line with most observers – found that a number of areas – including the administration and the judiciary, as well as the management of agricultural funds, food safety and aviation safety – remained highly problematic. The Commission therefore planned to use 'remedial measures' in these areas right from the start of membership to continue monitoring and, if necessary, to apply sanctions, such as withholding or cutting payments (Commission, 2006b). In mid-October, the Council officially approved of the admission of Bulgaria and Romania on 1 January 2007.

Turkey

In December 2006, the EU partially suspended the accession negotiations with Turkey, which had been opened in October 2005. What caused the new low in EU–Turkey relations? On the surface, the division of Cyprus is the main issue responsible for the persistently tense relationship over the past two years. On the one hand, the Republic of Cyprus (RoC), a new Member State since 2004, has consistently demanded that Turkey grant it full recognition as a precondition for opening accession negotiations. On the other hand, Turkey has blamed the Greek Cypriots for rejecting the UN Peace Plan for the reunification of the island and demanded international recognition the Turkish Cypriot community's independence, or at least an easing of its economic isolation, as a precondition of its recognition of the RoC. Yet, the conflict about Cyprus is often only the focal point for the persistent debate, in the EU and in Turkey, on whether Turkey should become a member of the EU at all. This fundamental debate has not gone away despite the decision to open accession negotiations.

An uneasy compromise paved the way for opening accession negotiations in 2005. On the one hand, Cyprus gave up its demand for early international recognition by Turkey. On the other hand, Turkey promised to implement the 'Additional Protocol' extending the Customs Union to Cyprus and open its ports and airports to Cypriot ships and planes (and those coming from Cyprus) before the end of 2006. In early 2006, Turkey offered to comply – but only in return for the abolition of EU restrictions on direct trade with northern Cyprus. This linkage was rebuffed by the RoC, but the EU released a financial package of €139 million for the benefit of the Turkish Cypriot community in February 2006, which Greece and Cyprus had blocked. By the time the screening process was completed and concrete negotiations were scheduled to begin in June 2006, Turkey had still not lifted its ban, however, and Cyprus threatened to veto the opening of the first negotiating chapter on science and research. In the end, Cyprus backed down when the EU once more admonished Turkey to comply by the end of the year.

The Regular Report on Turkey revealed a mixed picture. The Commission noted further progress in some areas, such as a new reform package that was introduced in April 2006, but criticized a slowdown in the overall pace of reform. The resurgence of PKK violence in eastern Turkey, the upcoming elections, a new hardline leadership of the Turkish military and an increasingly nationalist and anti-EU mood in the Turkish population – support for accession dropped from 75 per cent in 2004 to below 50 per cent in 2006 – reduced the government's room for manoeuvre to adopt further reforms and or make additional concessions to the EU. It was the issue of Cyprus, however, that caused the crisis in accession negotiations.

Attempts by the Finnish presidency to find a compromise solution on the opening of Turkish ports failed in the face of both Turkish and Cypriot intransigency. On 20 November, the EU therefore set Turkey a firm deadline of the end of the month to comply. When Turkey continued to uphold the link with ending the trade embargo against northern Cyprus, all of the member governments began to favour the imposition of sanctions. The supporters of Turkish membership, including the UK, Poland and some of the Nordic states, demanded only mild sanctions that would not jeopardize the continuation of accession negotiations. Others, such as Cyprus and members of the French government, wanted the EU to suspend negotiations altogether. On 29 November, the Commission proposed freezing eight trade-related chapters and preventing any other chapters from being declared provisionally closed until Turkey lifts the restrictions against Cyprus. The Commission, however, left sufficient room for the negotiations to continue (EU Rapid, 2006a). It was able to reject French and German calls for a deadline for compliance since these were not backed by most other governments and made sure that the Commission rather than the Council would review policy. A last-minute tactical concession by Turkey to open one of its ports and one of its airports did not prevent the foreign ministers from endorsing the Commission's proposal in early December. At the same time, they vowed to intensify their efforts to find a solution for Cyprus under UN auspices and to ease the economic embargo on the Turkish Cypriot community in order to break the deadlock in the relations between Cyprus, Turkey and the EU.

Croatia

Throughout most of 2006, Croatia's accession negotiations with the EU proceeded slowly and in step with Turkey's. The screening process was concluded in October, the science and research chapter was opened and provisionally closed in June. As a result of the partial freezing of negotiations with Turkey, however, the paths of the two countries parted. A second chapter (education and culture) was opened and provisionally closed on 11 December. In its summary assessment for the enlargement strategy, the Commission indicated that it was content with the start of the negotiations and expected negotiations 'to continue at a good pace'. It also demanded the acceleration of reforms, in particular in the same areas that proved most difficult for Bulgaria and Romania: 'judicial and public administration reforms, the fight against corruption and economic reform' (Commission, 2006a).

Serbia and Montenegro

Along with Turkey, Serbia saw the second major setback in the enlargement process in 2006 and, as in the case of Turkey, nationalist and territorial issues have got in the way of progress towards European integration. The first issue was the lack of co-operation with the International Criminal Tribunal for the former Yugoslavia (ICTY), in particular with regard to the indicted war-criminal Ratko Mladic. After complaints by the tribunal's general prosecutor, Carla del Ponte, that Serbia's co-operation had deteriorated since 2005, the EU threatened to interrupt the SAA talks with Serbia if Mladic was not arrested and extradited by the end of March 2006. New guarantees by the Serbian government persuaded the EU to give Serbia a new deadline, but when Mladic was not arrested by the beginning of May, the EU decided to suspend the SAA negotiations until Serbia fully co-operated with ICTY, which it did not do for the remainder of 2006.

The second issue impeding relations between the EU and Serbia was the referendum on the independence of Montenegro. Although the EU had not been in favour of independence initially, the referendum was part of a deal negotiated in 2003 by Javier Solana, the High Representative for Common Foreign and Security Policy (CFSP), to try to keep Serbia and Montenegro together. In 2006 the EU limited its role to setting the terms of the referendum by demanding a 55 per cent threshold (with a minimum of 50 per cent turnout) for the referendum to pass. After a vote of 55.5 per cent in favour of independence in May, the EU recognized Montenegro and opened SAA negotiations in September.

The future status of Kosovo was the third complicating issue. When the High-Level Meeting on the Future Status of Kosovo agreed in July failed in

September, UN Special Envoy Martti Ahtisaari was asked to draft his own plan. In order to pre-empt this move and avoid to be seen as 'losing Kosovo', the Serbian government called a referendum in October on a new constitution proclaiming Kosovo an inalienable part of Serbia and a parliamentary election for January 2007. The referendum was accepted, but declared irrelevant by the EU. These moves led Ahtisaari to delay the submission of his proposal until after the elections lest it fuel a further nationalist backlash in Serbia. In sum, the EU's hopes that its 'European perspective' would make the loss of Kosovo acceptable to Serbia have not materialized so far.

Other Western Balkan Countries

There were also setbacks in Bosnia-Herzegovina, where the process of state consolidation was disrupted by the failure of constitutional reform in April and the continuing obstruction of the centralization of police and security services by the Republika Srpska. As a consequence, the SAA negotiations were not finalized during 2006.

Otherwise, progress on the way to integration was slow but without major setbacks in the western Balkans. The SAA with Albania was signed in June, with the Interim Agreement (focusing on the trade-related aspects of the agreement) entering into force in December. Macedonia remained a candidate country, but was not invited to enter accession negotiations.

Finally, three developments for the region as a whole are worth mentioning. First, on 19 December, a new Central European Free Trade Agreement was signed in Bucharest, which will now include the western Balkans and Moldova. Second, the Energy Community Treaty, which was signed in Athens in October 2005 and entered into force in 2006, also links EU Member States, actual and potential candidate countries as well as countries without an officially acknowledged membership perspective in south-eastern Europe. It is a prime example of flexible horizontal integration in that it extends EU legislation concerning electricity and gas (and related environmental laws) to non-member countries. Third, in November, talks on visa facilitation and readmission agreements between the EU and the western Balkan countries were launched.

II. European Neighbourhood Policy

The second year of implementation of the European Neighbourhood Policy (ENP) was instructive regarding the potential and limits of a foreign policy based on the concepts and routines developed in the context of enlargement. The war in Lebanon, the deterioration of the Israeli–Palestinian conflict and the Presidential elections in Belarus raised questions about the relevance of the ENP in dealing with regional conflicts and non-co-operative authoritarian regimes. The weakness of the EU's responses to these events confirmed doubts about the ENP's potential to meet its proclaimed ambitions to promote peace and democratic change.

At the same time, the procedures established under the ENP were consolidated and further expanded. New Action Plans were concluded with Armenia, Azerbaijan, Georgia and Lebanon. An Association Agreement with Syria was pending ratification at the end of the year. On the sectoral level, the EU continued to deepen its co-operation with its neighbours. Progress on the implementation of the commitments under the Action Plans and Partnership or Association Agreements, however, has been mixed and has tended to confirm the disparities existing between different ENP countries. Whereas the *avant-garde* countries – Ukraine, Morocco, Israel and to some degree also Moldova – have confirmed their commitment to deepen their ties with the EU, progress with other countries – such as Tunisia, Egypt and the South Caucasus countries – has been more ambiguous.

The plurality of goals and strategies embedded in the ENP was bemoaned by the EP when it called on the Commission 'to define the purpose and clear priorities of the European neighbourhood policy, thus setting criteria for the evaluation of achievements' (European Parliament, 2006b, p. 2). While emphasizing 'the need to establish an effective monitoring mechanism and a readiness to restrict or suspend aid and even to cancel agreements with countries which violate international and European standards of respect for human rights and democracy' (European Parliament, 2006b, p. 2), the EP also calls for an enhanced sectoral co-operation through the greater organizational involvement of ENP countries, for instance as non-voting representatives to discussions in Council working groups in 'appropriate fields', Community programmes and agencies (European Parliament, 2006b, p. 3).

Towards the end of the year, the Commission presented its first evaluation of the ENP on the basis of the progress made implementing the Action Plans in place. Apart from country-specific evaluations, the Commission released three important documents taking stock and highlighting new avenues for future co-operation: the 'Communication on strengthening the European Neighbourhood Policy' (Commission, 2006c) and two accompanying Commission Staff Working Documents, one giving an 'Overall Assessment' (2006d) and a separate 'Sectoral Progress Report' (2006e). Together, these documents confirm the distinction inherent in the ENP between general foreign policy goals, such as democracy promotion and conflict resolution and sectoral co-operation, which may be interpreted as a form of flexible horizontal integration (Lavenex and Schimmelfennig, 2006) and external governance (Lavenex, 2004). Originally external governance under the ENP focused only on the expansion of the EU's *acquis*. In 2006, the EU took first steps towards coupling such policy-transfer with partial organizational engagement of ENP countries with EU agencies and programmes.

The First Evaluation of the ENP and Proposals for Innovation

The evaluation published in December reviewed the first 18 months of implementation of the ENP. Overall, the Commission gave a modest assessment of ENP's potential and its actual use in relations with individual countries. More interesting perhaps than the assessment of the individual countries' performance (see below) is the Commission's view on the policy as a whole, its means and capabilities, but also its incoherences. The Commission admits that 'the ENP could and should be strengthened, particularly when one considers the prohibitive potential costs of failing to support our neighbours in their reform efforts' (Commission, 2006c). The ENP's strengths are identified as its working methods, the concrete nature of the Action Plans and monitoring mechanisms, the principle of joint ownership and the fact that the ENP integrates previously distinct policies both geographically (linking all neighbours into one policy framework) and substantially (ranging from economic to governance and human rights issue as well as distinct policy areas such as migration or the environment).

The Commission stresses four weaknesses: the lack of impact on regional conflicts; the modest financial support – even under the new European Neighbourhood and Partnership Instrument (ENPI); the weakness of people-to-people exchanges and civil society participation in the ENP; and the asymmetry between the partners countries' demands and the EU's offers that do not immediately address their main concerns. In this regard, the Commission highlights the necessity of supporting better the needs and aspirations of partners in two areas: trade and migration.

In order to strengthen the policy, the Commission proposes a number of measures, some of which are more innovative than others. In order to enhance political co-operation it proposes extending and strengthening the possibilities for associating ENP partners with EU initiatives, such as CFSP declarations (as already granted to the eastern European partners); co-ordinating positions in international forums and greater parliamentary co-operation. In financial terms, it suggests introducing new financial instruments, such as an ENP investment fund and a Governance Facility. Concerning trade and economic co-operation, it confirms the aim to move towards 'deep and comprehensive free trade agreements'. Apart from free trade in goods and services and the elimination of non-tariff barriers, which are already included in the Action Plans, the Commission now stresses the need to *include 'those products of particular importance for our partners'* (Commission, 2006c, p. 4, own emphasis). Conceding that 'mobility of persons is also of the utmost importance for all ENP partners' and that 'the Union *cannot fully deliver on many aspects of the European Neighbour-hood Policy* if the ability to undertake legitimate short-term travel is as constrained as it is currently' (2006c, p. 5, own emphasis), the Commission proposes making it easier for certain types of visitors from ENP partners to the EU to acquire visas.

Apart from such incremental policy adaptation within individual ENP sectors and instruments, the Commission also proposes two amendments to the general set-up of the policy. The first is the enhancement of regional co-operation, including a new initiative for the Black Sea region, which now includes EU Member States (Bulgaria and Romania), a candidate (Turkey), ENP partner states (Georgia and Ukraine), as well as Russia. This initiative strengthens the links between the EU and already existing regional bodies, such as the Black Sea Economic Co-operation Organization (BSEC) and the Baku initiative on energy and transport and will facilitate addressing common priorities irrespective of the different formal contexts of the respective countries' bilateral relations with the EU.

The second important general innovation is the proposal to increase multilateral co-operation in key sectors through new functional 'thematic agreements' and eventually common institutional structures. The proposal suggests extending the South-East-European Energy Community (see above) to ENP countries and the establishment of similar networks, e.g. in transport, research or migration policy. In sum, these new proposals tend to strengthen the sectoral, functional dimension of the ENP by pro-moting the idea of expanded multilateral regimes in key areas of regional interdependence.

III. Eastern Europe

Ukraine

Ukraine continued to consolidate its path to democracy in 2006 with free and fair parliamentary elections in March and the removal of restrictions on the freedom of the media and civil society. However, the political paralysis following the elections prevented the formation of an effective government until August and the return to power of pro-Russian Viktor Yanukovych, revealed persistent deep political divisions in the country. These divisions also surfaced during Prime Minister Yanukovych's visit to Brussels in

September. While confirming his country's ambition to join the EU, he distanced himself from NATO accession, prompting immediate criticism by President Yuschchenko (Centre for European Policy Studies, 2006). This infighting also had an impact on economic policy and made it difficult to introduce sustained reforms. Through the end of 2006 the business climate had not really improved and risks for foreign investors remained high. The lack of independence of the judiciary also remains a problem. Further, although Ukraine joined the Council of Europe's group of states against corruption (GRECO) and passed new laws, little progress was made in reducing corruption. Nevertheless, at the EU–Ukraine Summit in October, both sides decided to start official negotiations on an Enhanced Agreement, including the 'deep' free trade area proposed by the Commission, in early 2007, conditional on Ukraine's entry into the World Trade Organization (WTO).

Intensified co-operation was also visible in foreign policy and on justice and home affairs (JHA). In foreign policy, Ukraine aligned itself with the vast majority of the EU's CFSP declarations. Ukraine did not, however, support the EU's sanctions on Belarus following the presidential elections in that country (see below). JHA activities focused on the negotiation of a readmission agreement for irregular migrants from the EU, which was finally initialled at the EU–Ukraine Summit in October after 12 rounds of contentious negotiations. As previously with Russia and Morocco (see below), the EU rewarded Ukraine for concluding the agreement with a facilitation of visa requirements for certain categories of Ukrainian citizens travelling to the EU. Ukraine, in a symbolic act, had abolished all visa requirements for EU citizens already in July 2005. The institutional basis of Ukraine's association with the EU's JHA policies was strengthened with the start of negotiations on co-operation agreements with the EU agencies Europol and Eurojust.

Last, but not least, energy relations remained high on the agenda. These were given new urgency with Gazprom's decision at the beginning of the year to nearly quadruple the price of gas exports to Ukraine and then to interrupt gas supplies when Ukraine refused to pay the new price. This interruption also left several Member States short of fuel, thus raising awareness of the EU's increasing energy dependence. In response, the EU decided to integrate Ukraine gradually into its internal energy market and to grant it observer status in its Energy Community Treaty (see above).

Finally, in 2006 instruments borrowed from enlargement, such as twinning and TAIEX, which involve the secondment of experts from Member States' administrations to Ukraine to foster the exchange of best practices for institution-building and legal approximation, were introduced.

Moldova

Like Ukraine, Moldova agreed to a strict monitoring system, including annual implementation tools and comprehensive sets of priorities and timelines, for the implementation of its ENP Action Plan. During 2006, it became clear that these may have been too ambitious and the Commission concluded in its ENP Progress Report that Moldova 'needs to concentrate resources in implementation and clearly prioritize action' (Commission, 2006f, p. 2). This statement holds both for the political dimension (corruption, freedom of the media, independence of the judiciary and human rights – although the Moldovan Parliament abolished the death penalty in June) and for the economy, which suffered greatly from increased gas prices and the closure of the Russian market, the traditional destination of Moldovan exports. Although officially declared for phyto-sanitary reasons, Russian import bans may have been motivated by Moldova's opposition against Russia joining the WTO. In order to support Moldova's implementation and absorption capacities, the Commission announced that it would double the volume of financial aid in the coming years.

JHA remained a focus of co-operation under the ENP, with the EU border assistance mission to Moldova and Ukraine (EUBAM) augmented to 101 EU experts. Negotiations progressed on a framework of co-operation with Europol and Moldova appointed contact persons to work with Eurojust. Moldova's hopes of starting negotiations on visa facilitation in 2006, however, were dashed. By contast, Moldova's flexible horizontal integration has progressed furthest in energy. Alignment with the internal energy market *acquis* continued and Moldova obtained observer status in the Energy Community Treaty.

South Caucasus

During 2006 ENP Action Plans were concluded with Armenia, Azerbaijan and Georgia. Generally less ambitious than earlier Action Plans concluded with other countries, these Action Plans also include symbolic elements, such as that the EU 'takes note of the European aspirations expressed by Armenia'. Talks with Azerbaijan were particularly difficult, as differences persist between the EU and Azerbaijan on how to address the status of Nagorno-Karabakh. These differences, however, were resolved during the negotiations: whereas Armenia's Action Plan mentions the need to take the principle of self-determination into account, Azerbaijan's Action Plan mentions the principle of territorial integrity! This concession may be seen as the EU compromising its own standards in exchange for access to Azerbaijan's vast energy reserves.

The EU's relations with Georgia were also complicated by territorial issues. In the first half of 2006, Georgia called for greater EU engagement in the solution of the conflict in South Ossetia and announced that it would expel Russian troops from the breakaway region. In October, Russia decided to cut all bilateral traffic connections and money transfers after Georgia arrested four alleged Russian military spies on its territory. In an attempt to neutralize Russia's sanctions, the Commission launched a study on a free trade area with Georgia, even though such a deal might have an adverse impact on the Georgian economy due to its lack of competitiveness.

In sum, developments in the South Caucasus highlighted once again the distinct challenges facing the ENP in this region and generated new pressure to tackle border disputes. Just as in the cases of Ukraine and Moldova, they also underlined Russia's enduring geopolitical influence in the region.

IV. Mediterranean Countries

Relations with the Mediterranean countries were also marked by increasing differentiation among ENP partners and coloured by increased instability in the Middle East. Although sectoral horizontal integration could make significant progress, especially with Israel and Morocco, the deterioration of conflicts in the Middle East stressed once again the tension between a policy aiming at functional co-operation and the need to address pressing foreign policy challenges.

Middle East

Co-operation with countries in the Middle East was overshadowed by the war between Israel and Hezbollah in Lebanon in July and the political stalemate following the formation of a Hamas-led Palestinian government in January. The devastating war in Lebanon and the ensuing destabilization of the country interrupted a promising start in ENP relations with the entry into force of the Association Agreement and the start of negotiations on an Action Plan in April. The war put to the test the EU's capacity to react and underlined the need for greater European involvement in the region. The EU's relatively rapid deployment of more than 7,000 peace-keeping troops from five Member States may be seen as a success when compared to earlier crises, e.g. in the Balkans. This success, however, is mitigated by the unseemly internal tug of war over troop numbers that preceded the deployment and by the minimal impact of the EU on the conduct of the combatants.

In the Palestinian Authority, the formation of the Hamas-led government followed an open and fair electoral process in January. Ironically, given what followed, the Commission judged these elections as great progress in 'the reinforcement of the democratic process in the Palestinian territories' (Commission, 2006g, p. 3). With Hamas's refusal to accept the Quartet principles – commitment to the principles of nonviolence, recognition of Israel and acceptance of previous agreements and obligations, including the Roadmap – the EU decided to suspend political contacts and co-operation with the new government. This move followed Israel's decision to stop transferring tax and customs revenue collected on behalf of the Palestinian Authority and most international donors' suspension of direct support to or through the government. These actions caused a severe financial crisis and an associated humanitarian crisis, which was intensified by new Israeli restrictions on movement and access. The humanitarian crisis prompted the EU in June to seek alternative ways to provide aid without passing through the Palestinian government. Under the umbrella of the Quartet and with the World Bank, the Commission set up a Temporary International Mechanism in June to channel allowances directly to vulnerable Palestinians and social facilities.

Quite separate from these regional problems, sectoral co-operation under the ENP made some progress, especially with Jordan and Israel and mainly on trade issues. Negotiations to liberalize trade in agricultural and progressed agricultural products were initiated with Israel and completed with Jordan. Both countries also started negotiations on liberalizing services, both provided across borders and through establishment. Israel also deepened its co-operation in JHA. Co-operation focused on terrorism and data protection in view of a future co-operation agreement with Europol. In addition, Eurojust established contact points in the country. Israel repeated its interest in more Community Programmes and Agencies, which prompted the Commission to review the possibility of opening these to third-country participation.

North Africa

Relations with north African countries were less complicated by regional conflicts, but did highlight the differential potential of the ENP for different countries. Morocco, true to its ambition for an 'advanced status' in its relations with the EU, made significant use of the Action Plan. Co-operation with Tunisia concentrated on mainly economic and social issues. Negotiations on trade in services and establishment were launched with both countries, while those on agricultural, processed agricultural and fishery products started with only Morocco. Morocco also engaged in political dialogue on foreign policy and was the first Mediterranean country to establish a human rights, democratization and governance sub-committee, which met for the first time in November. Morocco was also the first country to designate a contact point with the Council for external security co-operation and took part in the EU's military operation ALTHEA in Bosnia-Herzegovina. Co-operation also intensified in JHA. The first JHA twinning initiative in the Euro-Mediterranean Partnership (MEDA) region was launched, involving training activities for border control forces and a negotiation mandate was issued for a co-operation agreement with Europol. As of the end of the year, conclusion of a readmission agreement seemed imminent. These negotiations were linked to initial talks on visa facilitation and co-operation on a pan-African approach to migration management, which culminated in an EU-supported conference in Rabat on migration and development. Finally, there was significant progress on sectoral integration at the more technical level. Morocco and the EU initialled an aviation agreement on the gradual integration of aviation markets and concluded an agreement that enables Morocco to take part in the Galileo programme, the EU's satellite navigation system.

Co-operation with Tunisia, by contrast, was much more selective and tended to reflect Tunisian priorities. In particular, talks started on implementing the Action Plan clause on equal treatment of Tunisian nationals in the EU. Otherwise, little progress was made apart from on trade. By the end of the year, the two sides had still not agreed rules of procedure for the subcommittee on human rights and Tunisia's record on democracy and civil liberties remained poor. Although JHA is not such a priority issue in Tunisia, as it is not a major transit migration point, co-operation in migration, rule of law or police matters was still slow.

In addition, the EU's relations developed with other countries in north Africa. By the end of the year the conclusion of the Action Plan with Egypt was imminent and progress was made negotiating a 'Memorandum of Understanding' on energy co-operation with Algeria (Rapid Press Release IP/06/1679 of 4 December 2006).

V. Other Potential ENP Partners

2006 was also a year of significant events shaping EU relations with other would-be ENP partners. The war in Lebanon and concern about Syrian interference prompted conflicting reactions from the Member States. Some, such as Germany, called for the adoption of an association agreement (the agreement concluded in 2004 was never signed or ratified) to entice Syria back into the international mainstream. Others, such as France, argued that Syria must first comply with UN resolutions before the EU makes any firm commitments. Co-operation with Libya on migration and border controls intensified, despite major human rights violations and the imposition of death sentences on five EU-citizen nurses and a Palestinian doctor for allegedly deliberately infecting 400 children with HIV.

Finally, not much changed in the EU's relations with Belarus. Lukashenko's authoritarian regime was confirmed with almost 83 per cent of the vote in the presidential elections in March 2006. The Commission's proposal to impose economic sanctions in response to the flawed election was vetoed by Poland, Lithuania and Italy. At the end of the year, when tensions emerged between Belarus and Russia over increases in gas prices and trade restrictions, however, the EU started considering whether to offer Belarus closer economic and political ties.

VI. European Economic Area and Switzerland

Relations with the non-EU members of the European Economic Area (EEA) progressed smoothly during 2006. The main innovation was an agreement between the EU and Norway to set up a joint energy co-operation group. The group will consider energy developments between now and 2020 and will generate proposals to improve EU–Norway energy co-operation. In order to secure its energy supply, the EU would like to see greater involvement of EU companies and technologies in the Norwegian energy market. Norway supplies between 10 and 18 per cent of EU oil demand and around 15 per cent of its natural gas.

With Switzerland, 2006 was marked by the implementation of the second round of Bilateral Agreements (Church, 2006). In April, the agreement to extend the free movement of persons to the ten new Member States entered into force. Switzerland has also agreed to contribute €125 million per year over five years to social and economic cohesion in the enlarged EU. Following the example of Norway, which pays about €220 million a year, Switzerland requested channelling this money through bilateral binding agreements with the new Member States to finance projects it selects. A public referendum on the contribution, held on 26 November, obtained 53 per cent in favour.

In June, the Swiss Government released its second Europe Report on bilateral relations with the EU (Bundesrat, 2006). The report analyses the current state of bilateralism in EU–Swiss relations and discusses its advantages and disadvantages compared with other options such as membership in the EEA or the EU itself. Not surprisingly given the euroscepticism of broad sections of public opinion and of the political elites, it concludes that the bilateral approach, that is the conclusion of sectoral bilateral agreements with the EU, currently best serves Swiss interests, including preserving the key domestic political institutions of federalism and direct democracy.

Conclusion

When Enlargement Commissioner Olli Rehn presented the Commission's enlargement strategy and progress reports on 8 November, he warned that the EU accession process was 'a slow, slow train', more Orient Express than TGV (EU Rapid, 2006b). But what causes this slowness? Is it the EU, putting up red signals along the track and diverting the train onto a siding, as it were, or is it the situation in the would-be members themselves that slows down the process? The evidence from 2006 suggests that the EU is indeed raising the hurdles for new members. Growing scepticism towards enlargement is reducing the credibility of the membership promise that has proven an indispensable condition for spurring reform in neighbouring countries. However, the main causes for the setbacks in EU–Serbia and EU–Turkey relations and the slow progress in relations with the Western Balkans during 2006 were homemade. Unresolved territorial issues and nationalist reactions have raised the domestic political costs of compliance with EU demands to the point where the Turkish and Serbian governments rated their short-term political survival higher than the long-term benefits of membership. Moreover, the weak states and state administrations in the Western Balkans are an obstacle to quick and effective reform.

For the ENP, the main question arising from the developments in 2006 is the relationship between its sectoral approach, providing new opportunities for the flexible horizontal integration of neighbouring countries and its overarching foreign policy goals. How does enhanced sectoral co-operation relate to the promotion of democracy and human rights, or how does it contribute to preventing or pacifying regional conflicts? As our review has shown, especially with regard to Tunisia, Israel, Lebanon and the Southern Caucasus states, intensifying sectoral co-operation can progress independently from these traditional foreign policy concerns.

To conclude, in 2006 both developments with the remaining candidate countries and the EU's other neighbours highlighted a number of challenges for EU policies that are designed primarily upon the experience of earlier enlargement rounds. While it would be premature to judge the general potential of these policies, these countries' political systems and geopolitical situations pose particular challenges that might be beyond current approaches.

Key Readings

Commission (2006a) presents its enlargement strategy and includes its special report on the EU's integration capacity and the main conclusions from the progress reports on the potential new Member States. Commission

(2006c, 2006d, 2006e), together with the ENP Country Reports, give a first assessment of the implementation of the ENP.

Grabbe (2006) analyses the Europeanization mechanisms in the accession process with a focus on the free movement of persons and Schengen rules. She argues that the EU's influence did not realize its potential because of inconsistency among and lack of precision in the EU's membership criteria.

Schimmelfennig *et al.* (2006) examine the strategies of the EU, NATO and other European organizations and the conditions under which they have been able to generate compliance with international norms of democracy, human rights, minority and state building in eastern Europe and Turkey. They argue that the credibility of EU membership conditionality and the domestic power costs of the target governments have been the most relevant conditions of effective norms promotion.

Bundesrat (2006) is the Swiss government's evaluation of the pros and cons of the so-called 'bilateral approach', i.e. the negotiation of agreements in different sectors, from the perspective of Swiss interests and institutions.

References

Bundesrat (2006) Europabericht, Document 06.064, 28 June, Berne.

Centre for European Policy Studies (2006) European Neighbourhood Watch No. 19, September 2006, pp. 10–12, available at: «http://www.ceps.be/files/NW/NWatch19.pdf».

Church, C. (ed.) (2006) *Switzerland and the European Union* (London: Routledge).

Commission of the European Communities (2006a) 'Enlargement Strategy and Main Challenges 2006–2007', COM(2006) 649 final, 8 November.

Commission of the European Communities (2006b) 'Monitoring Report on the State of Preparedness for EU Membership of Bulgaria and Romania', COM(2006) 549 final, 26 September.

Commission of the European Communities (2006c) 'Strengthening the European Neighbourhood Policy', COM(2006) 726 final, 4 December.

Commission of the European Communities (2006d) 'Overall Assessment', Commission Staff Working Document Accompanying the Communication on Strengthening the European Neighbourhood Policy, SEC (2006) 1504/2, 4 December.

Commission of the European Communities (2006e) 'Sector Progress Report', Commission Staff Working Document Accompanying the Communication on Strengthening the European Neighbourhood Policy, SEC (2006) 1512/2, 4 December.

Commission of the European Communities (2006f) 'ENP Progress Report on Moldova', SEC (2006) 1506/2, 4 December.

Commission of the European Communities (2006g) 'ENP Progress Report on the Palestinian Authority', SEC (2006) 1509/2, 4 December.

Commission of the European Communities (2006h) Standard Eurobarometers Nos.
63–6, Spring 2005 to Autumn 2006.

Council of the European Communities (2006) Brussels European Council, 15–16
June 2006, Presidency Conclusions, 10633/1/06 REV1.

EurActiv.com (2006) 29 June.

EU Rapid (2006a) EU Rapid Press Release, 29 November 2006, IP/06/1652, available at: «http://europa.eu/rapid/».

EU Rapid (2006b) EU Rapid Press Release, 9 November 2006, SPEECH/06/663,
available at: «http://europa.eu/rapid/».

European Council (1993) European Council in Copenhagen, 21–22 June 1993. Conclusions of the Presidency, SN 180/93.

European Parliament (2006a) 'Resolution on the Commission's 2005 Enlargement
Strategy Paper', P6 TA (2006) 0096, 16 March.

European Parliament (2006b) 'Resolution on the European Neighbourhood Policy',
P6 TA(2006)0028, 19 January.

Grabbe, H. (2006) *The EU's Transformative Power. Europeanization through Conditionality in Central and Eastern Europe* (Basingstoke: Palgrave).

Lavenex, S. (2004) 'EU External Governance in Wider Europe'. *Journal of European
Public Policy*, Vol. 11, No. 4, pp. 680–700.

Lavenex, S. and Schimmelfennig, F. (2006) 'Relations with the Wider Europe'. *JCMS
Annual Review 2005*, pp. 137–54.

Schimmelfennig, F., Engert, S. and Knobel, H. (2006) *International Socialization in
the New Europe. European Organizations, Political Conditionality and Democratic Change* (Basingstoke: Palgrave).

JCMS 2007 Volume 45 Annual Review pp. 163–181

Relations with the Rest of the World

DAVID ALLEN
MICHAEL SMITH
Loughborough University

Introduction

During 2006, the EU was very active in its relations with the wider world. However, this activity, did not always add up to the development of consistent or coherent strategies and such a paradox has remained at the heart of the EU's international policies. One reason advanced for this 'strategy gap' has been the lack of institutional capacity and thus it is not surprising that the year saw continuing attention to institutional reform in foreign and security policy, despite the failure of the Constitutional Treaty. In economic affairs, the Doha Development Agenda (DDA) claimed a good deal of attention, but as will be seen below, it was not a very positive story and the allocation of blame for lack of progress became a prominent feature of EU trade politics. An increasing trend towards the negotiation of bilateral or inter-regional trade agreements became prominent and created the expectation that this might be a long-term feature. In terms of key relationships, the attempt to deal with the rise of China and India and the difficulties of dealing with a more assertive Russia were central, whilst relations with the USA continued to show the effects of multi-dimensional and increasingly politicized policy contexts.

I. General Themes

Foreign, Security and Defence Policy

The EU's common foreign and security policy (CFSP) and especially the European security and defence policy (ESDP) experienced a high level of activity in 2006 despite the impact of the loss of the Constitutional Treaty with its significant provisions for procedural changes in the external relations procedures such as the establishment of a European Foreign Minister (EFM), a European External Action Service (EEAS), an elected President of the European Council and a single legal identity for the European Union. Indeed during 2006, in anticipation of the German Presidency of the Council in early 2007, there were a number of moves designed to revive or resurrect the Constitutional Treaty or at least designed to implement the foreign policy provisions of the Constitutional Treaty without formally reviving it (Parker, 2006; Munchau, 2007). In particular, the Commission was keen to avoid the Council hijacking the notion of an External Action Service and made its own pitch to the June European Council for greater co-operation between the Commission, the Council and the Member States over diplomatic representation and the training of diplomats (Commission, 2006f). In November the Commission came forward with proposals for the establishment of 'common offices' to deal with the problems posed by the limited consular and diplomatic representations of many of the Member States. Of course, these plans were resisted strongly by those larger Member States that have extensive national diplomatic services and external representations (Duke, 2006). It would seem that the Commission's view of the External Action Service is focused mainly on the conversion of Commission Delegations into EU embassies, whilst the Council's vision, as articulated by the High Representative, is of an External Action Service drawn predominately from the existing diplomatic services of the EU Member States and concentrating mainly on the provision of what would effectively be a Foreign Ministry for the European Foreign Minister. By the end of 2006 it was the Council view that prevailed.

Under the CFSP no fewer than 69 joint actions and common positions were agreed in 2006, either initiating or continuing formal EU actions around the world (Commission, 2007, pp. 181–7). The ESDP was extremely active with a mix of civilian and military missions which reflected the proliferation of crises in the EU's neighbourhood (Iraq, Iran, Afghanistan, Palestine, Darfur, Somalia, Georgia, Belarus, Moldova, Kosovo and the Congo). It was perhaps noteworthy that the two military missions that involved the greatest number of armed forces from the EU Member States were not formally ESDP missions although those participating in both the International Security Force in Afghanistan and the UN force (UNIFIL 11) in the Lebanon (Dembinski, 2007) certainly discussed their roles within EU foreign and security policy circles. At present EU involvement in Kosovo is limited to a rule of law mission. There is the potential for further conflict in Kosovo as its future is determined which would provide the ESDP with a stern test.

In 2006 the ESDP added three new challenges to those laid out in the European Security Strategy (ESS). These were energy security, natural disasters and the security of the EU's external boundaries. The EU also confirmed that by the end of 2007 the much vaunted ESDP 'battle groups' would be ready for deployment (Lindstrom, 2007) and the European Defence Agency (EDA) published its *Long Term Vision* document (Institute for Security Studies, 2007, pp. 304–26) which sought to match defence procurement and capabilities to the threats, challenges and proposed actions laid down in the ESS. The problem for the ESDP as it develops so rapidly is that the missions are clearly growing faster than the capabilities (both material, institutional and procedural) and several Member States are now beginning to feel the strain of involvement in so many different missions. As long as the present decision-making and implementation institutions remain as they are and as long as the Member States continue to neither increase nor rationalize their defence expenditure, the ESDP will face a growing crisis of activity.

Despite the proliferation of CFSP joint actions, ESDP missions and EU special representatives, the EU continued to suffer from a lack of strategic vision and central direction, especially in its dealings with the other significant powers in the international system (Russia, China, the US, India etc.). The number of external relations actors and ongoing confusions, both within and outside the EU, about their roles and responsibilities ensured that coherence, consistency, and, above all, co-ordination, remained unattained objectives and continued to give ammunition to those who would seek to revisit the foreign policy provisions of the Constitutional Treaty for practical rather than ideological reasons.

As with other areas of EU activity, the enlargement of the EU to 25 and now 27 Member States has put great pressure on EU external relations decision-making and perhaps has made the larger Member States more inclined than before to pursue their external interests either unilaterally or in co-operation with other selected Member States. When this happens with the blessing of the entire EU – as was the case over the negotiating activities of the EU-3 (the UK, France and Germany) with Iran (although even here it probably took the reassuring addition of the High Representative to make it the EU-3+1 and thus carry the other Member States) – then it adds to the external capacity of the EU even if, as in the case of Iran, the EU's alternative strategy did not lead to a change in Iran's behaviour but to the EU joining with the US and others in 2006 to report Iran to the United Nations Security Council (UNSC). When it takes the shape of a unilateral action that appears to be in conflict with the interests of other Member States – as recent dealings with Russia by both Germany and Poland have appeared to be – however, then the external capacity of the EU is severely inhibited.

External Trade Policy

EU commercial policy in 2006 was largely dominated by continuing attempts to revive the World Trade Organization (WTO) negotiations in the 'Doha Development Agenda' (DDA). There was also a keen and growing concern with new forms of trade dispute and potential trade agreements. The DDA had come almost to a full stop after the Hong Kong Ministerial Meeting of the WTO in December 2005 and the first half of 2006 saw a series of efforts to create some momentum, working to a series of deadlines set by the parties and by the WTO itself. One mechanism used to try and manufacture some progress was restricted negotiations between the EU, the US and other major parties. Previously, this had entailed use of the 'Quad' (Japan, Canada, the EU and the US), but during 2006 there emerged the 'G-6', which brought India, Japan, Brazil and Australia into the mix alongside the two trade 'super-powers'. This was not the only forum used in the increasingly desperate effort to get a result: the G-8 augmented by India, China, Brazil and other major emerging economies, such as South Africa, was also used, as were other configurations within and outside the WTO itself.

In all of this, the EU presented itself as playing a core and constructive role – indeed, a key part of Trade Commissioner Peter Mandelson's strategy was to present the USA as the problem and the EU as part of the solution. As the year progressed, not only the USA but also agriculture came to be seen as the crucial obstacles to progress. But the effort to link agricultural market access (much desired by the emerging economies) with market access for industrial goods, investment and services (desired especially by the EU and the US) was eventually unsuccessful. The distribution of blame became one of the key features of the situation from April onwards (Beattie, 2006) and intensified after the failure to make progress against a G-8 imposed deadline in August. Although there were signs of movement on agriculture from both the EU and the US, the former was constrained by the absolute determination of France and others to give no ground, whilst the latter was increasingly constrained by the approach of mid-term elections in November. As a result, by the end of the year there was still essential deadlock, with the election of a Democrat-controlled Congress in the USA adding further to the gloom.

More challenging for the Union were disputes arising from the rapid shifts in the balance of world commercial power and especially those concerning China. During 2006, the 'bra wars' of 2005 were replaced at the centre of attention by the 'shoe war', in which the Union accused the Chinese (and the Vietnamese) of dumping certain types of footwear on the European market. Mandelson found himself on the horns of a familiar dilemma as a result: European manufacturers, led by the Italians, demanded protection and anti-dumping action, whilst European consumers and the 'free trade' Member States, especially Sweden, demanded the opposite. At the same time, the dispute became entangled with EU consideration of China's status as a 'non-market economy' and with the need to hold China to its commitments under the WTO, for which its transition period ended at the end of 2006. This was a highly politicized and intractable dispute, in which the eventual anti-dumping measures imposed by the EU were supported by only nine Member States, with 12 against and four abstentions. As the decision rules in anti-dumping require a majority of Member States to vote against a Commission proposal, abstentions counted as votes for the measures and they were imposed. This was certainly not the end of the story. The year also saw the beginnings of a major dispute arising from duties imposed by China on imports of car parts, with an unprecedented joint complaint to the WTO by the USA, Canada and the EU in September 2006.

During 2006, partly as a reflection of the tensions noted above, there were significant developments in the EU's overall commercial strategy. In the middle of the year, Mandelson publicly stated his desire to see the Union using its trade power more assertively – a position which could be interpreted as a response to lack of progress in the DDA. It then became apparent as the autumn progressed that the Commission was engaged in a search for bilateral trade agreements, especially with partners in Asia and Latin America and that Mandelson would be seeking a mandate from the Council to pursue such agreements as a matter of urgency even if the DDA did not completely stall.

This new orientation for EU commercial policy was formalized in the Commission Communication (Commission, 2006a) presented to the other institutions in October. The paper focused on the ways in which a 'more complete, more integrated and more forward looking' trade policy could enhance the Union's competitiveness and thus strengthen its internal economy. It set out an agenda for both internal and external action and prominent in the latter area was the pursuit of bilateral free trade agreements. Negotiations with the Association of Southeast Asian Nations (ASEAN), with Mercosur (the South American trading group) and with South Korea were already in train, but the communication called for new initiatives directed towards India, Russia and the Gulf Co-operation Council. In light of the continuing difficulties with the DDA, it might be expected that this thrust would become central to the 'new' EU commercial policy agenda. Although Mandelson presented the initiative as 'test driving' principles that could then be multilateralized, the consequences for the broader global agenda remain to be seen.

The second major formal initiative was the setting in train of a wide-ranging review of the EU's trade defence instruments. This can be seen largely as a response to the problems encountered with trade defence in a rapidly changing and globalizing world – a world in which, for example, the needs of consumers are as significant as those of EU producers and in which the outsourcing of production often means that trade defence measures can have perverse and unexpected consequences, such as the penalization of EU consumers and of major retailers. Relations with China (see below) are a case in point. Discussion and 'trailing' of this review began in the spring and was made more urgent by disputes such as those over shoes with China and Vietnam. In early December, the Commission adopted a Green Paper (Commission, 2006b) that set out the framework for consultation with a wide range of groups within the Community and was intended to lead to a set of legislative proposals during 2007.

Development Co-operation Policy and Humanitarian Aid

In 2006 the EU developed its plans for spending on development aid under the 2007–13 financial framework in a number of papers establishing four thematic programmes (Commission, 2007, pp. 167–8) Under this frame-work the EU will spend €16.9 billion on two 'mutually reinforcing' frame-works: the first of these is geographic and covers Asia, Central Asia, Latin America, the Middle East and South Africa. In addition the EU also agreed in 2006 to devote €21.9 billion in the 2008–13 period to the African, Caribbean and Pacific (ACP) under the 10th European Development Fund (EDF). This represents a small reduction of €700 million on the pro-grammes that were initially agreed in late 2005 and it is indicative of the growing supremacy of the Member States and the Council over the Com-mission, which had argued for an increase. The second spending framework is thematic and is open to all regions, including the ACP and is designed to strengthen regional programmes in response to particular needs such as education, health and migration. Finally a new financial instrument has been created (Instrument for Stability) that will devote €2 billion to dealing with crisis situations in non-EU states between 2007 and 2013.

There has been general dissatisfaction amongst the ACP countries about the EDF settlement and the way that the EU forces developing countries to liberalize their economies without adequate financial assistance. The ACP countries have been forced to remove almost all of their tariffs, thereby losing both protection and income. Further, the EU is insisting that they accept certain proposals in the Economic Partnership Agreements that were rejected in the DDA negotiations (Tendon, 2006).

There were some issues around the legality and propriety of some aspects of development spending in 2006, with the European Parliament taking exception to what it saw as the diversion of development aid funding to the African Peace Facility, a fund designed for peacekeeping and conflict prevention that has been used to support the African Union's efforts in the Darfur region of the Sudan. Similarly, the Commission was criticized for proposing that development aid to non ACP regions (i.e. other than the EDF) could be used to finance anti-terrorism measures. The Parliament's criticism is part of a much larger and ongoing argument between the Commission and the Council on the one hand and the Parliament on the other. The former seeks to better co-ordinate and merge development policy with other EU policies (on security, crime and immigration for instance) and the Parliament seeks effectively to ring-fence development spending where co-decision applies and prevent itself being by-passed.

During 2006 the EU delivered €671 million in Humanitarian Aid (Commission, 2007, p. 172), dealing with just under 100 incidents. The EU's swift and effective response to an earthquake in Java was typical (Crosbie, 2006), but, sadly, so too was the EU's decision to freeze humanitarian operations in some areas of the West Bank and Gaza Strip because of the danger to its personnel.

II. Regional Themes

Russia

2006 was not a good year for EU–Russian relations, with energy supply being added to an already considerable list of contentious issues. Russia's divide and rule strategy *vis-à-vis* the EU was aided by divisions amongst the EU Member States and institutions (Sweeney, 2006). Thus the Council and the Commission found themselves at odds over policy towards Russia and the larger states, led by Germany, demonstrated a preference for bilateral relations over EU solidarity. Towards the end of the year Poland vetoed the progression of talks designed to renew the EU–Russia Partnership and Co-operation Agreement (PCA). The official reason was Russia's refusal to accept Polish meat exports, but a more significant reason was to protest against German–Russian plans, first developed by then Chancellor Schröder and President Putin but continued by Chancellor Merkel, to build a gas pipeline under the Baltic bypassing both Poland and the Ukraine. Russia's hostility towards the EU has been increased by its unease at the growth of ESDP civilian and military activities, most especially on Russia's immediate borders in Central Asia (see below), in Georgia and in the Ukraine, Belarus and Moldova. Russia is also sensitive to the fact that, since 2004, the three Baltic States are now members of both the North Atlantic Treaty Organization (NATO) and the EU. NATO's meeting in Riga in November was tough for Russia to accept, although President Chirac played his part in a potential public relations disaster by apparently inviting President Putin to join him in Riga to celebrate his birthday! To the relief of all, Putin in the end declined because of his wish not to be received by the Latvian government. However, Russia's relations with the Baltic states were to take a more sinister turn when Russian objections to the re-siting of a Russian war memorial in Tallinn, Estonia, resulted in an interruption in Russian energy supplies as had also been the case earlier with Ukraine.

The question of the security of energy supply and of the possibility of Russian nationalization of EU-owned energy supply companies is, of course, a very important one for an EU which currently relies on Russia for 25 per cent of its oil imports and 35 per cent of its gas imports (*European Voice*, 2–8 November 2006, p. 19). Whilst the EU has failed to date to organize an effective common front for dealing with Russia over energy, it is, at the same time, criticized by those who feel that its concerns about energy lead it to be too soft on Russia as far as human rights abuses are concerned (Garton Ash *et al.*, 2006). Although the EU press cast suspicious eyes at Moscow over the death in London of Alexander Litvinenko, Putin once again avoided serious condemnation at the Helsinki EU–Russia summit mainly because the EU, thanks to Polish intransigence, was unable to agree on a common position despite the determination of the Finnish Presidency to move the EU's external focus from the Balkans under the Austrian Presidency to Russia (see Ojanen and Vuohula, this volume). Thus Putin was able, as before, to avoid discussion of corruption in Russia, of the treatment of minorities (here he was assisted by what he argued was the poor treatment of Russian minorities in the Baltic states) and of the situation in Chechnya. Some in the EU, such as the Baltic States and Poland, see Putin's behaviour in 2006 as a significant flexing of Russia's muscles and fear, in particular, further exploitation of its energy supplies. Others, like the UK and Germany, worry less about Russia's strength and more about its potential weakness. In particular they are concerned about Russia's ability to actually extract and deliver the energy supplies that the EU will need in the future. Concerns about the level of Russian investment in energy extraction and about the limitations of the broader Russian economy lead some in the EU to conclude that Putin's recent toughness towards the EU and some of its Member States is in some ways designed to compensate for an underlying weakness (*European Voice*, 2–8 November 2006, p. 21).

In the meantime the Council seems to be more relaxed about the delay in renegotiating the PCA than the Commission, but this is because the PCA process gives a major role to the Commission whilst more informal negotiations are more likely to be conducted by the Council in general and the High Representative, Javier Solana, in particular. Some observers, however, doubt whether it is necessary to negotiate an exact replacement for the PCA, citing the fact that the EU deals quite successfully with other major trading partners such as the US, India and China without the benefit of formal treaties. The issue of EU unity (best illustrated by the current differences between Germany and Poland over Russia) is probably a more serious barrier to an improved EU relationship with Russia than the nature of the documents that have or have not been negotiated to date (Munchau, 2006).

Africa

The refusal of the government of the Sudan to allow the UN to replace or further support the African Union peace-keeping force in the Darfur region frustrated the EU's attempts to do something about the plight of the region's inhabitants. By the end of 2006 the EU Special Representative for Sudan, Pekka Haavisto, expressed the view that the EU would need to finance the African Union AMIS force for at least another six months in 2007 before a long-term solution could be envisaged. The EU itself came under pressure to consider economic sanctions against Khartoum and to put pressure on China, the Sudan's major trading partner and supporter at the UN. Building on its Darfur experience the EU did take steps during the year to improve its relationship with the African Union both by reinforcing its presence at its headquarters in Addis Ababa and by seeking ways of speeding up the process whereby the EU launches its African security sector reform missions, such as that initiated in 2005 with the military of the Democratic Republic of the Congo (DRC). The European Security Strategy calls for EU action against failed states, organized crime and terrorism and weapons proliferation and Africa is increasingly seen as one of the central areas of concern in the contemporary international system.

In April the EU launched its fourth military mission, led by Germany, in the DRC and successfully provided support to the UN mission (MONUC) to ensure stability during the first democratic elections in the DRC for 40 years (Gegout, 2007). The EU also gave its support to negotiations initiated by the League of Arab States to try and bring peace to Somalia and organized a conference on 'good governance' in Brussels in November, attended by 16 African heads of state as well as the World Bank and the UN. However, as the EU pushed forward with its politico-security agenda for Africa and sought further ways to focus on conflict prevention and management, it faced problems in the economic area with east and central African countries threatening to frustrate plans for the second EU–Africa summit in 2007 because of their dissatisfaction with the EU's prioritization of trade over development issues. Specifically the African states are concerned about the apparent lack of EU funds available to finance the costs of adjusting to the trade reforms that the EU is demanding. They are, therefore, reluctant to develop further the EU's plans for EPAs for each of Africa's four designated regions that are meant to be in place by the end of 2007.

Asia

The 'rise of Asia' has become a predominant if not an obsessive concern for many EU officials, especially in commercial policy. One of the consequences of this rapid and fundamental shift in the 'terms of exchange' between the EU and Asian countries has been a real problem for the EU in setting priorities and deciding what its key targets and goals are in EU–Asian relations.

One response – sponsored by both the EU and Asian countries – has been the establishment of broad dialogue between the Union and its Asian partners in the context of the Asia-Europe Meeting (ASEM). This process has been institutionalized in a number of ways, with a range of dialogues and networks surrounding the biennial meetings of heads of state and government, but the institutionalization remains relatively thin and the obligations of those involved relatively informal. Thus, when the tenth anniversary of the ASEM was celebrated with the meeting in Helsinki (10–11 September), the meeting's focus was shaped not only by multilateral priorities shared by ASEM members, but also by broader global pressures and by narrower bilateral concerns. Global concerns with the price and availability of energy supplies were a central focus, but so were the new EU initiatives towards bilateral free trade agreements (see above).

At the meeting new members were proposed for the ASEM – India, Pakistan and Mongolia, bringing a South Asian dimension into the ASEM, as well as Bulgaria and Romania, because of their imminent accession to the EU. These changes – especially the South Asian members – are likely to have significant implications for the ASEM process, but only in the medium to long term.

In the realm of bilateral relations, China inevitably dominated. This review noted earlier that the EU and Commissioner Mandelson in particular, had called for greater assertiveness in holding China to its WTO obligations and in defending EU interests. Given the yawning and growing deficit in EU–China trade, this could be seen as a pragmatic response, but it also had a strongly strategic element, designed to contain China within a web of international obligations and to ensure that the EU was operating from a position of maximum strength in anticipation of disputes and challenges to come. A similar trend has been visible in US policies towards China and an indication of the convergence between EU and US policies can be seen in the joint complaint to the WTO over China's restrictions on imports of car parts (see above). The EU steadfastly refuses to cede to Chinese demands that they be accorded 'market economy' status in trade relations, whilst reminding China forcefully of its obligations under WTO membership. There is also still a majority in the EU (although a weakening one) in favour of maintaining the arms embargo established in the wake of the Tienanmen Square incident in 1989. But there is also a strong desire to establish a new framework for the development of what will become a dominant EU external relationship.

As a reflection of these strategic needs, the EU decided during 2006 to pursue a new trade and co-operation agreement with China. As part of the preparation for this, the Commission produced a Communication (Commission, 2006d) accompanied by a strategy paper (Commission, 2006e). These papers set out the Commission's priorities both in economic and political/ security terms for dealing with what has rapidly become one of the EU's key strategic partners. The broad framework was one of 'engagement and partnership' but also of fulfilment of international responsibilities and obligations.

The EU's second strategic partner in Asia is India and it is clear that EU–Indian relations are rather less mature even than those between the EU and China. It was noted above that India is becoming a member of the ASEM process and it is also clear that India has come to occupy a central position in the EU's approach to world trade via the DDA and the WTO. During 2006, the EU also achieved observer status in the South Asian Regional Co-operation Association (SARCA), giving it further access to policy debates about the region. Bilaterally, 2006 saw the sixth EU–India summit meeting and the initiation of an EU–India security dialogue, which was held for the first time in May 2006. In addition, as noted above, India is one of the EU's 'targets' for its new wave of bilateral free trade agreements. But it could still be powerfully argued that EU–India relations remained under-developed (Cameron, 2006) and that the EU had much to learn about the regional dynamics of South Asia as a whole. In this respect, the 'curve' of institutionalization and mutual learning in EU–India relations should develop rapidly during the next few years, as also should the potential areas of friction and dispute; the EU marked 2006 with calls for India to reduce its punitive tariffs on wines and spirits, lodging a WTO complaint and this is only the tip of the iceberg of potential trade tensions.

The EU also has a growing politico-security involvement in the affairs of the former Soviet Asian states and this in turn has attracted some hostile reaction from those in the European Parliament concerned about the abuse of human rights in these countries (Warkotsch, 2007). In 2006 the EU renewed sanctions against Uzbekistan for human rights infringements and contemplated a rule of law mission to Kirgizstan. It also made progress towards improved relations with both Kazakhstan, which has recently indicated a desire to participate in the EU's Neighbourhood Policy, and Turkmenistan – both of which have poor human rights records.

In Afghanistan, EU Member States provide considerable military support to the International Security Force, although it is perhaps significant that they choose Nato rather than the ESDP as the organizational framework for this mission. There are also significant tensions among the Member States about providing combat troops. If the EU does become involved in Afghanistan, it is likely to be via a policing and rule of law mission rather than a military mission.

Latin America

Latin America is the site for some of the more challenging political changes and confrontations of recent years, especially the rise of new nationalist/ socialist forms such as those represented by Hugo Chavez in Venezuela and Evo Morales in Bolivia. It is also the scene for indirect EU–US competition and for sustained engagement by some (though a minority) of EU Member States, such as Spain. In addition, it has spawned efforts at regional economic co-operation that perhaps come closest to those on which the EU is based. So there is a substantial basis for EU involvement and interest in the region. This involvement has been attempted at several levels: inter-continental via successive EU–Latin American summits, inter-regional through engagement with regional co-operation and integration efforts and bilateral through relations with key EU partners such as Brazil (the latter also important in terms of the WTO and global trade negotiations).

During 2006, all of these traits were in evidence, but with inconclusive outcomes. The fourth EU–Latin American summit was held in Vienna on 12 May, informed by an earlier Commission Communication (Commission, 2005 – adopted by the Council 27 February 2006); despite broader strategic aims, the summit was to a large degree hijacked by energy issues, especially those arising out of nationalization processes in Venezuela and Bolivia. There were continuing efforts to give new life to inter-regional negotiations, but those with Mercosur remained stalled, not helped by continuing tensions within Mercosur itself, whilst the inclusion of the Andean Community and the Central American Common Market in the list of targets for new free trade agreement negotiations was promise rather than performance during 2006. Bilaterally, the EU's relations with Cuba remained delicate in the wake of new measures against dissidents by the Castro regime, whilst those with key existing partners such as Chile and Mexico proceeded on established lines.

The United States, Japan and other Industrial Countries

The relationship with the USA is taken by many within and outside the EU institutions as a litmus test of the extent to which the EU has established itself as a key 'power' in the world arena and as a key indicator of the ways in which the Union has established a distinctive international role. This initial evaluation is well borne out by the events of 2006. Whilst the EU's relations with Japan were not without interest in 2006, especially in light of the growing 'China factor' in external policy-making in both Tokyo and Brussels, there is little of major significance to report from a relationship that seems to have matured and become more predictable year by year. In the same way, South Korea is of interest because of a number of ongoing trade disputes and because of the ways in which Seoul has become a target for the EU's bilateral free trade agreements initiative, but it cannot be said that it took a central place in EU external policies during 2006. After a few years of some activity and interest, Australia and New Zealand retreated well into the background during this year. The Union did adopt a Commission communication and a related new financial instrument relating to co-operation with advanced industrial countries (Commission, 2006c), which represented in many respects a globalization of measures that had been entered into with respect to the USA and Japan over the past decade and which covers a wide range of economic and social activities.

The United States, though, maintained its central role and importance, in a number of both established and new respects. Overall, 2006 might be seen as a year of some uncertainty but distinctly increased optimism about the direction of American policies. It was apparent throughout the year that the atmosphere was warmer and that this related to a perception in Europe that Washington had returned to more 'normal' directions in terms of diplomacy and global order. This did not mean that there were no tensions between Washington and Brussels; we have noted already the frictions generated by the WTO negotiations and there were others relating to specific commercial and political issues (see below). But there was a broad assumption that US policies had returned to a more readily recognizable path of co-operation and multilateralism. There were some who characterized this rather differently, as an attempt by the Bush Administration to 'export' some of its more worrisome international problems to the EU and other allies (Zaborowski, 2006), but in general there was a feeling that things were on the mend. There was also a related feeling that the EU's 'soft power' could gain more traction in the new circumstances and that attention could be paid to some of the issues arising from the evolution of the 'transatlantic architecture'. In the context of the annual EU–US summit meeting which took place in Washington during June, the European Parliament also passed a resolution calling for pursuit of a new 'Transatlantic Partnership Agreement' (European Parliament, 2006) and this seemed to sum up the more positive atmosphere.

One of the key areas of EU international diplomacy and of EU–US diplomatic interaction was the attempt to deal with Iran's nuclear programmes. One of the key elements in the policies pursued by the 'EU-3' has always been the desire to moderate US policies and above all to counter the push in some parts of the US Administration towards the use of force as a way of dealing with the problem. Thus during 2006, the EU-3 could be seen assembling and re-assembling packages designed to give the Iranian regime a way out of the impasse without selling the pass on the military aspects of nuclear power and also trying to assemble international support in the context of the International Atomic Energy Agency (IAEA) and the UNSC. Despite these efforts, as the issue was more thoroughly appropriated by the UNSC during the summer and autumn, the EU-3 seemed to become marginalized to a degree. Their offers of nuclear technology as part of an overall agreement were spurned by the Iranian government and whilst not obstructed by Washington, they were not wholeheartedly supported. As a result, by the end of the year the UNSC had voted for sanctions and the stage was set for potential escalation of the dispute – either through multilateral means or through action by the US and some of its allies.

Whilst Iran dominated EU–US diplomacy at the 'hard power' end of the spectrum, there were other security issues that claimed a good deal of attention during 2006. A cluster of issues either emerged or were sustained in the area of 'soft security', especially linked to the 'war on terror'. Throughout the year, the investigations by the Council of Europe and the European Parliament into the practice of 'rendition' (through which terrorist suspects were transported by the US's Central Intelligence Agency (CIA) via Europe to a variety of interrogation centres) rumbled on. An interim report of the European Parliament's investigation during April revealed the extent of the CIA's activity, whilst in June a Council of Europe report (2006) took the story further. Although it seemed to have been established that the flights took place (implicating Germany and Italy among others), there was little overall progress until late in the year when the newly-Democrat Congress began to put the pressure on the Bush Administration in the USA itself.

Alongside rendition, a series of other 'soft security' issues were the source of frictions and demands for EU action. In late May, the European Court of Justice (ECJ) ruled that the agreement between the Commission and the US Administration on the transfer and handling of airline passenger data (see Allen and Smith, 2006) was null and void, essentially because it had been constructed on an inappropriate legal base and gave the parties until 30 September to conclude a new agreement (see also Dougan, this volume). The European Parliament, which had referred the case to the ECJ in the first place, set out to obstruct any new agreement, whilst the US tabled new demands for access to and the retention of data. Eventually an agreement was made in early October, but this did not remove the causes of the initial tensions within the EU itself. There were related tensions over the transfer of financial services data to US authorities through the SWIFT interbank clearing system. In a related area, the EU pressed throughout the year for US action on the granting of visa waivers to some EU Member States (Greece and the 2004 new Member States except Slovenia, which had one), threatening to impose sanctions on Canada as a kind of indirect threat to the USA before hinting at more direct action. This is an area where the US is essentially limited by domestic legislation, which sets tests in respect of countries' record on such areas as overstaying or the commission of criminal offences, but it is also an area where EU officials have seen the importance of establishing some kind of parity and recognition of the results of enlargement.

The EU and the US were also involved in potentially far-reaching commercial negotiations and disputes during 2006. A number of important disputes persisted and some were exacerbated during the year. Most notable was that over genetically modified crops. Early in the year, a WTO panel judged that the EU's original rules – essentially constituting a moratorium on approval of such crops – were illegal (Grant and Minder, 2006). This ruling was seen as important not only in itself and in EU–US relations, but also in respect of potential access for GM crops to third markets such as those of Africa. However, the EU felt no real need to respond to the ruling since it had changed the rules in question and had started to approve at least some genetically modified products. This did not satisfy the Americans, nor did the persistence of a number of individual Member State restrictions. Later in the year, a new dimension of this issue emerged when it was discovered that US exports of rice to the EU had been tainted by contact with GM rice; the EU immediately imposed restrictions and testing requirements, eventually demanding that all US long-grain rice imports should be certified free of the GM strain.

Whilst this was perhaps the most pressing dispute, the mutual parallel complaints to the WTO between the EU and the USA in relation to the Airbus dispute (see Allen and Smith, 2006) also continued. There were arguments about the data provided by each side but with a subtle change in emphasis arising from the contrasting fortunes of Airbus and Boeing during the year (Boeing doing better, Airbus significantly worse). Meanwhile, the long-running dispute on 'foreign sales corporations' persisted and the EU remained anxious to ensure that previous disputes such as that over the so-called Byrd Amendment (which had given US firms the proceeds of actions against EU companies) were fully resolved; the Amendment was eventually fully phased out, but not before the EU exerted pressure to ensure it was eliminated.

Disputes are only part of the story of 'competitive co-operation' between the EU and the US and during 2006 the two partners moved forward on a highly significant international negotiation on creating 'open skies' in transatlantic air travel. The Commission, acting on a mandate from the Council, had established itself as a collective negotiator during previous years and in 2006 things came to a head in terms of the negotiations themselves. A provisional agreement reached at the end of 2005 had left some key issues unresolved, in particular that of Europeans' rights to invest in and take control of US-based airlines. There were other concerns, for example over the environmental implications of the agreement and over access to the 'domestic' markets of the EU and the US, but as time went on it was ownership that became central to the progress of the negotiations. Some US airlines and elements in Congress were ready to play the 'national security' card in arguing against any possibility of foreign control of US airlines. By the middle of the year, it appeared that protectionist pressures had stalled the negotiations and this feeling was underlined by the Democrat victory in the mid-term elections later in the year. As of the end of 2006, it appeared that only if either unexpected concessions were made by the US, or the EU was prepared to accept continuing restrictions on investment, could an agreement be contemplated on what had become a key issue for EU collective negotiations with the Americans.

By the end of 2006, therefore, EU–US relations held promise but also pitfalls. There were those who advocated a step change in EU leadership initiatives to take over from the US in important policy areas (Wallace, 2006). Equally, there were those on both sides who could see the opportunity for new and major steps in transatlantic collaboration (Stokes, 2006). It was questionable, though, whether leaderships on both sides of the Atlantic were ready to take major initiatives or capable of carrying them through in the face of domestic political pressures and more pressing international problems.

Key Readings

Commission of the European Communities (2007) provides a good review of the external activities of the EU (pp. 158–94) along with footnoted links to all the relevant EU documentation.

Institute for Security Studies (2007) brings together all the key documents on ESDP in 2006.

CFSP Forum is published bi-monthly by FORNET («http://www.fornet.info»). Volume 4 (2006) and Volume 5 (2007) contain numerous articles on current CFSP and ESDP activities.

Cameron (2007) provides useful background material for most aspects of EU external relations.

References

Allen, D. and Smith, M. (2006) 'Relations With the Wider World'. *JCMS Annual Review*, pp. 155–70.

Beattie, A. (2006) 'Doha Round Goes in Circles as Deal Remains Elusive'. *Financial Times*, 18 April, p. 6.

Cameron, F. (2006) 'When Will the EU Show up on India's Radar Screens?' *European Voice*, 2–8 March, p. 16.

Cameron, F. (2007) *An Introduction to European Foreign Policy* (London: Routledge).

Commission of the European Communities (2005) *A Stronger Partnership between the European Union and Latin America*, COM(2005)636 (Brussels: European Commission).

Commission of the European Communities (2006a) *Competing in the World – a Contribution to the European Union's Jobs and Growth Strategy*, COM(2006)567 (Brussels: European Commission).

Commission of the European Communities (2006b) *Global Europe: Europe's Trade Defence Instruments in a Changing Global Economy*, COM(2006)763 (Brussels: European Commission).

Commission of the European Communities (2006c) *Thematic Programme on Co-operation with Industrialized Countries under the Future Financial Perspective*, COM(2006)25 (Brussels: European Commission).

Commission of the European Communities (2006d) *EU–China: Closer Partners, Growing Responsibilities*, COM(2006) 631 (Brussels: European Commission).

Commission of the European Communities (2006e) *A Policy Paper on EU–China Trade and Investment: Competition and Partnership*, COM(2006)631 (Brussels: European Commission).

Commission of the European Communities (2006f) *Europe in the World – Some Practical Proposals for Greater Coherence, Effectiveness and Visibility*, Communication from the Commission to the European Council of June 2006, COM (2006) 278.

Commission of the European Communities (2007) *General Report on the Activities of the European Union*, 2006 (Brussels: European Commission).

Council of Europe (2006) 'Alleged Secret Detentions and Unlawful Inter-state Transfers Involving Council of Europe Member States' (Strasbourg: Council of Europe Parliamentary Assembly, rapporteur Mr Dick Marty, AS/Jur [2006]16, 7 June).

Crosbie, J. (2006) 'ECHO on Alert as Java Suffers Again'. *European Voice*, 1–7 June, p. 19.

Dembinski, M. (2007) 'Europe and the UNIFIL 11 Mission: Stumbling into the Conflict Zone of the Middle East'. *CFSP Forum*, 5/1, pp. 1–4.

Duke, S. (2006) 'Outcomes Before Dogma: Restarting the External Action Service Debate'. *CFSP Forum*, 4/6, pp. 8–11.

European Parliament (2006) 'Resolution on Improving EU–US Relations in the Framework of a Transatlantic Partnership Agreement'. Adopted 1 June. *Bulletin of the EU* 6-2006, point 1.33.20.

European Voice (2006) 2–8 November, pp. 8–9.

Garton Ash, T., Moisi, D. and Smolar, A. (2006) 'Europe Must not Trade its Principles for Russian Gas'. *Financial Times*, 10 July, p. 17.

Gegout, C. (2007) 'The EU and Security in the Democratic Republic of the Congo in 2006: Unfinished Business'. *CFSP Forum*, 5/1, pp. 5–8.

Grant, J. and Minder, R. (2006) 'Crop Resistance: Why a Transatlantic Split Persists Over Genetically Modified Food'. *Financial Times*, 1 February, p. 17.

Institute for Security Studies (2007) EU Security and Defence: Core Documents 2006, Compiled by Catherine Gliere, Vol. 11, Chaillot Paper No. 97 (Paris: EU Institute for Security Studies).

Lindstrom, G. (2007) *Enter the EU Battlegroups*, Chaillot Paper No. 97, February 2007 (Paris: EU Institute for Security Studies).

Munchau, W. (2006) 'Europe Needs a Joint Response to Russia'. *Financial Times*, 8 May, p. 17.

Munchau, W. (2007) 'Europe's Constitution May Not be Dead After All'. *Financial Times*, 27 January, p. 17.

Parker, G. (2006) 'Would a Constitution by Another Name Smell Sweeter?' *Financial Times*, 29 May, p. 4.

Stokes, B. (2006) 'Time to Think Big Across the Atlantic'. *European Voice*, 16–22 November, p. 13.

Sweeney, C. (2006) 'EU Disunity Plays into Putin's Hands'. *European Voice*, 30 November to 6 December, p. 14.

Tendon, Y. (2006) 'EU Brokering Unfair Deal With Poor States'. *European Voice*, 26 October to 1 November, p. 9.

Wallace, W. (2006) 'Europe Should Fill the Global Leadership Gap'. *Financial Times*, 27 September, p. 17.

Warkotsch, A. (2007) 'The Rhetoric–Reality Gap in the EU's Democracy Promotion in Central Asia'. *CFSP Forum*, 5/1, pp. 14–16.

Zaborowski, M. (2006) 'Softer Bush Exports Foreign Policy Dilemmas to Europe'. *European Voice*, 9–15 February, p. 13.

JCMS 2007 Volume 45 Annual Review pp. 183–211

Political Developments in the EU Member States

KAREN HENDERSON
University of Leicester
NICK SITTER
Norwegian School of Management, BI

Introduction

2006 was the second full year in which the European Union (EU) operated with 25 Member States. Across the EU, seven governments fell during 2006, four as the direct consequence of elections. Two parliamentary elections were held early because governments fell and seven were more or less on schedule. A number of these elections were close and resulted in protracted negotiations and in some cases grand coalitions. In two countries – France and Hungary – government initiatives have provoked sizeable demonstrations, which in France caused a policy reversal. In short, the patterns of elections, party competition and the making and breaking of governments varies across Europe, but not along an east–west axis. This chapter therefore adopts a comparative perspective on developments in the EU Member States. The central focus is on elections, changes of government and party system change. The latter includes both changes in political parties (their number, cohesion and policy profiles) and changes in their patterns of competition (alliances and bloc-building).

Although the crude distinction between old and new Member States may no longer be particularly useful, this chapter does not dispense with it completely. In what follows, developments in the EU Member States are analysed in a review that takes a roughly anti-clockwise sweep through the continent and groups states in four sets that reflect a combination of geography, political systems and accession dates. Section I covers five of the six original Member

States from the core of Western Europe, plus Austria. Section II turns to developments in the Mediterranean states, including original Member State Italy. Section III on eastern and central Europe discusses all the 2004 accession states except Cyprus and Malta. Section IV covers the Scandinavian Member States, the UK and Ireland.

The two *Eurobarometer* surveys of 2006 (see Table 1) show a general increase in popular support for the EU across the board, measured in terms of

Table 1: Share of Respondents Who Describe EU Membership as 'a Good Thing'

	2006		2005		2004	
	Autumn	*Spring*	*Autumn*	*Spring*	*Autumn*	*Spring*
Ireland	78	77	73	75	77	71
Luxembourg	74	72	82	80	85	75
Netherlands	72	74	70	77	75	64
Belgium	69	65	59	67	73	57
Spain	62	72	66	66	72	64
Lithuania	**62**	**59**	**57**	**59**	**69**	**52**
Poland	**62**	**56**	**54**	**53**	**50**	**42**
Denmark	61	65	56	59	61	54
Slovakia	**61**	**55**	**50**	**54**	**57**	**46**
Germany	58	57	53	58	60	45
Greece	57	53	54	56	61	71
Slovenia	**57**	**54**	**43**	**49**	**52**	**40**
Estonia	**56**	**51**	**41**	**48**	**52**	**31**
New Member States	*56*	*54*	*49*	*51*	*50*	*43*
EU-25	*53*	*55*	*50*	*54*	*56*	*47*
EU-15	*52*	*55*	*50*	*55*	*57*	*48*
Italy	52	56	50	56	57	54
Czech Republic	**51**	**52**	**44**	**49**	**45**	**41**
France	50	49	46	51	56	43
Portugal	50	47	54	61	59	55
Sweden	49	49	39	44	48	37
Cyprus	**47**	**49**	**41**	**43**	**52**	**42**
Malta	**45**	**44**	**43**	**40**	**45**	**50**
Latvia	**43**	**37**	**36**	**42**	**40**	**33**
Finland	39	39	38	45	48	46
Hungary	**39**	**49**	**39**	**42**	**49**	**45**
Austria	36	34	32	37	46	30
UK	34	42	34	36	38	29

Note: New Member States in bold.
Sources: *Eurobarometer Spring 2004: Joint Full Report of Eurobarometer 61 and CC Eurobarometer 2004:1* (July 2004), pp. B34, C50; *Standard Eurobarometer 62, Autumn 2004* (May 2005), p. 68; *Standard Eurobarometer 64, Autumn 2005: First Results* (December 2005), p. 12; *Standard Eurobarometer 65, Spring 2006* (January 2007), p. 76; *Standard Eurobarometer 66, Autumn 2006: First Results* (December 2006), p. 7.

the percentage of respondents who see EU membership as 'a good thing'. The average approval rate for the EU-25 increased from 50 per cent in the autumn of 2005 to 53 per cent a year later. Since the 2004 enlargement, this figure has held steady between 50 and 56 per cent. Only Luxembourg and Portugal showed a drop in support for the EU in both the spring and autumn surveys of 2006, though another five states showed a drop in one of the two surveys. The UK replaced Austria as the country with the lowest popular support for the EU. Comparing the present results to the 2004 data, there is no evidence of any kind of backlash against EU membership in the new Member States. Most of the Member States, new and old alike, show a marginal increase in popular support for the EU.

I. Central Western Europe

Two elections in central western Europe resulted in broad coalitions across the left–right divide. In both Austria and the Netherlands the elections of 2006 caused a return to grand coalitions, a common feature of their post-war histories, after a spell of centre-right government. In Austria this was a return to the 'red–black' coalitions of the consociational system. In the Netherlands it involved the centrist Christian Democratic Alliance changing coalition partners. France, Germany, Belgium and Luxembourg all ended 2006 more or less with the same government as they had started it.

Local elections in Belgium and state elections in Germany had only a limited impact on party politics. Germany saw the first tentative efforts of the Christian Democratic Union (CDU) and Greens to explore coalitions at the state (*Land*) level, but the five state elections generally reinforced the position of the two national coalition partners: the CDU and the Social Democrats (SPD). Although the CDU lost votes in four states and the SPD in three, both parties remained in their governing coalitions at the state level. In two cases (Mecklenburg-Western Pomerania and Saxony Anhalt) left- and right-wing coalitions were replaced by state-level grand coalitions between the CDU and SPD. The elections in Baden-Württemberg prompted the first ever coalition talks between the CDU and the Greens, although a renewed CDU-Free Democrat coalition was ultimately formed. The main political upset came in Mecklenburg-Western Pomerania, where the far-right (neo-Nazi) National Democratic Party crossed the 5 per cent threshold and won representation in the state legislature (the SPD lost more than ten percentage points). On the left of the German party spectrum, the socialist Labour and Social Justice (WASG), established in 2004, agreed a merger with the Left Party, due to take place in the spring of 2007. In

Belgium, Prime Minister Verhofstat's Liberals suffered losses in the local elections, while the far right Vlaams Belang performed well, polling more than 20 per cent in Dutch-speaking areas.

In France, the selection of candidates for the 2007 presidential election suggested considerable change: both the left and right selected candidates that claimed to stand for a break with traditional elitist French politics. Both the governing UMP (Union for a Popular Movement, which brought together Gaullist, Christian Democrat and conservative parties to support Jacques Chirac's successful presidential bid in 2002) and the opposition Socialists decided to select their presidential candidates by primaries.

On the left, the divisions over the Constitutional Treaty (see Taggart, 2006) prompted the Socialists to postpone their primary until November 2006. Ségolène Royal won the contest in the first round, polling more than 60 per cent of the vote. She cast herself as a modernizer of the Tony Blair type and an admirer of Nordic social democracy. Her victory owed more to her popular appeal with party members than to the traditional party machinery. Nicolas Sarkozy, the interior minister who emerged as the near-certain UMP candidate in 2006 (he won 98 per cent of the vote in the January 2007 primary), represented a victory for the party's liberal wing over the more traditional conservative prime minister, Dominique de Villepin. By the end of 2006, the two main contenders for the 2007 presidential election were campaigning on platforms that included 'modernization' (although a more old-fashioned third contender emerged when the centrist Union for French Democracy's François Bayrou declared his candidacy). The two main candidates diverged on the European question: Royal promising a referendum on a new version of the Constitutional Treaty; Sarkozy suggesting that a 'mini-treaty' might be passed by parliament.

Popular support for European integration remained fairly stable in central western Europe in 2006. The Netherlands, Belgium and Luxembourg score below only Ireland in terms of popular support for EU membership. Although the percentage of Luxembourg respondents who see EU membership as 'a good thing' slipped to 74 per cent, Luxembourg featured the second most pro-EU population in the EU. Figures in the Netherlands and Belgium were stable and even rose slightly, to nearly 70 per cent. With 58 per cent approval of EU membership, Germany remained above the EU average, while France's 50 per cent support put the country somewhat below average. Both saw relatively little change from 2005. Luxembourg and Belgium ratified the Constitutional Treaty in 2005, as did the German parliament (though the president had yet to sign it by the end of 2006), whereas French and Dutch voters had rejected the Constitutional Treaty by referendums in 2005 (see Taggart, 2006).

Austria: Back to Grand Coalition Politics

The 2006 election in Austria brought about the return to grand coalition politics: cooperation between the Social Democrats (SPÖ) and the conservative People's Party (ÖVP). Both the inconclusive election result and the grand coalition prompted immediate parallels to the 2005 election in Germany. In Austria, however, the two big parties had governed together for two long periods in the past, 1945–66 and 1986–99, while the previous German grand coalition had lasted only from 1966 to 1969. The strong electoral showing in the late 1990s of the right-wing Freedom Party (FPÖ) – it drew level with the ÖVP in 1999 – had generally been interpreted as a reaction to such 'grand coalition' politics and proportional power sharing, which extended to control over a number of public sector positions. Although the 1999 and 2002 elections resulted in centre-right coalitions and seemed to signal an era of left versus right coalitions, the 2006 elections brought this to an end. This was for want of other workable alternatives, however, as much as a conscious effort or strategic choice on the part of the two parties. Although six or seven parties were credible contenders, only five won parliamentary representation. The communists fell below the electoral threshold and (as in Sweden) a Eurosceptic movement that had performed very well in the 2004 European Parliament (EP) elections failed completely at the national level. The election took place on 1 October, eight weeks ahead of schedule, in order to secure a new government before the end of the year.

With this relatively large number of parties competing in the election and having a real chance of winning seats, polls indicated considerable support for the return of a grand coalition. Pre-election polls suggested a clear victory for Chancellor Wolfgang Schüssel's ÖVP, but he was running out of potential allies. The Austrian party system experienced a shock when the FPÖ left the coalition in 2004. Jörg Haider and much of the leadership remained in government and left the FPÖ to form the Alliance for the Future of Austria (BZÖ). However, the BZÖ's prospects for the 2006 election were poor and the result confirmed this (see Table 2). The Freedom Party performed better, but because it had split over whether to remain in the governing coalition with the ÖVP, it could hardly join a coalition in 2006. Personal animosity between Haider and FPÖ leader Heinz-Christian Strache in any case precluded a three-party centre-right coalition. Although the result was a surprise insofar as the SPÖ's victory was not expected (a scandal linked to the trade-union-owned bank Bawag eroded the SPÖ's initial lead in the polls in the spring), the grand coalition came as no surprise. The result left little other choice. The SPÖ ruled out a coalition with either of the two far right parties, the SPÖ and the Greens fell short of a majority and the Greens would not work with the

Table 2: Austrian Parliamentary Election, October 2006

	2006		2002	
	Votes (%)	Seats	Votes (%)	Seats
Social Democrats (SPÖ)	35.3	68	36.5	69
People's Party (ÖVP)	34.3	66	42.3	79
Greens (Grüne)	11.1	21	9.5	17
Freedom Party (FPÖ)	11.0	21	10.0	19
Alliance for the Future of Austria (BZÖ)	4.1	7	–	0
Others	4.2	0	1.7	0

Sources: Austrian Interior Ministry, available at: «http://www.bmi.gov.at»; Fallend (2007).

conservative ÖVP. The grand coalition was therefore left as the only sustainable majority alternative. However, it would take three months of negotiations, lasting into January 2007, to reach agreement on such a coalition, led by SPÖ Chairman Alfred Gusenbauer.

The 2006 Austrian election was a failure for the radical parties on the political periphery apart from the FPÖ. On the right flank, the hard-right (and Eurosceptic) FPÖ performed best, polling almost level with the Greens. As none of the three smaller parties were prepared to join forces to make possible a majority coalition with one of the two main parties, the three smaller parties were effectively marginalized. The two other somewhat extremist movements, the Communists and the Eurosceptic Hans-Peter Martin List, fell below the electoral threshold. Like the Eurosceptic list in Sweden, the List had performed well in the 2004 EP elections, scoring 14 per cent, but found little resonance in national politics.

The Netherlands: A Step to the Left and Back to 'Normal Politics'?

The 22 November election in the Netherlands was brought about by the fall of the centre-right coalition in June 2006; elections had not been due until the summer of 2007. As in Austria and the Czech Republic and in Germany in 2005, the results were inconclusive (see Table 3). The centre-right coalition was defeated, but no bloc emerged as the clear winner. The smaller parties on the left and the right flanks performed well, as did some of the smaller parties in the centre. The three big parties – Labour (PvdA), the Christian Democrats (CDA) and the Liberals (VVD) – polled less than 63 per cent of the vote, a loss of more than 11 per cent. Apart from the 'earthquake' 2002 election, when the right-populist Pim Fortuyn List (LPF) beat both the Liberals and Social Democrats and became the Netherlands' second largest party, this was the first time the big three parties (or their predecessors: the CDA was a merger of three religious parties in the 1970s) polled less than 70 per cent of

Table 3: Parliamentary Election in the Netherlands, November 2006

	2006 Votes (%)	Seats	2003 Votes (%)	Seats	2002 Votes (%)
Labour (PvdA)	21.2	33	27.3	42	15.1
Christian Democrats (CDA)	26.5	41	28.6	44	27.9
Liberals (VVD)	14.7	22	17.9	28	15.4
Democrats 66 (D66)	2.0	3	4.1	6	5.1
Socialists (SP)	16.6	25	6.3	9	5.9
ChristenUnie	4.0	6	2.1	3	2.5
Reformed Party (SGP)	1.6	2	1.6	2	1.7
Greens (Groenlinks)	4.6	7	5.1	8	7.0
Party for the Animals (PvdD)	1.8	2	–	–	–
Wilders/Freedom Party (PvdV)	5.9	9	–	–	–
Fortuyn (LPF)	0.2	0	5.7	8	17.0
Others	1.0	0	1.3	0	2.4

Source: Dutch Electoral Council, available at «http://www.kiesraad.nl».

the vote. The CDA and Labour reached a coalition agreement with the small Christian party ChristenUnie in early January 2007, a relatively short period of negotiations by Dutch standards. This CDA–Labour alliance was by no means new to Dutch politics: the Christian Democrats (and their predecessors) had taken part in every coalition since the Second World War, usually working with either the Liberals or Labour, until the two other parties formed the 'purple coalitions' between 1994 and 2002.

Although the Liberal–Labour coalitions of 1994–2002 broke new ground in Dutch politics by excluding the CDA, the shock that still resonates in Dutch politics was the strong performance of the populist LPF in 2002. The 2006 election confirmed the trend of a return to more traditional patterns of centre-left and centre-right coalition politics, but with a weaker role for the three big established parties. After the 2002 election the CDA's Jan Peter Balkenende had brought together a coalition with the Liberals and the LFP. This coalition proved short-lived, not least because of the problematic relationship with the LPF. The early election in 2003 brought a return to more normal patterns of party politics: the LPF was reduced to less than 6 per cent and a more traditional centre-right coalition was established by the CDA, the Liberals and the centrist Democrats 66. However, although D66 proved a more reliable partner than the LPF, the coalition was beset with tensions between D66 and the Liberals. At the same time, Labour leader Wouter Bos positioned the party closer to the CDA, hinting at a centre-left coalition after the next elections. D66 had threatened to leave the coalition in 2005 and early 2006 and matters came to a head over Liberal Interior Minister Rita

Verdonk's handling of a Somali-born Liberal MP's citizenship. When, in a television documentary, Ayaan Hirsi Ali admitted to giving false information in her asylum application (a fact disclosed to the Liberal party when she was selected for MP), Verdonk moved to have her citizenship revoked. Although Verdonk later backed down, D66 demanded her resignation and withdrew from the coalition when this was not forthcoming, thus causing early elections in November 2006. Neither of the two liberal parties, D66 and VVD, emerged well from this crisis.

The main winners in the 2006 Dutch elections were the small parties. The Socialist Party (which had opposed the Constitutional Treaty) nearly tripled its vote, largely at Labour's expense having attacked the party from the left. Geert Wilders's new Freedom Party emerged as a strong contender for the LPF's mantle on the populist right. The (Eurosceptic) ChristenUnie, which is somewhat better regarded than the fact that it derives its policies from the Bible might suggest, doubled its vote to 4 per cent and joined the governing coalition. Two smaller parties, the Calvinist SGP and an animal rights party contributed further to a fragmented parliament. The Liberals and D66, both of which had chosen new party leaders in 2006, were the main losers of the election. The CDA and Labour also lost votes and fell two seats short of a joint majority. Labour polled considerably worse than expected and among the main parties only Prime Minister Balkenende's CDA could claim any kind of victory. Although Bos had been working for the return to centre-left coalition government and this was the eventual outcome (this time with ChristenUnie participation), the new coalition was shaped partly by the success of the populist challengers on the right and left flanks of the party system.

II. Southern (Mediterranean) Europe

Southern Europe saw two elections in 2006, but only one change of government: Romano Prodi replaced Silvio Berlusconi as prime minister of Italy, while the Cypriot election returned the same three-party majority government. Apart from the election of a new president in Portugal in January 2006, the Portuguese, Spanish, Greek and Maltese governments remained more or less unchanged. Outside Italy the most notable political development was in Spain where the Basque separatist ETA's declaration of a 'permanent ceasefire' in March 2006. This peace process, however, received a severe set-back when ETA admitted responsibility for the explosion at Madrid airport in December that left two people dead.

Popular support for European integration remained fairly stable in the Mediterranean states in 2006 compared to 2005. Italy and Greece remained near the EU average; though in Greece this meant halting the erosion of support for the EU that occurred between 2004 and 2005. Spain remained among the top five states in terms of respondents who see EU membership as 'a good thing', whereas Portugal, Cyprus and Malta rank in the bottom third. Portugal postponed its referendum on the Constitutional Treaty pending agreement on a new text, whereas the other five states had ratified it in 2005.

Italy's Two-Bloc Election

The April election in Italy brought Romano Prodi and the centre-left back to power after five years in opposition. Prime Minister Silvio Berlusconi's reform of the electoral law, designed to secure his centre-right government a working majority even in the event of re-election by a narrow margin, back-fired. Prodi's left-wing *Unione* won with a small plurality of the votes and was rewarded with a large majority of the seats in the Chamber of Deputies and a more marginal majority in the Senate, where the seven life senators held the balance. Although the election saw the two main electoral alliances take almost all the votes, Italy's two-bloc party system remains fragile. Centre-left unity was tested soon after the election, as it had been time and again in the 1996–2001 parliament and Berlusconi's defeat raised questions about the future leadership of the Italian centre-right.

The electoral law of December 2005 provided the centre-left with a working majority in the Chamber of Deputies that far outweighed the 25,000 vote difference between the two blocs. This new law provided the main controversy of the 2006 election. Guerra and Massetti (2006, p. 3) argue that the new electoral law, which allows parties to run individually under a proportional representation (PR) system but awards a bonus to the biggest bloc, was tailor-made by and for the centre-right 'because its parties seem to perform much better when they fight elections independently than when they campaign together'. The left, on the other hand, generally suffers from disunity. As Table 4 indicates, the centre-left did indeed fragment into a larger number of parties, but this did not prevent a marginal victory for the *Unione* bloc (each bloc had to choose a leader and set out a common programme). In fact, the *Unione* attracted the liberal Radicals, which had fought the last election as part of the centre-right bloc but had joined the Socialists in the new *Rosa di Pugno* party. Moreover, the two main centre-left parties, the Left Democrats (DS) and the *Margherita*, fought the election for the lower house on the common *Ulivo* list within the *Unione*. They were joined in the government by six smaller parties that were part of the *Unione* bloc. Although the autumn of 2006 indicated that the centre-left might suffer from the same kind of divisions that brought down successive centre-left governments in the

Table 4: Italian Parliamentary Elections, Senate and Chamber of Deputies (CD),
April 2006

	2006			2002
	Senate seats	CD seats	CD votes (%)	CD votes (%)[a]
Prodi's l'Unione	**158**	**348**	**49.8**	–
Ulivo[b]	101	220	31.3	31.1
Rifondazione Comm.	27	41	5.8	5.0
Rosa nel Pugno	0	18	2.6	–
Others in Unione	30	69	10.1	–
Berlusconi's Casa delle Libertà	**156**	**281**	**49.7**	–
Forza Italia	78	137	23.7	29.4
Alleanza Nazionale	41	71	12.3	12.0
UDC	21	39	6.8	3.2
Lega Nord	13	26	4.6	3.9
Others in Casa	3	8	2.3	
Independents	**1 + 7**[c]	**1**		–

Notes: [a] PR list votes from the 2001 election; [b] Left Democrats and *Margherita* combined figures for the
Senate and for 2001; [c] 1 independent plus the seven unelected life senators.
Sources: Italian Ministry of Interior, available at elezioni.interno.it; Guerra and Massetti (2006); Newell
(2006).

1996–2001 parliament, the government survived through the end of the year.
Its main problem was discipline in the Senate, where its majority was marginal and it depended on the life senators. Early divisions on the left included
controversies over proposals for market liberalization, but the budget was
eventually passed in December with the help of five of the life senators. The
first substantial crisis came only in 2007 over foreign policy.

The electoral outcome left Berlusconi's centre-right *Casa delle Libertà*
(House of Freedoms) in somewhat greater disarray. As anticipated, other
centre-right parties picked up *Forza Italia's* 6 per cent loss. The defeat of the
76-year-old Prime Minister (and the prospect of a further corruption trial)
opened the question of the leadership of the centre-right, particularly if the
new centre-left government lasts the full five-year parliamentary term. Both
Gianfranco Fini of the *Alleanza Nazionale* and the Christian Democrat
(UDC) Pier Ferdinando Casini emerged as potential contenders. By December Casini was boycotting *Casa* leadership meetings and anti-government
rallies and even questioning the usefulness of the alliance. In particular, the
UDC was reluctant to criticize the government's removal of barriers to
entering some professions and its plans for further liberalization.

The longer term question raised by Italy's 2006 election is whether it
represents further movement towards a two-bloc system. Although the electoral result might seem to confirm this interpretation, as the two major blocs

took almost all the votes, the autumn of 2006 revealed that the divisions within both blocs remain as important as they have been throughout the 'second republic' (i.e. since 1992). Whether the centre-left sticks to its promise of reverting to the old (mixed) electoral law or not, the lesson from 2006 reinforces that from the 1990s: electoral reform can affect how parties compete and form pre-election blocs, but it is difficult to engineer change to a two-party system. The new electoral law and the electoral result that produced a new government notwithstanding, Italy ended the year with much the same party system and patterns of intra-bloc and inter-bloc competition as at the beginning of 2006.

Cyprus's Low-Volatility Election

The Cypriot election in May brought about little change in the party system, distribution of votes, or government composition, as shown in Table 5. As Charalambous (2006, p. 2) concludes, 'the stability of the major political actors and more broadly of the system itself was reconfirmed'. Presidential elections do not coincide with parliamentary elections (the last presidential election was in 2003) and the president only carried out a minor reshuffle after the election. The distribution of ministers between the three governing parties – the Communists, the Social Democrats and the Democratic Party – remained the same as before the election. The two largest parties, the governing Communists on the left and the opposition Democratic Rally on the right both lost about three percentage points, while the centrist parties in the governing coalition picked up similar shares. The balance of power thus shifted marginally to the centre, but this had limited implications for political competition. Two of the smaller parties exchanged a single seat in parliament, the winner being the newly formed European party that resulted from the merger of the far-right New Horizons and a splinter group from the Democratic Rally. Electoral volatility remained low compared to the European average, as it has done in Cypriot elections since the 1970s.

III. Central and Eastern Europe

In 2006 the parties and politicians of the eight post-communist new Member States in central and eastern Europe turned inward to focus their efforts on domestic party battles after the exigencies of achieving EU membership in 2004 and adapting to their new international status in 2005. This was particularly conspicuous because 2006 was, like 2002, a parliamentary election year in the four-year cycle of three of the four largest states concerned: Hungary, the Czech Republic and Slovakia. All three demonstrated turbulent

Table 5: Cypriot Parliamentary Elections, May 2006

| | 2006 | | 2001 | |
	Votes (%)	Seats	Votes (%)	Seats
Communists (AKEL)	31.1	18	34.7	20
Democratic Rally (DISY)	30.3	18	34.0	19
Democratic Party (DIKO)	17.9	11	14.8	9
Social Democrats (KISOS)	8.9	5	6.5	4
European Party (EK)	5.8	3	5.2	2
Greens (KOP)	2.0	1	2.0	1
United Democrats (EDI)	1.6	0	2.6	1
Others	2.4	0	0.2	0

Source: Charalambous (2006).

inter-party relations in their own idiosyncratic fashions. Ironically, given the consternation Slovakia's election result caused in the EP, harking back to its political pariah status in the mid-1990s, Slovakia demonstrated most domestic political stability in the wake of its election. Overall a gradual stabilization of the party system was notable, including in the Baltic states, where Latvia had parliamentary elections. The results, however, must be viewed in the context of the distinct rightward and nationalist shifts that took place in the post-accession elections in Slovenia in 2004 and Poland in 2005. Freed from the constraints of securing EU approval, some of the unresolved problems of post-communist political culture were able to manifest themselves.

EU issues did not feature strongly in central and eastern Europe in 2006. Since the Constitutional Treaty was largely dormant (see Dinan, this volume), there were no heated debates about referendums in Poland and the Czech Republic. When the Estonian parliament ratified the Treaty in May, the vote was uncontentious and it was passed by 73 to 1. The issue of joining the Schengen zone, which remained particularly sensitive in most post-communist states both because of the restrictions on travel under communist regimes and the humiliation often suffered at western borders thereafter, was largely settled in December 2006 with a decision that checks at land and sea borders be phased out at the end of 2007 and airport controls by March 2008. This did, however, require final confirmation at the end of 2007.

Public opinion on the EU generally showed positive trends as some of the benefits of membership, such as (albeit limited) free movement of labour and the greater availability of EU funds, began to be a feature of many people's daily lives. It is notable that the autumn 2006 *Eurobarometer* showed that whereas 53 per cent of EU citizens as a whole thought their country's membership of the EU was 'a good thing' (see Table 1), the percentage for the new Member States – 56 per cent – was four points higher than for old Member States. This contrasted with all previous *Eurobarometers*, in which new members were less positive than old, although they had gradually been catching up. Moreover, Poland, despite having one of the most Eurosceptic governments in Europe, was the only Member State in which support for EU membership has increased in every *Eurobarometer* poll since accession. The new Member States also remained the strongest supporters of further EU enlargement.

While citizens of the new Member States showed some characteristics of being 'good Europeans', in other respects value orientations were more worrying. Elections produced distinctly nationalist governments in Slovakia, Poland and Slovenia. In addition, *Eurobarometer* findings reveal strong illiberal strands in attitudes to social issues. On issues such as homosexual marriage, the legalization of cannabis and the severity of punishment of crimes, citizens of new Member States were markedly more conservative than those in old Member States. These attitudes are likely to change far more slowly than views on EU membership.

Hungary: Continuity and Instability

2006 demonstrated the way that Hungarian politics bucks the trend in the politics of central and eastern Europe in a number of ways. Hungary continued as the only state in the region not to have held an early election due to the collapse of the government, but it finally ended the pattern that every parliamentary election brought about an alternation of power. If anything, however, the Prime Minister remaining in power produced instability, as he announced a fiscal austerity programme shortly after the elections. Anti-government protests briefly turned violent in the run-up to the local elections.

Hungary was also rather idiosyncratic in popular attitudes to EU membership. While *Eurobarometer* surveys had shown Hungarians to be consistently strong supporters of EU membership throughout the accession process, this trend was reversed after 2004 – precisely the period in which positive views towards the EU increased in most other new members. Nonetheless, the EU barely surfaced as an issue in the election campaign.

In many respects, Hungary remained the model two-party system of central and eastern Europe: the (formerly communist) left-wing Hungarian Socialist Party (MSZP), which led the government from 1994–98 and 2002–06, versus the right-wing Fidesz, which was in power from 1998–02. Each had a smaller, more centrist coalition partner: the liberal Alliance of Free Democrats (SZDSZ) had twice ruled with the Socialists, while the centre-right Hungarian Democratic Forum (MDF) was a slightly less easy partner for

Fidesz, contesting the 2002 elections in coalition with the larger party, but deciding to stand alone and to profile itself by campaigning against both the Socialists and Fidesz, in 2006. Programmatically, however, the battle lines between the two main parties were less conventional. The 2002 election had been fought on the nationalist divide, with the conservative Fidesz pitted against the secular and more cosmopolitan Socialist Party, but in 2006 economics played a far more prominent role. The Socialists, although promoting a typically left-wing social welfare agenda, had also pushed through many of Hungary's major market-oriented reforms during its periods in government, while Fidesz had a strong element of populism in its economic policies. A further paradox was that the Socialist prime minister, Ferenc Gyurcsány, had in his youth been a Communist Party politician and then became a successful and extremely prosperous businessman before re-entering politics.

At the start of the election campaign, opinion polls indicated a close contest between the ruling Socialists and Fidesz, and there were doubts whether any of the smaller parties would cross the 5 per cent threshold in the PR parts of the election. A rather successful campaign by the MDF leader, Ibolya Dávid, however, generated a crucial 5.04 per cent of the list vote in the first round of the election on 9 April and SZDSZ also re-entered parliament (see Table 6). The second round on 23 April involved run-offs in single-member constituencies in which no candidate had obtained a majority of votes cast. Already in the lead after the first round, the Socialists benefited from their close collaboration with their coalition partner, whereas Fidesz suffered from its competition with MDF. Consequently, the ruling MSZP/SZDSZ coalition increased its majority by 12.

Although the election was not marked by the bitter polarization of the 2002 contest, the 68 per cent first round turnout was high by Hungarian standards. It is also notable that both the two main parties increased their

Table 6: Hungarian Parliamentary Elections, April 2006

	2006		2002	
	Votes (%)	Seats	Votes (%)	Seats
Hungarian Socialist Party (MSZP)	43.2	190	42.1	178
Alliance of Free Democrats (SZDSZ)	6.5	20	5.5	20
Fidesz-Christian Democratic People's Party (Fidesz-KDNP)	42.0	164	41.1[a]	164
Hungarian Democratic Forum (MDF)	5.0	11		24
Others	3.2	1	11.3	0

Sources: National Election Office, available at: «http://www.valasztas.hu»; Sitter and Batory (2006).
[a] Stood with Fidesz in 2002.

shares of the vote at the expense of the 'wasted votes' for parties that did not enter parliament, which indicated a further consolidation of the party system. The most turbulent events in Hungarian politics, however, occurred after the parliamentary election in the run-up to the October local elections and the fiftieth anniversary of the failed 1956 revolution. The background was Hungary's large fiscal deficit, which the government had done little to correct during its previous term in office for fear of damaging its election chances, but which now jeopardized the country's chances of joining the euro area. Gyurcsány's new government sunk rapidly in popularity as it introduced tough economic measures that had not featured in its election campaign. The problem exploded on 17 September with the leaking of a recording of a closed party meeting in May in which the prime minister had tried to prepare his party for the measures by pointing out that everyone had been lying about the state of the economy for years. The speech contained the fateful phrase 'we lied in the morning, we lied in the evening and we lied at night'. This triggered the most violent demonstrations since 1956, during which a group of right-wing extremists and football hooligans broke off from a large demonstration, attacked the police and tried to storm the state television building.

Although the local elections inevitably led to large defeats for the Socialists, Gyurcsány survived a vote of confidence in parliament the following week. The government's parliamentary majority and the Socialist Party's lack of a more popular figure to replace him, permitted the government to weather the storm.

The Czech Republic: The Politics of Stalemate

The Czech Republic had a Social Democratic Prime Minister for the eight years that covered almost the entire accession negotiations and the first two years of membership. As the June parliamentary election approached, the centre-right Civic Democratic Party (ODS), founded and led for over 11 years by Václav Klaus (Czech president since 2003), was expected to return to power. During its second term in government, the Czech Party of Social Democracy (ČSSD) had changed the Prime Minister twice, once following its disastrous EP election result in 2004 and again in 2005 following a corruption scandal. The new Prime Minister, Jiří Paroubek, had lacked a high political profile when he took over the party, languishing at around 10 per cent in the opinion polls. His goal of winning at least 30 per cent of the vote in the 2006 election – equal to its 2002 result – therefore seemed rather optimistic. In fact, the party achieved its highest vote ever, winning more than 32 per cent (see Table 7).

While the Social Democrats' election result was a personal triumph for Paroubek, the ODS under Klaus's successor, Mirek Topolánek, also achieved

Table 7: Czech Parliamentary Election, June 2006

	2006		2002	
	Votes (%)	Seats	Votes (%)	Seats
Civic Democratic Party (ODS)	35.4	81	24.5	58
Christian Democratic Union-Czechoslovak People's Party (KDÚ-ČSL)	7.2	13	14.3[a]	31[a]
Green Party (SZ)	6.3	6	2.7	0
Czech Party of Social Democracy (ČSSD)	32.3	74	30.2	70
Communist Party of Bohemia and Moravia (KSČM)	12.8	26	18.5	41
Others	6.1	0	9.8	0

Note: [a] Standing with the Freedom Union-Democratic Union (US-DEU).
Sources: Czech Statistical Office, available at: «http://www.volby.cz»; Hanley (2006).

its best result ever, with over 35 per cent of the vote. As in Hungary, the two-party system was consolidating, but unlike in Hungary, the left–right division was less ambiguous. The Social Democrats campaigned on a slogan of 'Security and Prosperity', while ODS supported a 'flat tax', continuing the clear left–right economic divide that was also underlined by a (less salient) divide over values. ODS projected itself as conservative and also had strongly Eurosceptic tendencies that had to be played down in the election campaign because they did not entirely accord with the aspirations of the party's many young, educated and urban voters.

The extraordinary debacle surrounding the forming of a government after the elections was due to the fact that, while the Czech Republic had been characterized by left–right two-party competition since the mid-1990s – far earlier than elsewhere in the region – the rest of the party system was idiosyncratic. The Czech Social Democrats are unique in post-communist Europe because they have their roots in interwar social democracy rather than being a reformed communist party. The attendant complication was that the country also had the region's only relatively successful unreformed communist party. Although the Communist Party of Bohemia and Moravia (KSČM) lost votes in 2006, it still had the support of nearly 13 per cent of the electorate. Together with the Social Democrats, they held 100 of the 200 parliamentary seats and while the Communists were not generally considered fit to participate in government, Paroubek was more open to collaboration with them than his predecessors.

The small centrist parties also complicated matters. The Christian Democrats (KDU-ČSL), which lost support but nonetheless obtained 13 seats, had previously participated in governments led by both the Social Democrats and ODS. The 2006 elections also saw the first entry of a new party into parliament since 1992: the Green Party (SZ). The Green Party is politically interesting because it represents the first 'post-materialist' party to emerge in a new Member State. Its supporters were demographically similar to those of the ODS – young, urban and educated – but rejected the materialist, conservative and Europhobe elements of ODS policy. They are modern, progressive voters, who incline to 'the left' in western Europe, but incline to 'the right' in central and eastern Europe, through enthusiasm for economic reform rather than conservatism. This dichotomy of values meant, however, that – like the Christian Democrats – the Green Party was a potential partner for both ODS and the Social Democrats.

President Klaus nominated the ODS's Topolánek as Prime Minister in August 2006. The Christian Democrats and the Greens were prepared to go into coalition with ODS, but the coalition did not command a parliamentary majority, having only 100 of 200 seats. This created a window of opportunity for the Social Democrats that the combative Paroubek was prepared to exploit, by withholding support for the coalition.

Consequently, with the legislatively demanding process of attaining EU membership already achieved, Czech politicians permitted themselves the extreme indulgence of spending the entire period from the June elections through the end of the year without a new government. Topolánek's government coalition, containing the ODS, the Christian Democrats and Greens, was not endorsed by parliament until two Social Democrat deputies abstained in a vote in January 2007.

Slovakia: a Victory for Left–Right Politics

By 2006 Slovakia had reinvented itself. After the turbulence of the 1990s, when 'Mečiarism' nearly led to its exclusion from the first wave of EU eastern enlargement, it had become a pillar of stability in central and eastern Europe; Prime Minister Mikuláš Dzurinda, who entered office after the crucial 1998 elections that defeated Vladmír Mečiar, was the longest serving leader of an EU Member State apart from Tony Blair. In addition, the country's image had changed from that of a nationalist and clientelist 'black hole' that discouraged foreign direct investment to an open and transparent flat-tax magnet for automobile companies and many other foreign investors (see Johnson, this volume). The shift in the government's priorities, however, had not been without social costs and the 2006 elections took place amid widespread popular disaffection with the growing regional and social disparities in wealth.

The parliamentary election took place three months early, on 17 June, after the fractious four-party centre-right government finally came apart. It was unlike most previous parliamentary elections because of two great uncertainties. First, which parties would succeed in crossing the 5 per cent threshold established by the country's PR election system and what would be their relative strengths? Second, the coalition preferences of virtually all the six parties most likely to enter parliament were uncertain. The latter uncertainty was of greater concern to journalists in the run-up to the election than the content of the parties' programmes.

The fluidity of coalition possibilities was caused by the fact that the traditional cleavage in Slovak politics – nationalists versus supporters of post-communist reform – had been eroded. The Movement for a Democratic Slovakia (HZDS) of Vladimír Mečiar, three times Prime Minister in the 1990s, had designated itself as a centre-right party in 2000, renaming itself the People's Party-Movement for a Democratic Slovakia (ĽS-HZDS) and now bent over backwards to be EU-friendly in the rather futile hope of being allowed to join the European People's Party (EPP) in the EP. The party did, however, succeed in becoming a possible coalition partner for serving Prime Minister Dzurinda's Slovak Democratic and Christian Union (SDKÚ). This option was attractive to SDKÚ, since – although an EPP member – it was basically a liberal party that strongly supported the free market. Indeed, the government had fallen because of its refusal to make concessions to the strong Catholic agenda of one of its coalition partners, the Christian Democratic Movement (KDH). The SDKÚ had also had a number of conflicts with its other longstanding coalition partner, the ethnically based Party of the Hungarian Coalition (SMK), which, like KDH, is also an EPP member.

The party that continually led opinion polls with about 30 per cent support was Smer-Social Democracy (Smer-SD), a Party of European Socialists (PES) member, which had led the opposition to the second Dzurinda government. Smer-SD's founder and dominant leader, Robert Fico, was determined to become prime minister and refused to exclude any of its competitors as a possible coalition partner. Fico and Dzurinda were mutually successful in framing the election as a left–right contest between Fico's image of a more socially sensitive state and Dzurinda's insistence that his government's flat tax policy was Slovakia's 'trade mark' and the key to international acclaim and national prosperity.

The election result (see Table 8) showed that these two leaders' agenda accorded with the voters' overriding concern with economic rather than national issues. Fico's opinion poll lead converted itself into votes on polling day (in contrast to 2002), giving him 29 per cent. Dzurinda came second with over 18 per cent, which (repeating 2002) was far higher than even the most favourable predictions for SDKÚ. It appeared superficially that the nationalist vote had increased alarmingly, with the nationalist right Slovak National Party (SNS)

Table 8: Slovak Parliamentary Election, June 2006

	2006		2002	
	Votes (%)	Seats	Votes (%)	Seats
Smer-Social Democracy (Smer-SD)	29.1	50	13.5	25
Slovak National Party (SNS)	11.7	20	7.0[a]	0
			(3.3/3.7)	
Movement for a Democratic Slovakia (HZDS)	8.8	15	19.5	36
Slovak Democratic and Christian Union (SDKÚ)	18.4	31	15.1	28
Party of the Hungarian Coalition (SMK)	11.7	20	11.1	20
Christian Democratic Movement (KDH)	8.3	14	8.3	15
Others	12.0	0	25.5	26

Note: [a] Includes votes for the breakaway 'True Slovak National Party' (PSNS), which later re-integrated.
Sources: Statistical Office of the Slovak Republic, available at: «http://www.statistics.sk»; Henderson (2006).

re-entering parliament with its highest vote since 1990. This success, however, was attributable largely to the efforts of the traditionally larger ĽS-HZDS to tone down its nationalist rhetoric and enter the mainstream. The vote for Mečiar's party declined radically: from having been the largest party in all four elections since 1992, it was now the second smallest of the six parliamentary parties.

Despite the clear realignment of Slovak politics to a left–right divide and the failure of all of the smaller parties that had hovered around the 5 per cent mark in opinion polls to enter parliament, the shape of the future government coalition remained an open question. Fico initially met with all other party leaders. SDKÚ – Smer-SD's major adversary on the left–right divide and the main critic of its policies – quickly emerged as the least likely coalition partner. A coalition with the two other centre-right parties was complicated by internal Christian Democrat divisions over whether to enter government with Smer-SD and the Hungarian SMK was highly reluctant to enter a government with Smer-SD if ĽS-HZDS rather than the Christian Democrats was the other party.

Although forming a government was expected to be a long drawn-out process, Dzurinda effectively forced Fico's hand by trying to form a four-party centre-right coalition with KDH, SMK and ĽS-HZDS, which would have excluded Fico from power. Within ten days of the election, Fico therefore opted for what many considered the 'nightmare scenario' of a left-nationalist government with ĽS-HZDS and SNS. This choice had been considered unlikely because of probable adverse reaction abroad toward the formation of a coalition with the nationalist right. In practice, however, the only sanction available to EU institutions in the wake of accession was to suspend the membership of Fico's party in the PES.

In the context of domestic politics, Fico's new government had a strong rationale. Smer-SD's two coalition partners had more compatible programmes than those of alternative parties and public opinion polls soon after the government's formation showed that it was the favoured option among voters of all three parties. EU membership also posed certain constraints on the government's actions. SDKÚ had been largely successful in establishing the idea that joining the euro area in 2009 is the litmus test of a Slovak government's ability to defend national interest. When a comment by Fico shortly after the election raised doubts about an early adoption of the euro, immediately causing the Slovak crown to sink, he hastily established entering the euro area as an absolute government priority. Likewise, he has so far left the previous government's flat tax policies essentially untouched. Even the nationalist rhetoric of SNS has been reined in to prevent too much adverse international publicity. The erosion of progress in areas such as the battle against corruption remains a considerable danger to the completion of the post-communist reform process in Slovakia.

Poland: An Unstable Coalition

While Poland faced no elections in 2006, the aftermath of the parliamentary and presidential elections of autumn 2005 was still being felt. The year began with Lech Kaczyński of the Law and Justice Party (PiS) as president. PiS was chaired by his twin brother Jarosław and led a minority government under Kazimierz Marcinkiewicz. An early parliamentary election remained a distinct possibility. In April/May, PiS formed a controversial coalition government with the agrarian – and ostensibly anti-EU – Self-Defence (*Samoobrona*) party and the nationalist right-wing League of Polish Families (LPR). This coalition gave the government a majority, but led to resignations in the Polish Foreign Ministry and considerable concern in the EU. Nor did much government stability ensue. Marcinkiewicz resigned in July after disputes with the PiS over the appointment of a new Finance Minister and he was replaced as Prime Minister by Jarosław Kaczyński. Poland was thus led by a president and prime minister who are identical twins.

While this situation lasted into 2007, the governing coalition was shaky. *Samoobrona* left the coalition in September after Prime Minister Kaczyński dismissed its leader Andrzej Lepper as Deputy Prime Minister and Agriculture Minister. PiS briefly led a minority government until the original coalition was restored, but party defections again left it a minority government, albeit with the informal support of other deputies.

The government remained controversial both within Poland and in the EU at large. Domestic accusations and criticism focused on corruption and its extreme social conservatism. Problems in Polish–German relations and EU criticism of the Kaczyński's' support for the death penalty, meant that Poland – by far the largest of the 2004 accession countries – was scarcely a model new Member State.

The Baltic States: Fluid and Unstable Party Coalitions

The Baltic states had long had the most erratic party systems among the new Member States, with the frequent entry of completely new parties into both parliament and government and rather unstable governing coalitions. This fluidity notwithstanding, they continued to perform well in terms of economic reforms and growth rate in the wake of EU enlargement (see Johnson, this volume).

Only one of the three states – Latvia – had a general election in 2006. A three-party minority government comprising the People's Party (TP), the Latvia First Party (LPP) and the Union of Greens and Farmers (ZZS) had been in office since April following the departure of its fourth partner, New Era (JL). The election was preceded by several corruption scandals involving both money and votes.

As shown in Table 9 the result of the Latvian election on 7 October showed a degree of stabilization of the party system in two respects. First, Aigars Kalvitis became the first Latvian prime minister to return to office after an election. The three parties that had participated in the pre-election minority government now had the narrowest of majorities (51 of 100 seats) and consequently added a fourth partner, the Fatherland and Freedom Union (TB/LNNK). Second, the election was the first in which no new party had been standing in order to capitalize on disillusioned Latvian voters. There was, however, one new entrant to parliament: Harmony Centre (SC), which eclipsed For Human Rights in a United Latvia (PCTVL) as the major representative of the country's Russian minority – the largest in the EU. While PCTVL had been the major left-wing party in Latvia, Harmony Centre was more moderate and centrist, although also emphasizing Russian language rights.

The Latvian party system remained somewhat curious, however, in terms of the programmatic differentiation of parties. The divide between right and left still largely coincided with the national divide. All five ethnically Latvian parties that returned to parliament identified themselves as right of centre, so that the distinction between them was largely in the issues on which they chose to profile themselves: economic interests (TP); anti-corruption (JL); rural issues (ZZS); social conservatism (LPP); and national identity

Table 9: Latvian Parliamentary Election, October 2006

	2006		2002	
	Votes (%)	Seats	Votes (%)	Seats
People's Party (TP)	19.5	23	16.7	20
Union of Greens and Farmers(ZZS)	16.7	18	9.6	12
Latvia First Party-Latvian Way (LPP-LC)	8.6	10	14.5[a]	10[a]
			(9.6/4.9)	(10/0)
Fatherland and Freedom Union (TB/LNNK)	6.9	8	5.4	7
New Era (JL)	16.4	18	24.0	26
Harmony Centre (SC)	14.4	17	–	–
For Human Rights in a United Latvia (PCTVL)	6.0	6	19.1	25
Others	11.4	0	16.2	0

Note: [a] The two parties stood separately in 2002.
Sources: Central Electoral Commission, available at: «http://www.cvk.lt»; Keesing's Record of World
Events, News Digest for October 2006, p. 47545.

(TB/LNNK). The crowded nature of the right of the political spectrum caused both the fluidity of the coalition-forming process and the importance of the potential for personality politics. It also suggests that more changes in the Latvian party system are likely before it finally stabilizes.

Estonia demonstrated lack of institutional stability in another fashion: difficulties in electing a president; a largely ceremonial post. The president is supposed to be indirectly elected every five years in a ballot of the 101 members of parliament, in which a successful candidate requires two-thirds of the possible votes. This method requires a high degree of consensus-building and compromise between parties that has never been forthcoming. When no candidate obtains the required majority, an electoral college is convened, which contains not only the 101 members of parliament but also a majority of local representatives (246 in 2006). Consequently, parties whose favoured candidate stands a better chance in the electoral college have no incentive to compromise in parliament.

In 2006, the incumbent president, the 78-year-old Arnold Rüütel – a communist-era politician who had supported independence and later chaired the People's Union – clearly stood a better chance of election in an electoral college ballot. He therefore failed to stand in the parliamentary ballots and members of the two parties who supported him abstained. In the electoral college he was eventually defeated by Toomas Hendrik Ilves, an MEP for the opposition Social Democrat Party who had lived abroad for most of his life, but was more strongly supported by younger and ethnic Estonian voters. The election of former émigrés as president thus continued in the Baltic states. In addition, the conduct of Rüütel's supporters in the electoral process is likely to increase pressure for a constitutional change enabling direct election of the president. The fluidity of party systems and the attendant low level of institutionalized inter-party consensus-building has made the direct election of presidents lacking executive powers increasingly common in post-communist EU Member States.

Finally, although no elections took place in Lithuania, the country was also characterized by the government instability characteristic of states with complex and shifting coalition politics. After losing one member of the four-party government coalition in April, the government finally collapsed in May with the withdrawal of the Labour Party (DP), whose Russian-born leader Viktor Uspaskich returned to Russia after accusations of corruption. Parliament finally approved a new minority government in July.

IV. Northern Western Europe

There was only one election and one change of government in northern western Europe in 2006: the September election in Sweden resulted in a change from a centre-left to centre-right government. This change of electoral fortunes was far from ordinary, however. The governing Social Democrats suffered badly, defeated by four opposition parties that joined forces before the elections and adopted a moderate, centrist electoral strategy. The Danish, Finnish, British and Irish governments ended the year more or less as they started it and there was little party, or party system, change. The Finnish and Irish parties began to position themselves for the 2007 elections, but without major changes to the patterns of party competition. In Denmark party competition remained in a stable mid-term pattern. In the UK, however, Prime Minister Tony Blair's announcement that he would resign at some point during 2007 affected party politics.

Popular support for European integration remained stable in all five states. Ireland and the UK scored top and bottom in the rankings respectively, with 78 per cent of Irish respondents rating EU membership as a 'good thing', against a mere 34 per cent of those in the UK. Denmark remained in the top third of the table, with 61 per cent approval for the EU, very much in line with the pattern of the last two years and a marginal increase on 2005. Sweden and Finland both remained in the bottom third in terms of approval of EU membership, but with support increasing somewhat in Sweden and decreasing in Finland. The EU Constitutional Treaty was ratified by the Finnish Parliament in December 2006, by 125 to 39 votes, whereas the other four states had suspended the ratification process after the French and Dutch referendums of 2005.

An 'Earthquake' Election in Sweden

The September election in Sweden saw the governing Social Democrats defeated by a unified non-socialist bloc, the four-party 'Alliance for Sweden'. This result was the Social Democrats' worst since universal suffrage was introduced in 1921. For the first time the non-socialist parties fought the election as a united bloc, providing Sweden with its first majority government since 1981. It must therefore, as Bolin and Aylott (2006, p. 1) argue, 'count as something of an electoral earthquake'. The share of the votes that went to the Social Democrats and their two supporting parties on the left declined from 52.9 per cent in 2002 to 46.2 per cent in 2006, whereas the four non-socialist parties increased from 44.1 to 48.2. With 5.7 per cent of the votes going to small parties that failed to cross the 4 per cent threshold for electoral representation, this was sufficient to secure the centre-right an absolute majority: 178 seats to the centre-left's 171.

At the time of the 2006 election the Social Democrats had governed Sweden for all but nine years since 1932 (albeit in coalition with the agrarian Centre party in the 1930s and 1950s and a grand coalition during the Second World War). During the past two parliaments, however, the party had come to rely on increasingly close co-operation with the two smaller (and more Eurosceptic) left-wing parties, the Greens and the formerly communist Left Party. In the 2002 parliament, this co-operation was extended so far as to permit the two small parties advisers in some government departments. The ensuing debate about coalition politics played an important part in weakening the left as a whole. Whereas the centre-left had long enjoyed an advantage as the most credible government alternative, this had changed by 2006. Social Democrat Prime Minister Göran Persson ruled out a coalition with the far Left, whose leader Lars Ohly had caused much debate in 2005 by refusing to

Table 10: Swedish Parliamentary Election, September 2006

	2006		2002	
	Votes (%)	Seats	Votes (%)	Seats
Left Party (V)	5.9	22	8.4	30
Greens (MP)	5.3	19	4.6	17
Social Democrats (S)	35.0	130	39.9	144
Centre (C)	7.9	29	6.2	22
Liberals (FP)	7.5	28	13.4	48
Christian Democrats (KD)	6.6	24	9.2	33
Conservatives (M)	26.2	97	15.3	55
Others	5.7	0	3.1	0

Sources: Swedish Election Authority, available at: «http://www.val.se»; Bolin and Aylott (2006).

distance himself from communism. The Greens, however, demanded a coalition, while the Left said it would not lend external support to a Social Democrat-Green coalition from which it was excluded. The centre-left's second weakness could be found in the governing Social Democratic party itself and its track record. After 12 years in power (ten under Persson's leadership), the party was increasingly seen as running out of steam. Three important examples are its poor handling of issues related to the many Swedish tourists caught up in the 2004 Asian tsunami; a few minor scandals; and the Foreign Minister's forced resignation in March (related to the 'cartoons crisis', see below) did not help. The Social Democrats' third weakness was its complacent electoral campaign. Bolin and Aylott (2006) suggest the crucial point was Persson's failure to address the employment question: impressive economic growth had not generated many additional jobs. The centre-right would not overlook this mistake.

The clear winners of the election were the four centre-right parties in general and the conservatives Moderates in particular. Taking a leaf out of Tony Blair's electoral strategy book, the party decided to move clearly toward the centre after badly losing the 2002 election. It even re-labelled itself the New Moderates and polled its best result in seven decades. Although both the Christian Democrats and the Liberals lost votes (both parties' support has been volatile over the past two decades), the four-party bloc did well. The Centre party increased its support by a quarter and the Moderates reaped the biggest absolute single-party increase in Swedish politics ever. The centre-right's success mirrored the centre-left's defeat: as a bloc it presented a more credible and unified governing alternative; the biggest party repositioned itself closer to the centre; and the alliance campaigned successfully. The four parties had negotiated agreement on a series of issues before the election, some of which included major compromises. More to the point, the Moderates played down their earlier support for market liberalism and adopted a somewhat more social democratic stance. This in turn allowed the four parties to campaign effectively on the employment question, on which they presented a clear (albeit somewhat liberal) plan while the centre-left had none.

The election thus both reflected and contributed to a sea change in Swedish politics. Its impact on the party system, however, was less than it might have been. The main development was the uniting of the centre-right parties in an alliance that will be tested in government. Within two weeks two ministers had resigned for failing to pay taxes, including the culture minister (in charge of public-service broadcasting) who had failed to pay her TV licence fees for years. On the left, Persson resigned after the election and was eventually succeeded by Mona Sahlin in January 2007. None of the three new parties that might have caused greater party system change fared particularly well. The far-right Sweden Democrats, which had published the Danish cartoons of the Prophet Mohammed on a website in February, polled 2.9 per cent. (Foreign Minister Laila Freivalds's denial of prior knowledge of the security service's move to ask the web host to remove these pictures prompted her resignation in March.) The Feminist Initiative, which split off from the Left, polled a mere 0.7 per cent. The eurosceptic June list, which had come third in the 2004 EP elections and entered Swedish national politics to protest against the lack of a referendum on the Constitutional Treaty, polled less than 0.5 per cent. In short, therefore, the Swedish election saw significant changes for the established parties on both sides, but on the extreme left and right wings the challengers failed, as did the Eurosceptic challenge.

Blair's Ten-Year Limit

In 2006 the longest-serving leader in the EU, UK Prime Minister Tony Blair, finally stated that this year's Labour party conference would be his last as party leader (and therefore as Prime Minister). Speculation about the precise timing of his departure had long been intense since Blair had made clear before his third general election victory in 2005 that he would not lead his party into a fourth general election. The decision came in a year in which the Blair's leadership suffered criticism on several counts, including the continuing problems in Iraq, Blair's reluctance to call quickly for a cease-fire in Lebanon, the Labour Party's poor results in the May local elections (where the party came third in terms of voters, behind the Liberal Democrats and the Conservatives) and the 'cash for peerages' investigation into whether the Labour Party nominated four people for places in the House of Lords in return for their making large loans to the party. Blair's announcement was precipitated by a week of public feuding among the leadership, which the *Financial Times* (2006) labelled 'civil war' and Blair himself described as 'not our finest hour'. Retirement from the Prime Minister's office in mid-2007 would leave Blair with a ten-year tenure in 10 Downing Street.

Blair's announcement prompted considerable speculation that a serious contender might emerge to challenge Chancellor (Finance Minister) Gordon Brown for the leadership of the Labour Party. After a cabinet reshuffle in May, which included changes of foreign, home and defence secretaries, the new Home Secretary John Reid emerged as a possible challenger to Brown for a period in the autumn. The subsequent rapprochement between Blair and Brown, however, made the latter's prospects of succeeding Blair as party leader and Prime Minister seem very strong by the end of 2006.

David Cameron, who took over the leadership of the Conservatives in 2005, strengthened his position as the main challenger to the new Labour leader, since the Conservative Party improved in public opinion polls in 2006. Cameron's decision not to follow through immediately on his promise in the party leadership campaign to take the Conservatives out of the EPP meant that 2006 became a less momentous year for the European question in British politics than it might have been. As of the end of 2006 Cameron was looking for partners from another four EU states to form a new centre-right group in the EP in 2009, focusing on conservative parties in the new Member States.

Danish, Finnish and Irish Parties Position Themselves for the Next Elections

2006 was a stable political year in Denmark, despite the controversies linked to the publication of cartoons of the Prophet Mohammed in the paper *Jyllands-Posten* in September 2005. The re-publication of the cartoons in a Norwegian magazine triggered major political protests across the Middle East in 2006, including assaults on Scandinavian embassies. A number of politicians, both in Scandinavia and elsewhere in the EU (including French President Jacques Chirac), suggested that the publication of the pictures was a provocation and therefore regrettable. The Danish centre-right government treated the row over the cartoons as a matter of freedom of expression; Prime Minister Anders Fogh Rasmussen did not condemn the cartoons and the public prosecutor ruled that there was no basis for prosecuting *Jyllands-Posten*. Nevertheless, the crisis provided a boost for the far-right Danish People's Party (DF). The DF continued to provide external support for the Conservative-Liberal minority coalition throughout 2006, as it had done since the 2005 election, but began to position itself for participation in government after the next election. On the left of the political spectrum, the Social Liberal party began to question its long-standing close ties with the Social Democrats and announced that it would present a candidate of its own for prime minister in the next election. It hinted that it might even lend support to a centre-right coalition. Thus, although both government and party politics in Denmark remained stable in 2006, some groundwork was laid on both the right and the left for possible changes to coalition politics at the next electoral contest, due in 2009.

2006 saw the Finnish and Irish parties prepare for the 2007 election. Finland's Social Democrat President Tarja Halonen narrowly saw off a challenge from Sauli Niisto of the conservative National Coalition, in a campaign that foreshadowed some of the changes expected in the 2007 parliamentary election. Prime Minister Matti Vanhanen of the Centre Party controversially backed Niisto, the candidate of the main opposition party, rather than his Social Democratic coalition partner. By the end of 2006, the Finnish parties had thus opened the question of whether the 2007 election might lead to a realignment of Finnish coalition politics. In Ireland the parties' positioning before the 2007 election was more predictable. The two-party Fianna Fail-Progressive Democrat coalition government remained in power, with only a minor reshuffle. The two main opposition parties, Fine Gael and Labour, developed a joint programme and announced that they would fight the 2007 election on a joint platform.

Conclusion

EU issues did not play a prominent role in any of the Member States in 2006. After the shock of the failed referendums on the Constitutional Treaty in France and the Netherlands in 2005, there were no major controversial decisions to be taken. The impending accession of Bulgaria and Romania and relations with the potential candidates in the Western Balkans (see Lavenex and Schimmelfennig, this volume) scarcely impinged on domestic politics.

Rather, every Member State faced its own domestic political issues. Nearly a third changed their government in the course of the year; mostly as a result of the routine parliamentary electoral process. The changes were more marked in the eight post-communist Member States, but only because half of them had elections scheduled. Although the formation of new governments was a tortured process in some cases and the end product was not always welcomed by other Member States and EU institutions, the 'new Europe' was also marked by signs of a gradual stabilization of the relevant party actors. Generally, the political representatives chosen by the very diverse electorates of the EU managed to work together constructively at the international level. Nonetheless, the sheer frequency with which governments change in an EU of 25 Member States creates some problems for the smooth functioning of its most intergovernmental institutions, the Council of Ministers and European Council (see Dinan, this volume).

Key Readings

On politics in Europe in general, see Heywood *et al.* (2006) and on the politics of East Central Europe, see Lewis and Mansfeldová (2006) and Šaradín and Bradová (2007). On public opinion in the Member States of the EU, see Eurobarometer (2006).

References

Bolin, N. and Aylott, N. (2006) 'The Swedish Parliamentary Election of September 2006'. EPERN Election Briefing No. 30 (Brighton: Sussex European Institute).

Charalambous, G. (2006) 'The Parliamentary Elections of May 2006 in the Republic of Cyprus'. EPERN Election Briefing No. 29 (Brighton: Sussex European Institute).

Eurobarometer (2006) *Standard Eurobarometer 66, Autumn 2006: First Results* (Brussels: CEC).

Fallend, F. (2007) 'Europe and the National Parliamentary Election in Austria, October 1, 2006', EPERN Election Briefing No. 31 (Brighton: Sussex European Institute).

Financial Times (2006) 8 September.

Guerra, S. and Massetti, E. (2006) 'The Italian Parliamentary Elections of April 2006'. EPERN Election Briefing No. 25 (Brighton: Sussex European Institute).

Hanley, S. (2006) 'Europe and the Czech Parliamentary Elections of 2–3 June 2006'. EPERN Election Briefing No. 27 (Brighton: Sussex European Institute).

Henderson, K. (2006) 'Europe and the Slovak Parliamentary Election of June 2006'. EPERN Election Briefing No. 26 (Brighton: Sussex European Institute).

Heywood, P.M., Jones, E., Rhodes, M. and Sedelmeier, U. (eds) (2006) *Developments in European Politics* (Basingstoke: Palgrave).

Lewis, P.G. and Mansfeldová, Z. (eds) (2006) *The European Union and Party Politics in Central and Eastern Europe* (Basingstoke: Palgrave).

Newell, J.L. (2006) 'The Italian Election of May 2006'. *West European Politics*, Vol. 29, No. 4, pp. 802–13.

Šaradín, P. and Bradová, E. (2007) *Visegrad Votes: Parliamentary Elections 2005–06* (Olomouc: Palacký University).

Sitter, N. and Batory, A. (2006) 'Europe and the Hungarian Elections of April 2006'. EPERN Election Briefing No. 28 (Brighton: Sussex European Institute).

Taggart, P. (2006) 'Keynote Article: Questions of Europe – The Domestic Politics of the 2005 French and Dutch Referendums and their Challenge for the Study of European Integration'. *JCMS Annual Review 2005*, pp. 7–15.

JCMS 2007 Volume 45 Annual Review pp. 213–230

Economic Developments in the Euro Area

AMY VERDUN
University of Victoria

Introduction

2006 was characterized by increased economic growth for the Member States of the euro area in a world economy that continued to show strong growth, with an overall growth rate projected to be about 5 per cent of world Gross Domestic Product (GDP) (IMF, 2006). Whereas 2005 was dominated by the reform of the Stability and Growth Pact (SGP), in 2006 the pact played a very minor role due to the stronger economic outlook of countries of the euro area. Whether the revised SGP will 'bite' will only be tested in the years to come, most likely following a downturn in the economy.

The euro area's growth did not occur during a calm time, however. Oil prices continued to increase in the first half of 2006, reaching a peak in early August. A number of factors contributed to a sense of uneasiness about the world economy: continued uncertainty about the state of the United States' (US) economy, particularly its current account deficit and mounting public debt, a risk of a rapid cooling of its housing market and the onset of economic slowdown; continuing unrest in the Middle East and US foreign policy in the region; and continued strong growth of the economies of China and India. In 2006 there was a concern about rising inflation rates as a result of these developments and central banks (including the European Central Bank, ECB) responded by raising interest rates. In currency markets the real effective exchange rate of the euro strengthened by 2.8 per cent *vis-à-vis* other currencies as a whole, but appreciated more sharply against the US dollar (11 per cent) and the yen (9 per cent) (OECD, 2007, p. 56). The analysis of the Organisation for Economic Co-operation and Development (OECD) shows that the euro is close to its average of the 1990s and thus this appreciation for now should not be considered a problem for export competitiveness. As was the case in 2005, these developments came against the background of a euro area economy that was still not performing as strongly as those of non-euro area EU Member States (see Johnson, this volume) or other advanced industrialized societies (see Tables 1 and 2 below). The euro area economies, however, did perform considerably better than in previous years, although there was wide variation among the 12 Member States of the euro area.

This article looks at the economic developments in the euro area by highlighting a few core characteristics of the euro area as a whole and those of the largest five economies of the euro area (Germany, France, Italy, Spain and the Netherlands). Section I provides some key economic performance indicators. Section II examines the policy of the ECB and briefly discusses progress in the SGP, before reviewing the external dimension of the euro. Section III looks at the five selected countries. Section IV offers a reflection on the developments with Economic and Monetary Union (EMU) over the reviewed time period. Section V closes with a brief summary and outlook for 2007.

Table 1: Overview of World Economic Outlook Projections (Annual % Change)

	2004	2005	2006 projections	2007 projections
World	5.3	4.9	5.1	4.9
Advanced economies	3.2	2.6	3.1	2.7
United States	3.9	3.2	3.4	2.9
Euro Area	2.1	1.3	2.4	2.0
Japan	2.3	2.6	2.7	2.1
United Kingdom	3.3	1.9	2.7	2.7
Canada	3.3	2.9	3.1	3.0
Other advanced economies	4.6	3.7	4.1	3.7
Central and eastern Europe	6.5	5.4	5.3	5.0
Commonwealth of Independent States	8.4	6.5	6.8	6.5
China	10.1	10.2	10.0	10.0
India	8.0	8.5	8.3	7.3
European Union	2.4	1.8	2.8	2.4

Source: IMF (2006, p. 2, Table 1.1).

Table 2: Annual Average % Change in GDP for the EU-15, 1992–2007

	1997–01	*2002*	*2003*	*2004*	*2005*	*2006* *projected*	*2007* *projected*
Euro Area Member States:							
Belgium	2.6	1.5	1.0	3.0	1.1	2.7	2.3
Germany	2.1	0.0	−0.2	1.2	0.9	2.4	1.2
Greece	4.0	3.8	4.8	4.7	3.7	3.8	3.7
Spain	4.4	2.7	3.0	3.2	3.5	3.8	3.4
France	3.0	1.0	1.1	2.3	1.2	2.2	2.3
Ireland	9.9	6.0	4.3	4.3	5.5	5.3	5.3
Italy	2.1	0.3	0.0	1.1	0.0	1.7	1.4
Luxembourg	6.3	3.8	1.3	3.6	4.0	5.5	4.5
Netherlands	3.7	0.1	0.3	2.0	1.5	3.0	2.9
Austria	2.6	0.9	1.1	2.4	2.0	3.1	2.6
Portugal	3.8	0.8	−1.1	1.2	0.4	1.2	1.5
Finland	4.6	1.6	1.8	4.4	2.9	4.9	3.0
Euro Area	1.9	0.9	0.7	2.0	1.3	2.6	2.1
Non-Euro Area Member States:							
Denmark	2.4	0.5	0.7	1.9	3.0	3.0	2.3
Sweden	3.2	2.0	1.7	3.76	2.7	4.0	3.3
UK	3.1	2.1	2.7	3.3	1.9	2.7	2.6
EU-25	2.9	1.2	1.3	2.4	1.7	2.8	2.4

Source: Commission (2006, p. 133, Table 1).

I. Economic Developments in the Euro Area:
Main Economic Indicators

Economic Growth

In September, the International Monetary Fund (IMF) reported that the average rate of economic growth for advanced economies in the year 2006 was projected to be 3.1 per cent, which is up a little from 2.6 per cent the year before (IMF, 2006, p. 2). As was the case in previous years, the euro area, however, continued to perform less well than the advanced economies as a whole, performing particularly badly in 2005 but recovering in 2006 (see Table 1). The recovery in the euro area in 2006 closed the performance gap with other leading nations, such as the US and Japan, albeit not quite catching up (see Table 1). Furthermore, even the EU as a whole performed better than the euro area.

In January 2007 the OECD concluded that recovery has finally taken hold of the euro area. It estimated euro area GDP growth for 2006 at 2.6 per cent, compared to considerably weaker growth in previous years, namely 1.5 per cent in 2005 and 1.7 per cent in 2004 (OECD, 2007, p. 25, Table 1.3).

In 2006 some of the euro area economies that had performed particularly poorly in 2005, such as Germany and Italy, picked up. The *European Economy* autumn forecast (Commission, 2006) estimated the GDP growth in 2006 for Germany at 1.7 per cent and France at 3.1 per cent. EU-15 countries that are not part of the euro area did a little better than the average of the euro area countries (2.6 per cent). For example, growth in the United Kingdom (UK) was estimated at 2.7 per cent, Denmark at 3.2 per cent and Sweden at 3.4 per cent. Table 2 sets out the European Commission's latest estimates of GDP growth in the euro area plus Denmark, Sweden and the UK and the forecast for 2007.

Employment

The employment situation in the euro area also continued to improve, as had been the case in 2004 and 2005. Stronger than expected economic growth throughout 2006 contributed importantly to the improved employment performance and forecast. The forecasted figures for 2006 suggest that the euro area's employment performance is catching up to that of the other countries of the EU-25. Table 3 shows that the average unemployment in the euro area is now the same as that of the EU-25. Note the continuing buoyancy of Ireland, but also the strong performance of Austria and the Netherlands. High unemployment still exists in Belgium, Germany, Greece and France, although the situation in Germany has improved markedly compared to last year.

Inflation

Looking at the Harmonized Index of Consumer Prices, we find that inflation rates in the euro area countries have, on average, stayed more or less the same over the past three years. The performances of individual countries, however, continue to diverge a little, with the same countries being the high and low inflation performers as in 2005. The average inflation rate of the euro area countries in 2006 was 2.2 per cent, with a maximum of 3.6 per cent (Spain) and a minimum of 1.3 per cent (Finland) (see Table 4).

If we compare the inflation performance of the euro area countries with those in the rest of the EU we find that inflation rates still diverged between the euro area Member States and the three EU-15 'outs' and the new Member States, although the average inflation rate for the EU-27 was close to that of the euro area (see Table 4). Much discussed in 2006 was the decision by the European Commission and the ECB not to allow Lithuania to join the euro area in 2007 as it missed the inflation criterion by less than 0.1 per cent, whereas Slovenia was allowed in (see Johnson this issue).

Table 3: Percentage of the Civilian Labour Force Unemployed in the EU-15, 1992–2006

	1997–2001	2002	2003	2004	2005	2006 projected	2007 projected
Euro Area Member States:							
Belgium	8.1	7.5	8.2	8.4	8.4	8.6	8.5
Germany	8.1	8.2	9.0	9.5	9.5	8.9	8.4
Greece	11.0	10.3	9.7	10.5	9.8	9.3	8.9
Spain	13.1	11.1	11.1	10.7	9.2	8.1	7.9
France	10.1	8.9	9.5	9.7	9.6	9.3	8.9
Ireland	6.3	4.5	4.7	4.5	4.3	4.3	4.5
Italy	10.5	8.6	8.4	8.0	7.7	7.1	7.0
Luxembourg	2.4	24.5	4.7	5.1	4.5	4.6	4.4
Netherlands	3.4	2.8	3.7	4.6	4.7	3.9	3.0
Austria	4.0	4.2	4.3	4.8	5.2	5.1	5.1
Portugal	4.9	5.0	6.3	6.7	7.6	7.6	7.7
Finland	10.6	9.1	9.0	8.8	8.4	7.7	7.4
Euro Area	10.6	9.1	9.0	8.8	8.4	7.7	7.4
Non-Euro Area Member States:							
Denmark	4.8	4.6	5.4	5.5	4.8	3.8	3.5
Sweden	7.1	4.9	5.6	6.3	7.8	7.3	7.4
UK	5.8	5.1	4.9	4.7	5.7	5.3	5.0
EU-25	9.1	8.8	9.0	9.1	8.8	8.0	7.6

Source: Commission (2006, p. 146, Table 28).

Public Finances

Public finances in the EU stabilized somewhat during 2006, mostly because of better growth performance. As a result, the budget deficit as a percentage of GDP improved in most Member States. Average deficit in the euro area in 2006 is projected to be 2.0 per cent, down from 2.4 per cent in 2005. The only two countries still above the 3.0 per cent threshold in 2006 were Italy and Portugal (see Table 5).

II. Developments Surrounding the Stability and Growth Pact

Last year's review discussed in some detail the 2005 reform of the Stability and Growth Pact (SGP) and what its main aim was, namely to serve as a disciplining mechanism once Member States were in the third stage of EMU (Verdun, 2006). In a nutshell, the SGP aims to ensure that Member States keep their fiscal policies under control once in EMU. The 2005 reform made the original SGP rules less mechanical so as to include more scope for

Table 4: Harmonized Consumer Price Index (Annual % Change)

	2000	2001	2002	2003	2004	2005	Projected 2006
Belgium	2.68	2.44	1.55	1.51	1.86	2.53	2.34
Bulgaria	10.32	7.36	5.81	2.35	6.15	6.04	7.42
Czech Republic	3.95	4.54	1.43	−0.07	2.55	1.60	2.09
Denmark	2.71	2.30	2.38	1.98	0.90	1.70	1.85
Germany	1.40	1.90	1.35	1.03	1.79	1.92	1.78
Estonia	3.94	5.62	3.59	1.39	3.03	4.11	4.44
Ireland	5.25	3.99	4.72	4.00	2.30	2.18	2.70
Greece	2.90	3.65	3.92	3.44	3.03	3.48	3.31
Spain	3.48	2.83	3.59	3.10	3.05	3.38	3.56
France	1.83	1.78	1.94	2.17	2.34	1.90	1.91
Italy	2.58	2.32	2.61	2.81	2.27	2.21	2.22
Cyprus	4.86	1.98	2.79	3.96	1.90	2.04	2.25
Latvia	2.64	2.52	1.95	2.94	6.19	6.90	6.57
Lithuania	1.08	1.55	0.34	−1.08	1.16	2.66	3.79
Luxembourg	3.78	2.40	2.06	2.54	3.23	3.76	2.96
Hungary	9.96	9.08	5.24	4.68	6.77	3.48	4.03
Malta	3.04	2.51	2.61	1.94	2.73	2.53	2.58
Netherlands	2.34	5.11	3.87	2.24	1.38	1.50	1.65
Austria	1.96	2.29	1.70	1.30	1.95	2.11	1.69
Poland	10.08	5.31	1.95	0.71	3.59	2.18	1.27
Portugal	2.80	4.41	3.68	3.26	2.51	2.13	3.04
Romania	45.68	34.47	22.52	15.27	11.89	9.07	6.61
Slovenia	8.95	8.56	7.46	5.69	3.66	2.46	2.54
Slovakia	12.20	7.16	3.50	8.43	7.47	2.80	4.26
Finland	2.94	2.67	2.01	1.30	0.14	0.77	1.27
Sweden	1.30	2.67	1.93	2.34	1.02	0.82	1.50
United Kingdom	0.79	1.24	1.26	1.36	1.34	2.06	2.33
Euro Area[a]	2.12	2.36	2.26	2.08	2.14	2.18	2.18
EU-27	3.46	3.20	2.54	2.14	2.27	2.28	2.30
EU-25[b]	2.44	2.49	2.13	1.95	2.14	2.16	2.20
EU-15[c]	1.90	2.19	2.08	1.96	1.96	2.14	2.19

Notes: [a] Euro area with 12 countries; [b] Former EU-25; [c] Former EU-15.
Source: Commission (2007b).

economic judgement and consideration of country-specific conditions. Many observers have pointed to the flexibility of the reformed SGP and have questioned whether it will still have the disciplining effect it originally was aimed to have (Buiter, 2006; Buti, 2006; Calmfors, 2005; Heipertz and Verdun, 2006; Šabić, 2006).

In 2006 the countries that were still judged by the Commission and Council as having excessive deficits (above 3 per cent of GDP) were Germany, Greece,

Table 5: Net Lending (+) or Net Borrowing (−) of General Government as a Share of GDP in EU-15, 1992–2008

	1997–2001	2002	2003	2004	2005	2006 projected	2007 projected	2008 projected
Euro Area Member States:								
Belgium	−0.5	0.0	0.0	−2.3	−2.3	−0.2	−0.5	−0.5
Germany	−1.6	−3.7	−4.0	−3.7	−3.2	−2.3	−1.6	−1.2
Greece	−4.7	−5.2	−6.1	−7.8	−5.2	−2.6	−2.6	−2.4
Spain	−1.8	−0.3	0.0	−0.2	1.1	1.5	1.1	0.9
France	−2.1	−3.2	−4.2	−3.7	−2.9	−2.7	−2.6	−2.2
Ireland	2.3	−0.4	0.3	1.5	1.1	1.2	0.9	0.4
Italy	−2.2	−2.9	−3.5	−3.4	−4.1	−4.7	−2.9	−3.1
Luxembourg	4.5	2.1	0.3	−1.1	−1.0	−1.5	−0.5	−0.3
Netherlands	0.0	−2.0	−3.1	−1.8	−0.3	0.0	0.1	0.3
Austria	−1.5	−0.5	−1.6	−1.2	−1.5	−1.3	−1.2	−1.0
Portugal	−3.3	−2.9	−2.9	−3.2	−6.0	−4.6	−4.0	−3.9
Finland	2.8	4.1	2.5	2.3	2.7	2.9	2.9	2.9
Euro Area		−2.5	−3.1	−2.8	−2.4	−2.0	−1.5	−1.3
Non-euro Area Member States:								
Denmark	1.8	1.2	1.1	2.7	4.9	4.0	4.3	4.2
Sweden	2.2	−0.2	0.1	1.8	3.0	2.8	2.4	2.5
UK	0.8	−1.7	−3.3	−3.2	−3.3	−2.9	−2.8	−2.5
EU-25		−2.3	−3.0	−2.7	−2.3	−2.0	−1.6	−1.4

Source: Commission (2006, p. 151, Table 37).

Italy and Portugal. Although Germany's and Greece's deficits are forecast to have fallen below the 3 per cent threshold by the end of 2006, the other two are still above the threshold. Italy has until 2007 to correct its excessive deficit, while Portugal has until 2008 (Commission, 2007a).

Leaving these four countries aside, the other EU Member States are not reducing their levels of public debt as one might expect in a year of improved economic performance. Instead, the OECD survey of the euro area shows that public debt in EU Member States is projected to stay high, albeit declining somewhat during the period 2005–10 (OECD, 2007, p. 95, Table 3.1).

Some of the challenges that the Member States are facing include ageing populations (thereby higher pressures on pensions and healthcare in the future) and non-demographic pressures on health care services (such as increasing technological progress and an increase in desire for healthcare services related to an increase in wealth). In other words, Member States will need to account for these pressures in the present in order to maintain responsible public debt and budgetary deficit positions in the future.

It is clear, however, that Member States have not put in the effort that is needed to avoid difficulties in the future. The SGP did not have an effect in this regard during 2006 in part because economic growth enabled countries to keep their deficits below the 3 per cent without taking action, even though Member States are supposed to keep their budget deficits 'close to balance or in surplus' in the medium term (the 'medium term objective', MTO). Although some Member States – such as Belgium, Finland, Ireland, the Netherlands and Spain – have already reached their MTOs, others are either not targeting that objective or are not doing so successfully (OECD, 2007, p. 99 and Table 3.3).

III. Policies of the European Central Bank

The Governing Council of the ECB sets the key interest rates for the euro area. Since its creation, the ECB has taken the euro area as a whole as its reference point. In determining policy the Member States' economies are weighted proportionally to their economic size in the euro area economy. There were no changes in policy by the ECB in 2006 (for a general discussion of ECB policy see Verdun, 2006). During 2006 the ECB raised interest rates five times, each time by 25 basis points (from 1.25 per cent on 6 December 2005 to 2.50 per cent on 13 December 2006). This increase in interest rates is unprecedented for the ECB. As was discussed in last year's review (Verdun, 2006), when the ECB raised its interest rates in December 2005 it was the first time it had done so since 2003. The ECB has typically not been responsive to outside pressures. It has usually kept its interest rates unchanged when commentators were pointing to weak economic growth or the value of the euro (either over or undervaluation). These interest rate increases in 2006 were a response to a threat of increasing inflation, driven primarily by higher prices for energy and raw commodities. Despite the sharp increases, the ECB's interest rate at the end of 2006 was still 100 basis points (i.e. 1 per cent) lower than that of the US Federal Reserve.

IV. External Dimension of the Euro

The euro gained considerably in value against other major currencies during 2006. Even though the euro had been deemed by the media to have been overvalued in 2004 and to a lesser extent 2005, in 2006 (see Figure 1) there was less emphasis on the euro being overvalued, but concern focused on the decline of the US dollar. The concern was that a sharp decline in the US dollar might undermine the competitiveness of the euro area economy. Towards the

Figure 1: US–Euro Exchange Rates January 1999 – January 2007

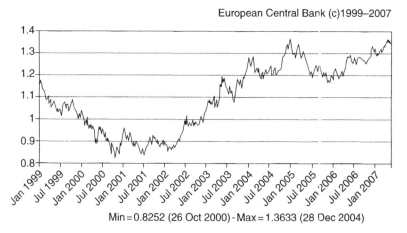

European Central Bank (c)1999–2007

Min = 0.8252 (26 Oct 2000) - Max = 1.3633 (28 Dec 2004)

Source: European Central Bank.

end of 2006 the depreciation of the Japanese yen emerged as another concern. In addition to the height of the exchange rate, there was concern about the euro's volatility. During 2006 it fluctuated between roughly $1.20 and $1.30, for example. However, if put in historical perspective the euro (or in the past the Deutschmark) exchange rate *vis-à-vis* the US has often fluctuated this much or more.

Given the appreciation of the euro throughout 2006, the ECB came under some pressure to act. The ECB, however, considers the value of the euro only insofar as it might contribute to inflation. Ministers of Finance of the EU are the ones responsible for setting any exchange rate regime. To date the euro has been freely floating. In other words, although the mandate of the ECB is to secure price stability (defined as 2 per cent inflation) and it has also to consider the overall economic performance of the EU, the ECB has not targeted the exchange rate in 2006. However, the President of the ECB, Jean-Claude Trichet, signed a G-7 Communiqué in Singapore stating that 'Excess volatility and disorderly movements in exchange rates are undesirable for economic growth' (Trichet, 2006). This statement suggests that the ECB might consider interventions in the exchange rate in the future.

V. Developments in Selected Member States of the Euro Area

Since EMU is an asymmetrical monetary union (Verdun, 1996), with a strong central authority responsible for monetary policy whereas fiscal policy is conducted decentrally by national governments, more than in any other monetary union, its success depends on the economic performance of Member States. Some of the criticisms of the euro area have been that its economic growth has lagged behind, in particular that of the largest countries (Germany, France and Italy). The performance of the larger Member States is important as the ECB sets monetary policy based on a weighted average of the economies of the euro area and the largest economies weigh the most. Let us now turn to a discussion of some economic developments in the largest five Member States of the euro area and assess what the differences in performances are of these countries on a number of characteristics, such as growth, investment, employment, public finances, inflation and the forecast for the next year.

Germany

Economic growth in Germany in 2006 was stronger than expected. Measured as annual percentage of change at previous year prices, 2005 saw only 0.9 per cent growth compared to a projected 2.4 per cent in 2006 (Commission, 2006, p. 58). Exports were seen to be the main driver, although the German government's announcement that it would increase value-added tax (VAT) from 16 to 19 per cent on 1 January 2007 caused consumption to be brought forward to 2006. The football World Cup during the summer also generated growth, in particular through its effect on the service sector.

The consumer confidence index, an indicator of how likely consumers are to make larger purchases, went up very strongly in 2006 (Commission, 2006, p. 56). Overall investment was also up, with investment in the housing sector getting a boost in advance of the 2007 VAT increase and some policy changes, such as subsidies on energy-saving construction measures, that offered stimuli in this sector. Corporate investment was encouraged by some depreciation rules that would be valid only until the end of 2007.

Employment was up in Germany in 2006 in terms both of number of people employed and number of hours worked. Although in past years Germany has seen a strong increase in so-called 'flexible jobs', in 2006 growth occurred in more traditional jobs; for the first time in years there was even an increase in jobs subject to social insurance contributions.

Having had problems since 2002, public finances in Germany finally did better in 2006. The fall in the government budget deficit to 2.3 per cent of GDP in 2006 was due to increased revenue (mostly via direct taxes) from increased economic activity. The government is keeping general government expenditure under control. As total expenditure grew by 0.8 per cent (spring projection) in 2006, the unexpectedly high GDP growth reduced expenditure as a share of GDP by one percentage point. At the same time, the improved employment situation reduced the amount needed to pay unemployment insurance. The budget deficit is forecast to fall further in 2007 to 1.6 per cent of GDP (see Table 5), in part because of the increase in VAT on 1 January 2007. Public debt is forecast to remain roughly unchanged (67.9 per cent of GDP in 2005 to 67.7 per cent of GDP in 2008).

Inflation in Germany has been lower than in other euro area countries and at 1.8 per cent was slightly lower in 2006 than in 2005. Although Germany is a large economy that has the greatest impact on the policies of the ECB, this does not mean that euro area interest rates exactly reflect economic conditions in Germany. In 2006, as in the recent past, inflation in Germany would have merited a lower interest rate than that set by the ECB. As a consequence, German economic growth has occurred despite a relatively tight monetary policy.

The economic forecast for Germany in 2007 is favourable. The planned VAT increase will cause inflation to increase slightly, which will mean that the ECB's monetary policy will be more appropriate for the Germany economy, although inflation is forecast to come down again in 2008. GDP and employment growth are also forecast to continue to grow in 2007. According to the Commission's (2006, p. 58) annual forecast, unemployment is projected to come down to 8.4 per cent in 2007 (from 8.9 in 2006). Last but not least, Germany's public finances seem finally to have improved and are forecast to stay below the SGP's 3 per cent reference value in 2007.

France

As in Germany, economic growth in France in 2006 was stronger than expected and significantly higher than the year before. Measured as annual percentage of change at previous year prices, 2005 only saw 1.2 per cent growth, whereas 2006 was projected to be at 2.2 per cent (Commission, 2006, p. 668). Increased domestic demand was the main driver of this increased growth, although exports also improved. Strong import growth, however, meant that the contribution of net exports to growth was close to neutral (in 2005 it had been negative).

Investment in the French housing sector also got a boost following the implementation of new mortgage financing conditions. Investments by companies were also strong. In part corporate expenditures reflect the economic cycle; an increase in economic growth following a period of weak growth causes companies to invest to replace their equipment.

The employment situation in France in 2006 also showed improvement and finally employment levels began to catch up to those of the other EU

Member States. In 2005 job creation was about 0.2 per cent, whereas the projected increase in jobs in 2006 was 0.8 per cent. Similarly, whereas the rate of unemployment was 9.7 per cent in 2005, the forecast for 2006 was 9.3 per cent, with further reductions envisaged in the years to come.

Having famously had problems since 2002, public finances in France started to improve in 2005. The budget deficit fell to 2.9 per cent of GDP, with a further decline projected to be at 2.7 per cent of GDP in 2006 (see Table 5). Most of the reduction in the budget deficit was due to stronger economic growth (that is, improved revenues and reduced expenditures). The increase in revenue was largely due to strong consumption growth and thus higher revenue collected through indirect taxes. In addition, increased corporate profits led to higher corporate tax revenue and increased employment contributed to more revenue collected through income taxes. In terms of expenditure, the cost of healthcare fell as a result of reforms. In addition to these improvements related to the economic cycle, the French government also relied on some one-off measures (Commission, 2006, p. 67). The public debt to GDP ratio is forecast to fall slightly from 66.6 per cent of GDP in 2005 to 64.7 per cent in 2006 and 63.9 in 2007.

Inflation in France has been steady and marginally lower than in other euro area countries. Inflation in 2006 was projected to be 2.0 per cent, compared to 1.9 per cent in 2005 and is expected to fall to 1.8 per cent in 2007. Because inflation in France is close to the average of that of the euro area as a whole, the ECB's interest rate policy is appropriate for France.

The economic forecast for France for 2007 is favourable. After years of sluggish domestic demand, it is expected that the next years will be better largely because of strong demand, especially private consumption (Commission, 2006, p. 66). Inflation should stay stable at just below 2 per cent. Being so close to the projected average inflation rate of euro area Member States will mean that ECB monetary policy will be 'just right' for France. GDP and employment growth are also forecast to continue in 2007. According to the Commission's autumn annual forecast, France's unemployment rate, although still relatively high compared to other EU Member States, is projected to come down to 9.0 per cent in 2007 from 9.3 in 2006 (Commission, 2006, p. 58). Finally, France's budget deficit seems to have stabilized at just below the SGP's 3.0 per cent threshold. It is forecast to be at 2.6 per cent in 2007 and 2.2 per cent in 2008.

Italy

As in Germany and France, economic growth in Italy in 2006 was stronger than expected and markedly better than in previous years. Measured as annual percentage of change at constant prices, the economy stagnated in 2003 and 2005 (0.0 per cent in both years) and grew only slowly in 2004 (1.1 per cent), whereas for 2006 growth was projected again to be 1.7 per cent (Commission, 2006, p. 73). As in France, increased domestic demand was the main driver. Following from the increased growth in the euro area and the rest of the EU, Italian exports picked up, but they seem not to have grown as much as could be expected if keeping in pace with increased demands in their export markets. The problem is, that with relatively high prices and wages, Italy is not as competitive as its neighbouring countries (Commission, 2006, p. 36).

The employment situation in Italy has improved in 2006 (Commission, 2006, p. 35). Italy recorded one of the stronger rates of job creation in the euro area in 2006, with employment increasing by 1.3 per cent. Some of these jobs are related to net immigration and there has been strong growth in so-called 'flexible jobs'. Unemployment also went down from 8.0 per cent in 2004 to 7.7 per cent in 2005 and is projected to have been 7.1 per cent in 2006. It is forecast to stay at roughly that level in the coming years (Commission, 2006, p. 73).

As was mentioned earlier, Italy was one of those countries that ran an excessive deficit in 2006, despite the government's significant efforts to bring it below the 3 per cent SGP threshold. An important reason for the disappointing budgetary situation in 2006 was related to a recent European Court of Justice ruling that allows companies to claim VAT refunds for company cars, which has had a considerable impact on Italian public finances, estimated to be the equivalent of 1 per cent of GDP (Commission, 2006, pp. 41 and 72). Nevertheless the forecast for 2007 is that the deficit will drop just below 3 per cent of GDP. The public debt to GDP ratio is forecast to increase slightly to 107 per cent in 2006, compared to 104.3 per cent in 2003, 103.9 per cent in 2004 and 106.6 per cent in 2005. In 2007 and 2008, however, the debt as a proportion of GDP is forecast to come down gradually (Commission, 2006, p. 73).

Inflation in Italy over the past few years has been around 2.3 per cent and is expected to go down to 2.0 per cent in 2007 and 1.9 per cent in 2008. Italy, like France, has an inflation rate that is close to the average of that of the euro area as a whole. As a consequence, the ECB's interest rate policy is appropriate for Italy as far as price stability is concerned.

The economic forecast for Italy for 2007 is quite favourable. Domestic demand is on the rise and is expected to continue to be positive in the coming years, albeit at a slower pace than in 2006 (Commission, 2006, p. 71). Inflation is forecast to come down slightly to 2.0 per cent in 2007 and 1.9 per cent in 2008. GDP is forecast to grow by 1.4 per cent in both 2007 and 2008. Job creation is not expected to be as strong as in 2006, but is still positive (forecast to be 0.5 per cent in both 2007 and 2008). According to the Commission's annual forecasts, unemployment is projected to come down to 7.0 per cent in both 2007 and 2008 (Commission, 2006, p. 73).

Spain

Growth in Spain was faster than in most Member States of the euro area. Measured as annual percentage of change at previous year prices, 2005 saw 3.5 per cent growth, whereas 2006 is projected to be at 3.8 per cent, well above the euro area average (Commission, 2006, p. 65). Again, increased domestic demand was an important driver. In Spain net exports are contributing negatively to growth but less so than in 2005 (Commission, 2006, p. 63). With strong job creation and easy monetary conditions, Spain is benefiting from the strong economic performance.

The employment situation in Spain is still looking very good, confirming a remarkable success story. A country that had double digit unemployment in the 1990s now serves as an example of job creation and low unemployment. Employment increased again in Spain in 2006. In 2005 the job creation rate was about 3.1 per cent, whereas the projected increase in jobs for 2006 was 3.2 per cent. Similarly, whereas the rate of unemployment had been 9.2 per cent in 2005, the forecast for 2006 was 8.1 per cent, with further reductions envisaged in the years to come (to 7.9 per cent and 7.4 per cent in 2007 and 2008, respectively).

Spain has not had problems meeting the SGP deficit criteria. In 2005 Spain ran a budget surplus equivalent to 1.5 per cent of GDP and it was projected to be even larger (1.9 per cent) in 2006 (see Table 5).

Inflation in Spain has been steady and tended to be a little higher than that in other euro area countries. Inflation in 2006 was projected to be at 3.6 per cent, compared to 3.4 per cent in 2005 and projected to come down to 2.8 per cent in 2007. In 2006, as in the recent past, the inflation rate in Spain is the second highest in the euro area as a whole. Thus the interest rate policy of the ECB is not ideal for Spain.

For Spain the economic forecast for 2007 is once again favourable. Growth in 2007 and 2008 is expected to be similar to, but not quite as high, as was projected for 2006 (Commission, 2006, p. 65). Inflation will gradually come down to about 2.8 and 2.7 per cent in 2007 and 2008, respectively. With Spain growing faster in terms of both GDP and employment and with an overall higher inflation than the euro area average, ECB monetary policy is rather too loose for Spain.

The Netherlands

After three years of economic decline, the Dutch economy began to recover in 2005 and economic growth accelerated in 2006. Measured as an annual percentage change at the previous year's prices, 2005 saw 3.5 per cent growth, whereas growth in 2006 was projected to have been at 3.8 per cent, well above the euro area average (Commission, 2006, p. 65). Domestic demand is an important driver in the Netherlands, with private consumption doing a lot of 'catching up'. Exports also grew but as imports grew at a similar pace, the impact of net exports remained unchanged (Commission, 2006, p. 86).

The employment situation in the Netherlands has improved with the economic recovery. In 2005 and 2006 the Netherlands was among the countries with the lowest rates of unemployment of the euro area countries; 4.7 per cent in 2005, dropping to 3.9 per cent in 2006 (Commission, 2006, p. 87). Although there was no increase in new jobs in 2005, 2006 is thought to have seen growth, with an increase in new jobs of 1.6 per cent. Although growth has accelerated and jobs have been created, there has been no sign of a considerable wage increase. The implication is that the productivity of Dutch labour has gone up.

The Netherlands has performed admirably lately with regarded to the SGP's budget deficit criterion. Whereas it was considered to have an excessive deficit in 2003, the Netherlands was in surplus in 2006 (see Table 5), a very rapid turnaround.

Inflation in the Netherlands has been dropping since the early 2000s, falling to 1.5 per cent in 2005, but is expected to have increased to 1.6 per cent in 2006 and is forecast to continue to increase gradually to 2.3 per cent in 2008. Thus, in 2006, as in the recent past, inflation in the Netherlands has been low. With the forecast gradual increase, however, one could conclude that the interest rate policy of the ECB is fine for the Netherlands.

The 2007 economic forecast for the Netherlands is positive. Since the recovery finally took hold in 2005, private consumption is back and productivity growth appears strong as well (Commission, 2006, p. 36). Overall, the Netherlands is doing very well indeed.

VI. An Assessment of Economic and Monetary Union in 2006

EMU has done well in 2006. After a number of years of speculation about whether it was good for the Member States, criticisms of EMU were much less frequent in 2006. In part this improved perception of EMU is due to the improvement of the economic performance of the larger economies of the euro area (in particular Germany's). In recent years the economic performances of the countries in the euro area have been compared unfavourably to those Member States that stayed out; in fact it was argued that those who stayed outside EMU were faring better. Such comments were much rarer in 2006.

The reality is that, on average compared to the period prior to 1999, EMU enables the euro area countries to benefit from the lower cost of borrowing money (i.e. better financial circumstances, in particular low interest rates, low inflation and easy access to money). Other benefits of EMU are the ease in comparing price levels which should promote trade and investment into the euro area. Finally, the dynamic effects of EMU are such that other imperfections of market integration, such as shortcomings in the integration of financial services, are now coming to the surface and are being discussed. This year was characterized by an overall acceptance of EMU, rather than any major reflection on whether EMU's institutional design needs any adjustment. The only major institutional change was the accession of Slovenia (see Johnson, this volume).

Conclusion

The economic developments in the euro area countries during 2006 were overwhelmingly positive. The concerns about the lack of economic growth in the euro area that dominated 2005 have withered away. The differences between the 'ins' and the 'outs' did not get larger and the larger economies in the euro area made clear improvements. Moreover, although the euro area Member States' economies still perform differently, the differences among them are not very large and are shrinking. Some larger Member States that performed worse in earlier years are now experiencing stronger economic growth.

EMU as a whole seems to enjoy the support of citizens in the EU. The year 2006 saw no major discussion of the institutional structure. Criticism of the Stability and Growth Pact was subdued in 2006, in part because the improved economic performances meant that its restrictions bit less. The commitment of the euro area countries to EMU and the SGP still seems strong, but a clear assessment of that commitment can be made only after their economies have been tested by a recession.

The ECB has been very active in 2006 changing interest rates in response to increasing inflationary pressures. Yet interest rates in the euro area are still considerably lower than elsewhere, notably the United States.

The outlook for the euro area economy in 2007 is good. It is likely that economic growth in 2007 will be slightly weaker than 2006, but the prospect is that countries will still experience strong economic growth, improvement in job creation and drops in unemployment. The countries in the euro area may look ahead to another good year.

Key Readings

Buiter (2006) argues that old criticisms of the Stability and Growth Pact survive intact, but emphasizes two further features. First, the Pact imposes constraints on national fiscal autonomy, but there are no clear cross-border externalities that warrant debt and deficit limits. Second, the Pact cannot address E(M)U-wide stabilization and the fiscal-monetary policy mix.

El-Agraa's (2007) textbook is designed for readers from all disciplines studying the EU, its economics and policies and the effects of economic integration. It offers an overview of economic policies and principles (including chapters on theories of economic and on monetary integration) and touches on various policy-making areas. It is among the most useful textbooks for those mainly interested in the economics of the EU (for a discussion of De Grauwe 2005, see last year's review).

Puetter (2006) is the first study on the work of the Eurogroup – monthly informal meetings between euro area Finance Ministers, the Commission and the European Central Bank. It examines how this group of senior decision-makers shapes European economic governance through a routinized informal policy dialogue. It shows how an understanding of the interplay of formal provisions and informal processes is pivotal to the analysis of euro area governance.

Torres *et al.* (2006) explore issues of economic and political governance in the European Economic and Monetary Union. Combining the perspectives of economics, law, political science and historical research, it provides an up-to-date analysis of the development of the Eurozone and assesses the prospects for the economic and political sustainability of the euro.

References

Buiter, W.H. (2006) 'The "Sense and Nonsense of Maastricht" Revisited: What Have We Learnt about Stabilization in EMU?' *Journal of Common Market Studies*, Vol. 44, No. 4, pp. 687–710.
Buti, M. (2006) 'Will the New Stability and Growth Pact Succeed? An Economic and Political Perspective'. *European Economy, Economic Papers*, No. 241, January.
Calmfors, L. (2005) 'The Revized Stability and Growth Pact: A Critical Assessment', Institute for International Economic Studies, available at: «http://www.iies.su.se/~lcalmfor/slovbankj.pdf».

Commission of the European Communities (2006) 'Economic Forecasts'. *European Economy*, No. 5, Autumn.

Commission of the European Communities (2007a) 'Stability and Growth Pact and Fiscal Surveillance Excessive Deficit Procedure' (last updated 16 March 2007) available at: «http://ec.europa.eu/economy_finance/about/activities/sgp/edp_list_en.htm».

Commission of the European Communities (2007b) 'Harmonized Index of Consumer Prices'. Made available by the Commission services DG Ecfin in March 2007.

El-Agraa, A. (2007) *The European Union: Economics and Policies* (Cambridge: Cambridge University Press).

Grauwe, P. de (2005) *Economics of Monetary Union*, 6th edition (Oxford: Oxford University Press).

Heipertz, M. and Verdun, A. (2006) 'The Dog That Would Bark But Never Bite? Origins, Crisis and Reform of Europe's Stability and Growth'. In Torres, F., Verdun, A. and Zimmermann, H. (eds) *EMU Rules: The Political and Economic Consequences of European Monetary Integration* (Baden-Baden: Nomos), pp. 115–35.

IMF (2006) *World Economic Outlook* (Washington, DC: International Monetary Fund).

OECD (2007) *OECD Economic Survey of the Euro Area* (Paris: Organisation for Economic Co-operation and Development), September.

Puetter, U. (2006) *The Eurogroup: How a Secretive Circle of Finance Ministers Shape European Economic Governance* (Manchester: Manchester University Press).

Šabić, A. (2006) 'Reform of the Stability and Growth Pact'. *Financial Theory and Practice*, Vol. 30, No. 3, pp. 283–93.

Torres, F., Verdun, A. and Zimmermann, H. (eds) (2006) *EMU Rules: The Political and Economic Consequences of European Monetary Integration* (Baden-Baden: Nomos).

Trichet, J.-C. (2006) 'Interview with Jean-Claude Trichet, President of the European Central Bank', conducted on 11 December by I. Chrysolora (*Ta Nea*), M. Döbler (*Der Tagesspiegel*) and P. Leyers (*Luxemburger Wort*), published on 18 December. Available at: «http://www.ecb.int/press/key/date/2006/html/sp061218.en.html».

Verdun, A. (1996) 'An "Asymmetrical" Economic and Monetary Union in the EU: Perceptions of Monetary Authorities and Social Partners'. *Journal of European Integration*, Vol. 20, No. 1, pp. 59–81.

Verdun, A. (2006) 'Economic Developments in the Euro Area'. *JCMS Annual Review 2005*, pp. 199–212.

Developments in the Economies of Member States Outside the Euro Area

DEBRA JOHNSON
Hull University

Introduction

In 2006 the non-euro area EU Member States faced the most benign economic outlook for years. Real world trade growth was 9 per cent and world real gross domestic product (GDP) grew an estimated 5.1 per cent (Commission, 2006; IMF, 2006). Growth was relatively balanced among the world's regions and, apart from in the Middle East and Africa (Commission, 2006), was above the levels of 2005, itself a year of buoyant economic expansion. This world economy remained strong despite high oil prices, which peaked in August and which, although falling back towards the end of the year, remained relatively high.

The US economy, long one of the main drivers of the world economy, remained strong, although growth did slow towards the end of 2006 as the housing market cooled and, with it, consumer spending. However, high levels of corporate profitability and investment plus some employment growth have helped sustain US growth, suggesting the economy is in for a soft rather than a hard landing.

However, even if the US economy does less well than expected, the performance of Asia, which has increased in relative importance to the EU as a trading partner in recent years, will go some way to compensate. After many disappointing years, Japan has begun to register unspectacular but steady growth. China once more grew at over 10 per cent in 2006 and large parts of the rest of the continent grew by over 8 per cent. Other regions demonstrating improved performance in 2006 include the Commonwealth of Independent States, several of which have benefited from higher energy prices and strong domestic demand and Latin America where both domestic and external demand have been strong.

In Europe, the recovery of the euro area continued to pick up speed as a result of buoyant domestic demand and good export performance, thereby contributing to growth in the non-euro area members. Despite this recovery, the euro-outsiders continued to outperform the euro area. This is particularly true of the 2004 accession states, who continue to play catch up and whose export sectors benefited from the economic recovery in the rest of Europe.

I. Overall Economic Performance

Despite real GDP growth reaching 2.6 per cent for the euro area as a whole in 2006, up from 1.4 per cent in 2005, growth rates in Member States outside the euro area, apart from Malta, continued to outstrip those of the euro insiders. The Baltic states grew particularly strongly with double digit growth in Estonia and Latvia and growth approaching 8 per cent in Lithuania. Most other countries grew at rates similar to or higher than those of 2005. Poland's rebound from its 2005 slowdown was particularly notable (see Table 1).

Growth has been healthy in both the old and new euro-outsiders for some years to the extent that reports of emerging capacity constraints and fears of

Table 1: Real GDP Growth (% Annual Change) – Non-Euro Area

	1997–01	2002	2003	2004	2005	2006 estimate	2007 forecast
Czech Republic	1.2	1.9	3.6	4.2	6.1	6.0	5.1
Denmark	2.4	0.5	0.7	1.9	3.0	3.0	2.3
Estonia	6.2	8.0	7.1	7.8	10.5	10.9	9.5
Cyprus	4.2	2.1	1.9	3.9	3.8	3.8	3.8
Latvia	6.2	6.5	7.2	8.6	10.2	11.0	8.9
Lithuania	5.0	6.9	10.3	7.3	7.6	7.8	7.0
Hungary	4.6	4.3	4.1	4.9	4.2	4.0	2.4
Malta	3.6	2.2	–2.4	0.0	2.2	2.3	2.1
Poland	4.4	1.4	3.8	5.3	3.2	5.2	4.7
Slovenia	4.2	3.5	2.7	4.4	4.0	4.8	4.2
Slovakia	2.7	4.1	4.2	5.4	6.0	6.7	7.2
Sweden	3.2	2.0	1.7	3.7	2.7	4.0	3.3
UK	3.1	2.1	2.7	3.3	1.9	2.7	2.6
Euro Area	2.8	0.9	0.8	2.0	1.4	2.6	2.1

Source: Commission (2006).

overheating have been voiced regarding a number of them, including the UK, Denmark, Slovakia, Estonia and Latvia. Emerging labour shortages and upward pressure on prices, notwithstanding the fall in oil prices towards the end of 2006, reinforce these fears and open up the possibility that real wage increases, which in most instances have so far been constrained, will push up prices further and undermine recent competitive improvements.

In all countries under discussion, growth received a major boost from domestic demand. The contribution of the external sector, however, was mixed. Although real export growth accelerated in many countries as a result of the good performance of major export markets, in many cases the buoyancy of domestic demand, both in terms of household consumption and investment, boosted import growth even more. In many cases, this either reduced the positive contribution of exports to GDP growth or, in the case of the Baltic states, turned a positive contribution from the external sector into a negative one. It was only in the cases of Sweden, Slovenia and Slovakia that the positive contribution of the external sector to growth increased.

Apart from in the UK and Hungary, labour markets continued to tighten in all of the euro outsider countries in 2006. In Poland, Slovakia and the Baltic states the falls in unemployment were large and significant (see Table 2). In most countries, lower unemployment was also accompanied by higher levels of employment.

Table 2: Unemployment (as a Percentage of the Civilian Labour Force) – Non-euro Area

	1997–01	2002	2003	2004	2005	2006 estimate	2007 forecast
Czech Republic	6.4	7.3	7.8	8.3	7.9	7.4	7.1
Denmark	5.1	4.6	5.4	5.5	4.8	3.8	3.5
Estonia	10.5	10.3	10.0	9.7	7.9	5.4	3.8
Cyprus	5.0	3.6	4.1	4.6	5.3	5.4	5.5
Latvia	15.6	12.2	10.5	10.4	8.9	7.4	7.2
Lithuania	13.9	13.5	12.4	11.4	8.3	5.9	5.2
Hungary	8.0	5.8	5.9	6.1	7.2	7.3	7.7
Malta	6.4	7.5	7.6	7.4	7.3	7.0	7.0
Poland	12.6	19.9	19.6	19.0	17.7	13.9	12.2
Slovenia	7.0	6.3	6.7	6.3	6.5	6.1	6.1
Slovakia	14.5	18.7	17.6	18.2	16.3	14.3	13.3
Sweden	8.0	4.9	5.6	6.3	7.8	7.3	7.4
UK	6.4	5.1	4.9	4.7	4.7	5.3	5.0
Euro Area	9.8	8.3	8.7	8.9	8.6	8.0	7.7

Source: Commission (2006).

Economic growth and higher domestic demand have been the main drivers of these labour market improvements. It has taken some time for labour markets to respond fully to the consistent and healthy growth that most of the central and eastern European countries have been experiencing for a few years. In part, this is because the transition process and the restructuring that these states have undergone initially resulted in the shedding of large quantities of labour, and later dealt with increasing labour demand by increasing productivity rather than by job creation. This stage is now coming to an end and a more conventional relationship between growth and labour demand appears to be emerging.

Several worrying trends, however, are coming to the fore. Large differences in regional employment have been reported for many years in central and eastern Europe and these continue. Moreover, a growing number of skills shortages are being reported in many parts of the region. This is partly a result of increased labour demand and partly of increasing outward migration. Consequently, even countries that have what would ordinarily be regarded as high levels of unemployment, such as Poland, could find themselves subject to capacity constraints resulting from labour market inflexibility and skills mismatches. An unfortunate consequence of this is that as business comes up against labour constraints, real wages, which so far have remained remarkably restrained, could start to ease upwards and exceed ongoing productivity improvements. In the long run, real wages need to grow in central and eastern Europe in order to enable these countries to catch up with the rest of Europe. This needs to be done, however, without undermining the region's competitiveness.

High growth and capacity constraints induced by labour market constraints are pushing up inflation rates. High energy prices were behind this trend through much of 2006, but overheating inspired price increases plus further increases in regulated prices took over as a major source of inflationary pressure during the second half of 2006 in most of the old and the new euro-outsiders (see Table 3).

It is inflationary concerns in particular that have resulted in delays in plans to adopt the euro. Whilst Slovenia was being given the go-ahead for euro membership from January 2007, Lithuania's request was turned down because it failed to meet the inflationary criterion (by less than 0.1 per cent) and because of concerns that inflation was on an upward trend, which subsequently proved to be the case. Lithuania's case demonstrated that the European Commission intends to interpret the Maastricht criteria strictly when it comes to considering requests to adopt the euro – unlike the assessment of the suitability of the original euro area members. Moreover, it is questionable whether inflation is such an intractable problem for rapidly

Table 3: Inflation – non-euro area
Harmonised index of consumer prices

	1997–01	2002	2003	2004	2005	2006 estimate	2007 forecast
Czech Republic	5.6	1.4	–0.1	2.6	1.6	2.5	2.7
Denmark	2.1	2.4	2.0	0.9	1.7	2.0	2.0
Estonia	6.1	3.6	1.4	3.0	4.1	4.4	4.2
Cyprus	3.7	2.8	4.0	1.9	2.0	2.4	2.0
Latvia	3.9	2.0	2.9	6.2	6.9	6.7	5.8
Lithuania	3.9	0.3	–1.1	1.2	2.7	3.8	4.6
Hungary	12.3	5.2	4.7	6.8	3.5	3.9	6.8
Malta	3.1	2.6	1.9	2.7	2.5	3.0	2.6
Poland	9.8	1.9	0.7	3.6	2.2	1.4	2.5
Slovenia	8.0	7.5	5.7	3.7	2.5	2.5	2.5
Slovakia	8.5	3.5	8.4	7.5	2.8	4.5	3.4
Sweden	1.5	1.9	2.3	1.0	0.8	1.5	1.6
UK	1.3	1.3	1.4	1.3	2.1	2.4	2.2
Euro area	1.7	2.3	2.1	2.1	2.2	2.2	2.1

Source: Commission (2006).

growing economies that are endeavouring to catch up with the economies of the EU-15 as it was for the EU-15 themselves.

Because of inflation, public deficits, or, as in the case of Poland, the election of a less pro-euro government, several countries have pushed back their target dates for adoption of the euro. The Baltic states, for example, talk of joining as soon as possible, but acknowledge it is unlikely to be before 2010 and Hungary has quietly dropped its 2010 target without setting another. Poland never set a target but its likely entry date is receding into the future. In reality, the earliest the bigger central and eastern European countries will be able to join the euro is 2011–12. In the interim, the possibility of waning enthusiasm and political changes could make euro entry less attractive for the 2004 and 2007 accession countries, which can point to the precedent of Sweden as a country that made a commitment to join the euro area upon accession but has managed to remain outside.

II. Economic Developments in the Old Euro-Outsiders

The United Kingdom

The UK is in the throes of one of its longest periods of continuous economic growth free from the boom and bust of yesteryear, thereby limiting damaging swings in business and consumer confidence. These dampened variations in UK economic fortunes continued into 2006. After growth slowed down in 2005 to 1.9 per cent (down from 3.3 per cent in 2004), it picked up again in 2006 to reach 2.75 per cent.

The main boost to growth in 2006 came from domestic demand, especially from private consumption, which was helped by a growing labour market and by a robust housing market. The latter had shown signs of weakness in 2005, but rebounded in 2006 when house prices increased by an average 10 per cent, below the boom levels of the early 2000s, but significant nevertheless. Constraints on household spending included a slight acceleration in inflation in 2006, high levels of household debt, higher interest rates towards the end of the year and a slight increase in unemployment. Higher public spending also contributed to growth, but in the longer term the Treasury plans to rein in public spending and forecasts of stronger revenues should result in a return to budget surplus in the medium term.

Investment growth in both the public and the private sectors also played a key role in GDP growth. Private investment, which had been relatively weak in 2005, showed the greatest improvement. This was the result of healthy corporate profitability and low capital costs – costs which increased with the interest rate rises in August and November, but which were still relatively low by historical standards.

All aspects of business and financial services remained buoyant in 2006 and other service sectors demonstrated growth. In 2006, however, the fortunes of manufacturing turned around; after falling in 2005, manufacturing growth resumed in 2006, bolstered by strong growth in key export markets. Despite this positive export performance, the growth of imports was even stronger, resulting in a marginally negative impact of the external sector on GDP. Nevertheless, given the appreciation of sterling, the export sector performed well and benefited from the robustness of the world economy and, in particular, from the stronger growth of the euro area, which constitutes the UK's biggest market.

Labour issues attracted a lot of political attention in 2006. This debate took place against the background of a sharp rise in labour supply, reflected in both higher employment and unemployment figures. This increase had two components: first, unprecedented net immigration helped by the large inward movements from the 2004 accession states; and second increased labour force participation by older workers concerned about their retirement incomes. Despite the greater availability of labour, it is still not unusual for employers to report difficulties in filling vacancies. This phenomenon has both a regional and a skills dimension, implying that labour flexibility remains an issue for the UK economy. In response to concerns about increased immigration, the government adopted a restrictive stance on migration from Bulgaria and Romania after their accessions.

Despite falling energy prices towards the end of 2006, inflationary pressure remained a concern and the Bank of England twice raised interest rates towards the end of 2006. Containment of inflation, however, was helped by subdued wage pressure, by productivity improvements, by generally lower inflationary expectations following many years of low, single-digit inflation and by the influx of migrant workers who increased competition for jobs. The risk of accelerating inflation has not disappeared, however, and the Bank of England has shown its readiness to act against this threat with its unexpected interest rate rise in January 2007. The absence of new energy price hikes and continuing wage moderation is essential for continuing price restraint.

The outlook for the UK economy continues to be encouraging, but it does face certain risks. These include the nature and extent of the US economic slowdown; the sustainability of the euro area recovery; the future path of energy prices and trends in UK business and consumer confidence. Moreover, the Bank of England (2006) consistently reported emerging capacity constraints during 2006, giving rise to the risk of overheating and rising prices if the supply side tightens further.

Denmark

In 2006 Denmark turned in a strong, well-balanced performance, which, according to Finance Minister Thor Pedersen, reflected 'high employment, record high fiscal surpluses, current account surpluses [and] a moderate inflation rate' (Ministry of Finance, 2006). This rosy picture reflected the gradual acceleration of GDP growth from a low point in 2002 to an estimated 3 per cent in 2006. Growth was driven by domestic demand. Private consumption growth reached almost 4 per cent with assistance from rising employment, falling unemployment, relatively low interest rates and a booming housing market. Signs of a softening property market, however, emerged in the summer. Investment growth, which accelerated sharply in 2005, continued to pick up in 2006, encouraged by the low cost of borrowing and emerging capacity constraints.

Both imports and exports registered double digit growth in 2006, but the absolute contribution of imports was greater, leading to a negative contribution to GDP growth from the external sector. The strength of imports came from private consumption growth, a marked propensity to import by the export sector and tightening capacity constraints.

Labour market developments have been positive in terms of boosting employment to record levels and bringing unemployment down below 4 per cent. Many sectors, however, have begun to report labour shortages, a trend that began in construction but has spread. Prices edged upwards slightly in 2006, but inflation remained below the euro area average. Inflationary expectations are generally low and wage demands have accordingly remained moderate. Tightening labour markets and capacity constraints, however, have the potential to destabilize this situation.

Sweden

In 2006 real GDP growth of 4 per cent was the fastest in Sweden for several years. This growth was broadly based, with significant contributions from both the domestic and external sectors. Bolstered by strong consumer confidence and by improvements in the labour market, household consumption accelerated and although households have taken on more debt, there has been a positive wealth effect as a result of rising equity and house prices.

Investment growth peaked in 2005, but was still at the relatively high level of 7.3 per cent in 2006. This growth was underpinned by relatively low real interest rates and high levels of corporate profitability. Construction, particularly house building, was the main factor in the investment boom for a while, but growth has subsequently increased in manufacturing and commercial investment, pushed by high capacity utilization. As new capacity comes onstream, investment in industrial machinery will decline. Public investment plans, especially for major road and rail initiatives, however, remain ambitious.

The external sector has also played its role in Swedish growth. Export growth, which has been marked in both goods and services, has been helped by the positive global economic situation and especially by the euro area's recovery. Recently Swedish exports have benefited from productivity improvements and a long-term weakening of the krona (although the government expects it to appreciate in the short term). Imports have also shown a marked growth as a result of the strong domestic demand and the high import content of exported goods, but their growth has been restrained somewhat by a drawdown of stocks.

Labour markets improved noticeably in 2006: employment grew by 1.6 per cent and unemployment fell from 7.8 to 7.3 per cent. These improvements were stimulated by GDP growth and by new work incentives from tax and benefits changes. Although tighter, labour markets remain relatively weak, a factor which has helped contain wage demands and contributed positively to the subdued level of inflation (1.5 per cent in 2006). There is a slight upward risk to inflation from strong growth and labour markets but the expected krona appreciation will act as a restraint.

III. Economic Developments in the New Euro-Outsiders

Poland

The economic recovery that began in Poland in late 2005 continued throughout 2006, with real GDP growth reaching 5.2 per cent, up from 3.2 per cent in 2005. This recovery has brought significant improvements in labour markets, healthier public finances, accelerating industrial production and, for the time being at least, lower and stable inflation.

Growth is strongly rooted in domestic demand. Private consumption has been buoyant and helped by the improved labour market situation and by real wage growth – a position that is sustainable if productivity growth continues. Investment growth, which itself helps productivity, was over 10 per cent in 2006, the highest level since 1998 and was boosted by the small firm sector, healthy corporate profitability and by construction growth. Investment growth has also benefited from the emergence of physical capacity constraints. Higher inward foreign direct investment (FDI) and inflows of EU funds will further contribute to investment providing that Poland's capacity to absorb EU funding improves.

Import and export growth both accelerated to 17 per cent in real terms in 2006. Exports benefited from lower exchange rate volatility, EU economic recovery and increased Russian and Ukrainian demand for imports. Imports were drawn into Poland by strong investment and high levels of private consumption. The combined impact of these trends on growth was neutral, but given that strong domestic demand growth is expected to continue, the external sector's growth contribution is forecast to turn slightly negative in 2007 and 2008.

The most marked change in Polish economic fortunes has been in the labour market. Although employment remains low and unemployment high by European standards, the upturn in the former and the downturn in the latter are substantial. Employment grew by over 3 per cent in 2006. Job creation was boosted by increasing early retirement. Unemployment fell from 17.7 per cent in 2005 to 13.9 per cent in 2006 in part as a result of more people staying in education longer and a significant net outward migration, a development which may in the long term deprive Poland of much needed skills.

Poland has been growing for some years but 2006 was the first year that growth has had a significant impact on labour markets (previous improvements had been slow and limited). The earlier limited labour market response to growth was related to ongoing restructuring and the propensity for increased demand for labour to be absorbed by increased labour productivity – an important factor if Poland is to maintain its competitiveness against a background of probable real wage increases. The greater responsiveness of labour markets to economic growth in 2006, however, implies that restructuring is coming to an end. The OECD (2006), among others, is concerned that the physical constraints alluded to above could be accentuated by labour market constraints, despite continuing high unemployment. These constraints would come from the low levels of skills among the unemployed and the limited territorial and vocational mobility of the labour force. The OECD is therefore urging Poland to pay greater attention to education and training and to fiscal reform.

Hungary

Despite a relatively strong overall economic performance, Hungary did not meet any of the Maastricht convergence criteria in 2006. Indeed, if anything, it moved further away from them. Consequently, the government dropped its 2010 target for euro adoption and has not replaced it. Nevertheless, the official position remains that meeting the conditions for euro entry remains a policy priority (Magyar Nemzeti Bank, 2006).

Real GDP growth of 4 per cent originated from both the domestic and external sectors. Net exports in particular have become a major driver of growth. Imports grew strongly (9.6 per cent) in 2006, but were exceeded by exports, which benefited from a depreciating forint and the recovery of the EU market, which accounts for over three-quarters of Hungarian exports. Domestic demand made a positive contribution to growth in 2006, but both consumption and investment growth decelerated during the year. Consumption has been increasingly affected by the fiscal consolidation strategy, the dampening impact of which began to be felt towards the end of 2006.

After several years of missed targets, public sector finances appeared to be almost spiralling out of control in 2006. The public sector financial deficit, already 7.8 per cent of GDP, reached 10 per cent in 2006 compared to a target of 6.2 per cent. Government debt also exceeded 60 per cent of GDP in 2005, reaching nearly 68 per cent in 2006 and is forecast to continuing rising until 2008 at least (Magyar Nemzeti Bank, 2006). In response to the need to sort out its public finances if euro entry is to become a reality, the government introduced a fiscal consolidation strategy, which helped to shape the 2007 budget. The budget entails increased taxes and higher regulated prices, especially for public transport and energy. Although implementation of this strategy will apply the brakes to the economy in the short run, the government maintains that it will provide a platform for sustained growth. It may, however, prove difficult for the government to push through its proposed cuts in health care and the public sector wage bill.

The fiscal strategy could also temporarily put a stop to the slight improvements seen in the labour markets. In 2006 employment increased marginally because of increasing participation rates – which nevertheless remain low (55.4 per cent) by international standards – but projected public sector redundancies are likely to inhibit further employment increases.

Inflation fell slightly in the first half of 2006 before picking up again. This is also partly linked to the fiscal strategy, which pushed up some taxes and regulated prices and partly to the depreciation of the forint. Inflation for the year was almost 4 per cent, compared to 3.5 per cent in 2005. The 2006 trends and the measures taken in 2006, however, imply that inflation may accelerate to almost 7 per cent in 2007. In short, inflation and other relevant indicators have a long way to go before EMU entry becomes possible.

Czech Republic

The Czech Republic's real GDP growth of 6 per cent in 2006 was only marginally down on 2005. The composition of growth, however, has shifted. In 2005 growth was driven mostly by the external sector whereas in 2006, although net exports remained positive, domestic demand became the main contributor to growth. Strong growth is expected to continue into 2007 and 2008, albeit at slightly lower levels and to be driven by investment and private consumption.

In 2006 export growth remained strong and even accelerated as a result of the euro area recovery. Import growth, boosted by investment and household led demand, however, was even stronger, thereby reducing the impact of net exports to growth. These effects were reinforced by the appreciation of the koruna.

Increasing domestic demand came from both private consumption and investment. The former benefited from rising household income, helped by labour market improvements and lower income taxes. Favourable borrowing conditions in the form of easier credit and low interest rates also boosted household demand and private investment, a large part of which took the form of export-oriented FDI.

Industrial production has made a considerable contribution to recent Czech growth. Since 2004, the growth of value-added in manufacturing has been in double figures, stimulated by structural changes brought about by foreign capital. Production has increased as a result of new production facilities in the manufacture of vehicles, transport equipment and electrical and optical equipment. Double-digit growth has also occurred in the manufacture of machinery and equipment, base metals and fabricated metal products and rubber and plastics products. Production has been falling in the food industry, chemicals, pulp, paper and paper products and in publishing and printing (Czech National Bank, 2007).

Growth has helped reduce unemployment from 7.9 per cent in 2005 to 7.4 per cent in 2006 and employment has increased by almost 1 per cent. Further labour market improvements are anticipated, but the rate of improvement is hampered by structural factors, particularly the mismatch between the professional and skills structure of the unemployed and labour market demand. This inflexibility explains and is reflected in two characteristics of the Czech labour market: a marked increase in the number of foreign workers and a relatively high proportion of long-term unemployed (over 50 per cent), even if the numbers are falling overall.

Tighter labour markets plus an increase in the statutory minimum wage increased real wages. This increase has been largely counterbalanced by productivity growth, which has kept unit labour costs down and contributed to a relatively stable inflationary environment. Although prices did increase early in 2006, the pressure on prices was partially relieved by currency appreciation, itself a response to the attractiveness of the region to foreign investors. A sharp slowdown in the growth of regulated prices (especially housing and utilities) also helped bring inflation down sharply towards the end of the year.

Slovakia

Real GDP growth in Slovakia continued to accelerate in 2006, reaching an estimated 6.7 per cent. Domestic demand, especially private consumption and investment, continued to be the main drivers of growth, but the external sector also began to make a positive contribution. The prospects for growth remain buoyant in 2007 and there are fears about potential overheating of the economy.

High levels of private consumption were sustained in 2006 as a result of a combination of real wage increases, strong credit growth and marked improvements in the labour markets. Employment in 2006 rose by 2.6 per cent and unemployment fell two percentage points to 14.3 per cent in 2006. Thus, although still extremely high by the standards of the rest of Europe, Slovakian unemployment finally seems to be demonstrating a rapid and sustainable decline. New job opportunities came from new export capacity, particularly in the auto and related industries. Labour market improvements are, however, uneven: whilst western Slovakia is booming with rapidly rising property prices and emerging skills shortages, unemployment of 20 per cent or above is the norm in parts of eastern Slovakia. It is this structural inflexibility in the labour markets that has contributed to the co-existence of strong real wage increases and high levels of unemployment.

Large private sector projects kept investment levels high but they are forecast to fall as the big auto projects in particular come to fruition. Production at two major car plants – at PSA Peugeot-Citroen's plant in Trnava and at Kia's plant in Zilina – began in 2006. Production of the motor vehicle industry increased 75 per cent in 2006 and by 2007 vehicle exports will contribute 30 per cent of total exports. With production reaching 850,000 cars per year, Slovakia is set to become the highest per capita producer of cars in the world.

Following its November 2005 entry into Exchange Rate Mechanism (ERM) II, Slovakia's target remains adoption of the euro by 1 January 2009. Attainment of this objective was not helped in 2006 by an acceleration of inflation to 4.5 per cent, largely brought about by an increase in regulated prices at the end of 2005. The impact of these rises, however, disappeared within a year and by December 2006, inflation was clearly on a downward trend, registering 3.7 per cent compared to December 2005. This improvement also came from tighter monetary policy, which saw the Central Bank increase interest rates and encourage appreciation of the koruna.

In 2006 the budget deficit also rose above the Maastricht target to 3.4 per cent of GDP. Nevertheless, the deficit was lower than forecast as a result of strong growth and labour market improvements. Full implementation of the 2007 budget could bring the deficit below 3 per cent, but this will require widespread and unpopular cuts in education and social welfare. So far, despite pre-election rhetoric the government elected in June 2006, has, with some exceptions, decided against dismantling the previous government's reforms and has remained committed to the target of 2009 euro adoption. Continuing high levels of growth will ease the pressure on the government to push forward further cuts to help meet this target.

Slovenia

In 2006, as a result of its continuous, often unremarked economic progress since the start of transition and the degree of real and nominal convergence with its EU partners, Slovenia became the first of the 2004 accession states to become eligible for euro area membership. Consequently on 11 July, the Council of Ministers (ECOFIN) abrogated the Slovenian derogation and the euro-tolar exchange rate was irrevocably fixed prior to adoption of the euro on 1 January 2007.

This steady performance continued into 2006. Real GDP growth peaked at 5 per cent early in the year, the highest level since 1999, before falling back to 4.8 per cent for the year as a whole. Growth was driven by domestic demand, particularly investment. Investment demand originated from machinery and equipment, construction (especially house building) and improvements to transport infrastructure. For the second year, net exports made a positive contribution to growth following the improved performance of Slovenia's major trading European partners.

Since first meeting the Maastricht inflation criterion in November 2005, inflation has remained stable. During 2006 Slovenia experienced some upward price pressure as a result of oil price increases, but inflation for year still worked out at only 2.5 per cent. So far the positive economic situation, which has led to moderate increases in employment and small falls in unemployment, has not resulted in increases in real wages. Indeed, it appears that productivity gains are outstripping price rises. Nevertheless, Slovenian inflation does remain vulnerable to pressure from oil prices. The gradual phasing out of payroll taxes will continue to foster further improvements in labour markets.

Estonia

Growth in the Baltic states has outstripped that in other European countries for some time. Upward revisions of Estonian GDP imply growth of 10.5 per cent and 10.9 per cent in 2005 and 2006 respectively. By the end of 2006 Estonia had experienced seven consecutive quarters of double digit growth. There is a growing consensus, however, that growth peaked in the first half of 2006 and that it will subsequently decelerate. Nonetheless, growth forecasts of 8–9 per cent for both 2007 and 2008 do little to stem concerns about overheating.

Growth in 2006 was essentially driven by domestic demand. Household consumption was boosted by higher real wages and tighter labour markets. Indeed, in the third quarter, retail sales grew by almost 20 per cent. Investment responded to this strong final demand and to a favourable monetary stance. Although exports, boosted by the economic success of its main trading partners, continued to perform well, imports were stimulated by domestic demand and performed relatively better, leading to the previous positive contribution to growth turning negative in 2006.

Robust economic growth continued to promote employment growth in 2006 and contributed to the lowest unemployment level (5.4 per cent) for many years. Indeed, an increasing number of sectors – including construction, wholesale and retail trade, manufacturing and transport, storage and distribution – are reporting labour shortages. These shortages have been accentuated by outward migration. Remaining unemployment, however, could be difficult to shift because of the skills mismatch between those of the unemployed and those required by employers.

Although tightening labour markets have resulted in rapid increases in real wages, productivity growth has not kept pace. This has two main consequences. First, some foreign investors are concerned about these rising costs and are reportedly considering relocating to cheaper Belarus or Ukraine (*International Herald Tribune*, 2007). Second, wage increases reinforced the inflationary pressure from energy prices and high growth. Inflation was 4.4 per cent for the year as a whole and the government does not expect to fulfil this particular Maastricht criterion until 2008 at the earliest. Estonia has no trouble however with the Maastricht fiscal criteria; strong growth in 2006 boosted revenue, resulting in a budget deficit of 2.5 per cent and the national debt is in low single figures as a share of GDP.

Latvia

Latvia continued to experience the fastest growth (11 per cent) in the EU in 2006. Indeed, its growth in 2006 was the fastest since it broke away from the Soviet Union. The expected growth slowdown did not materialize and signs of overheating are giving cause for concern. The main factor behind growth in 2006 was domestic demand, particularly real private consumption, which grew by 12.6 per cent and investment, which grew by over 18 per cent. Consumption benefited from easy access to credit, high levels of consumer confidence, labour market improvements and real wage increases, reportedly in double figures in 2006. Investment was driven by construction, notably transport infrastructure and house building and by investment in machinery and equipment.

The external sector's small positive contribution to growth in 2005 became decidedly negative in 2006 as a result of accelerating import and decelerating export growth. Imports were sucked in to satisfy booming domestic demand whereas growth of exports, although still strong, were lower than expected, in part because of problems in one of Latvia's major manufacturing sectors – the wood industry.

Latvian labour markets, stimulated by strong growth, registered big improvements in 2006. In previous years, productivity growth had limited the impact of growth on employment but by 2006, although productivity growth remained impressive, sufficient demand remained in the system to result in a 2.6 per cent growth in employment and a fall in unemployment from 8.9 per cent in 2005 to 7.4 per cent in 2006. Labour market participation rates have increased, but significant outward migration and a diminishing population of working age have helped counterbalance the rise in labour supply. Overall, although economic growth is forecast to ease, it will remain high by most standards and continue to promote labour market improvements. Unemployment, which has been falling steadily for some years, still has scope to fall further, but there are potential problems due to skills mismatches. Indeed, labour shortages have already been reported in some sectors.

Inflation has been creeping up since 2004 and remains the biggest threat to Latvia's economy. Initially prices were driven up by regulated prices, pre-accession inflationary expectations and indirect tax harmonization. The main inflationary drivers in 2005 and into 2006 were fuel prices. High domestic demand, rapidly increasing real wages and credit growth have subsequently taken over as major inflation pressures. As a result, inflation was slightly below 7 per cent for the year as a whole. This undermined Latvia's aspirations for euro adoption in 2008 and caused the government to consider a new target date. Strong growth and the attendant fears of overheating pose the biggest single obstacle to euro zone membership. Latvia's fiscal position, however, is favourable and is helped rather than hindered by strong growth.

Lithuania

Although lower than that of its Baltic neighbours, Lithuanian real GDP growth in 2006 was still a healthy 8 per cent. Domestic demand – both in terms of consumption and investment – underpinned this growth. Private consumption grew 11.5 per cent due to large real wage increases, substantial improvements in labour market performance and income tax cuts. These factors, together with major credit expansion, combined to boost consumer confidence and contribute further to consumer demand. Investment growth remained strong in 2006 and is expected to continue in double figures for at least the next two years. Construction has flourished for many years and the positive picture for income and employment should help to sustain this sector.

Real export growth registered over 14 per cent in 2006, reflecting strong demand from major markets and the relative competitiveness of domestic industry. However, accelerating import growth resulting from strong domestic demand led to an increase in the negative contribution of the external balance to GDP growth in 2006.

Continuing strong growth and outward migration lie behind the rapidly tightening Lithuanian labour market: unemployment in 2006 fell below 6 per cent, less than half the level of three years previously and employment grew by almost 2 per cent. Consequently, there are increasing reports of labour shortages, especially of key skills, which in turn are driving up wages more quickly than productivity, with, among other things, unfortunate consequences for inflation.

Lithuania's inability to adopt the euro in January 2007 as hoped was due to inflation. When the European Commission rejected its application in May 2006, Lithuania's inflation was running at an annual average rate of 2.6 per cent, less than 0.1 per cent above the euro area's reference level. Since then inflation has moved upwards as a result of increases in wages, excise duties and energy, food and health prices. Inflation is forecast to peak in 2007 before moving towards compatibility with the euro area.

Despite its disappointment with the Council's strict application of the Maastricht criteria, the Lithuanian government has reasserted its commitment to the goal of euro adoption, stating in a recent resolution, 'Lithuania will make efforts to join the euro area as soon as possible. According to the available data, the best period for joining the euro starts in 2010' (Government of Lithuania, 2006).

Malta

The improvements in Malta's economic performance first seen in 2005 continued into 2006. Domestic demand was the main driver behind real GDP growth of 2.3 per cent. Private consumption grew at the same rate and was boosted by job creation and consumer credit expansion. The strongest component of domestic demand, however, was investment, which increased 7.5 per cent in 2006. Infrastructure projects partly financed by the EU's Structural Funds have also kept investment high. As the big projects, particularly the Mater Dei hospital (which accounted for 56 per cent of government investment expenditure in 2005), near completion investment contribution to growth will fall.

Real export performance improved in 2006, but high levels of domestic demand also pulled in imports with the result that, although the external balance moved in the right direction, its overall contribution to growth remained negative. Further external sector improvements are forecast for 2007 and 2008 as a result of a more favourable outlook for the electronics and pharmaceutical sectors. Tourism, however, traditionally a mainstay of the economy and a big foreign currency earner, has been a relatively weak performer.

Improvements in labour markets (reflected in a 1 per cent increase in employment and a fall in employment from 7.3 per cent in 2005 to 7 per cent in 2006) were helped considerably by opportunities provided by public sector construction projects. Further job creation is forecast for the pharmaceutical,

IT and financial services sectors. These new jobs will help to offset falling employment in manufacturing, which is encountering stiff competition from low cost producers.

Inflation, driven by higher energy prices, hit 3 per cent in 2006, but was falling by the end of the year. The budget deficit fell below 3 per cent of GDP to meet the Maastricht criteria, following lower current expenditure and continuing fiscal consolidation. Government debt, at almost 70 per cent of GDP in 2006, remains above the Maastricht limits but is moving downwards.

Cyprus

Estimated real GDP growth in Cyprus in 2006 was 3.8 per cent, similar to 2004 and 2005 and a level of growth which is forecast to continue into 2007 and 2008. This healthy and stable growth rate has been and continues to be based mainly on strong domestic demand.

Private consumption growth in 2006 was marginally below that of 2005 but remains essentially healthy. Its buoyancy is based on credit expansion, helped by low interest rates and on increasing employment and real wage growth. In 2006 higher social spending increased the contribution of public consumption to growth. Private investment growth has also accelerated, helped by favourable credit conditions and by high levels of business confidence. Construction, especially in the housing sector, has been instrumental in investment growth, but investment in machinery and equipment has also rebounded. Net exports, however, continue to make a negative contribution to growth.

Labour markets generally remained tight in 2006. Total employment continues to grow but higher participation rates and inflows of foreign workers, currently 16 per cent of the workforce, have combined not only to prevent a fall in unemployment but also to push joblessness up slightly. The inflow of foreign workers was in part a response to labour shortages in important sectors, including hotels and restaurants, trade and construction and in technical and low skilled jobs generally (Ministry of Finance and Central Bank of Cyprus, 2006).

Although labour markets were tight, the influx of foreign workers helped restrain sector wage growth. The continuation of these trends will help with ongoing efforts to contain inflation as part of the government's preparation for adoption of the euro by January 2008 (Ministry of Finance and Central Bank of Cyprus, 2006). The preparations appear to be going well: although inflation moved up early in the year as a result of high oil prices, it fell back in the second half of the year as oil prices retreated. The fiscal convergence criteria, helped by growth, are continuing to improve: the budget deficit fell to below 2 per cent in 2006 with further improvements forecast for 2007.

National debt remains above 60 per cent, but has been steadily falling since 2004 and the official forecast that the national debt will fall below 60 per cent by 2008 is not unrealistic.

References

Bank of England (2006) *Minutes of the Monetary Policy Committee Meetings* – published monthly on the Bank of England website: «http://www. bankofengland.co.uk».

Commission of the European Communities (2006) 'Economic Forecasts: Autumn 2006'. *European Economy*, No. 5.

Czech National Bank (2007) *Inflation Report*, January.

Government of the Republic of Lithuania (2006) 'Resolution No. 1230 of 8 December 2006 on the Convergence Programme of Lithuania of 2006'.

IMF (2006) *World Economic Outlook*, Autumn (Washington, DC: International Monetary Fund).

International Herald Tribune (2007) 13 February.

Magyar Nemzeti Bank (2006) *Analysis of the Convergence Process* (Budapest: Magyar Nemzeti Bank).

Ministry of Finance (Denmark) (2006) Press release accompanying publication of the December 2006 *Economic Survey*, available at: «www.fm.dk/1024/ visNyhed.asp?artikelID=8986».

Ministry of Finance and Central Bank of Cyprus (2006) 'Convergence Programme of the Republic of Cyprus 2006–10'.

OECD (2006) *Economic Survey of Poland* (OECD: Paris).

JCMS 2007 Volume 45 Annual Review pp. 251–255

Chronology: The European Union in 2006

ARANTZA GOMEZ-ARANA
University of Glasgow

At a Glance

Presidencies of the EU Council: Austria (1 January–30 June) and Finland (1 July–31 December).

January

27	'Sound of Europe' celebration of European integration in Salzburg.
31	European Court of Justice Decision in *Commission v. Spain*.

February

1	Commission White paper on European Communication Policy.
8	Commission presented the fourth 'national' communication, from the European Community under the United Nations Framework Convention on Climate Change.

March

11	Informal meeting of the foreign ministers of the EU Member States, the acceding states (Bulgaria and Romania), the candidate states (Croatia and Turkey) and the potential candidate countries of the Western Balkans on the reaffirmed European perspective for the Western Balkans. ('Salzburg Declaration').
15	European Parliament/Council Regulation establishing the Schengen Borders Code.

15   European Parliament/Council Directive on the retention of
           telecommunications data.

April
9   First Round of parliamentary elections in Hungary.
23   Second Round of parliamentary elections in Hungary.
27   Parliamentary elections in Italy.

May
3   The Commission decided to suspended negotiations of the
           stabilization and association agreement with Serbia pending
           full co-operation with the International Criminal Tribunal for
           the former Yugoslavia.
4–5   International Conference on Internal Security, Vienna,
           involving the Interior Ministers of the EU Member States,
           candidate countries, European Economic Area partners,
           countries of the Western Balkans, countries of the European
           Neighbourhood, Russia and the United States of America.
           Addressed the role of internal security in relation between the
           EU and its neighbours. Signature of 'Convention on Police
           Co-operation for South Eastern Europe'.
9   Estonia ratified the Constitutional Treaty.
9   Maltese Parliament ratified the Constitutional Treaty.
10   Commission communication: a Citizens' Agenda: Delivering
           Results for Europe.
12   Fourth EU–Latin America summit held in Vienna.
16   European Court of Justice decision in *Watts*.
21   Parliamentary elections in Cyprus.
26   EU–Russia Summit in Sochi.
29   Council political agreement on the Services directive.
30   European Court of Justice decision in *Parliament v. Council
           and Commission* (annulled passenger name records agreement
           with the United States).

June
2–3   Czech parliamentary elections.
9   Belgium ratified the Constitutional Treaty.
12   Stabilization and association agreement with Albania signed.

15–16   European Council Brussels. Agreed two-track approach to pursuing institutional reform: use of existing treaties to deliver concrete results while preparing the ground for continuing the reform process. Approved the Integrated Guidelines for Growth and Jobs 2005–08; the report by the Presidency, the Secretary-General/High Representative and the Commission on the implementation of the Strategic Partnership between the EU and the Mediterranean region and the Middle East; the Presidency report on the European Security and Defence Policy; and the Presidency report on EU activities in the framework of conflict prevention and stressed the need to continue work in this area.

17   Parliamentary elections in Slovakia.

21   EU–US summit meeting in Vienna.

July

4   Roberto Fico became Prime Minister of Slovakia.

4   European Court of Justice Decision in *Adeneler*.

7   Kazimierz Marcinkiewicz (Prime Minister of Poland) resigned and was replaced by Jarosław Kaczyński.

10–11   Euro-African ministerial meetings on 'Migration and Development' in Rabat.

11   Council (ECOFIN) accepted Slovenia's application to join the euro area on 1 January 2007 and rejected Lithuania's.

12   Court of First decision in *Ayadi*.

17   FRONTEX co-ordinated the HERA I deployment of experts from France, Germany, Italy and Portugal to the Canary Islands to provide support for identifying the migrants and establishing their countries of origin.

18   European Court of Justice decision in *De Cuyper*.

24   The Council adopted a mandate for the negotiation of a stabilization and association agreement with Montenegro.

August

11   Operation HERA II, which provided help with maritime surveillance between the West African coast and the Canary Islands, began.

17   Mirek Topolanek became Prime Minister of the Czech Republic.

September
9   EU–China Summit in Helsinki.
10–11   Asia–Europe meeting in Helsinki.
12   European Court of Justice decision in *Eman and Sevinger*.
15–16   Presidents of the Visegrad countries object to delays to their
           full integration into Schengen.
18   Parliamentary elections in Sweden.
21–22   Informal meeting of justice and home affairs ministers in
           Tampere.

October
1   Parliamentary elections in Austria.
3   European Court of Justice decision in *Cadman*.
4   Commission Communication 'Global Europe: Competing in
           the World'.
5   Council Decision establishing a mutual information
           mechanism concerning national asylum and immigration
           measures.
6   Council Framework Decision on the application of the mutual
           recognition principle to confiscation orders.
7   Parliamentary elections in Latvia.
13   EU–India Summit in Helsinki.
17   Council approved accession of Bulgaria and Romania on 1
           January 2007.
20   Informal meeting of heads of state and government in Lahti
           focused on competitiveness.
24   European Parliament and the Council Framework programme
           for Competitiveness and Innovation.
26   G-6 ministers (from France, Germany, Italy, Poland, Spain
           and the UK) agreed to co-operate more closely in combating
           terrorism.

November
8   Commission communication 'Enlargement Strategy and Main
           Challenges 2006–07'.
22   Parliamentary elections in the Netherlands.
23   European Court of Justice decision in *Joustra*.
22–23   Euro-African ministerial meetings on 'Migration and
           Development' in Tripoli.

24	Implementation of the Strategy and Action Plan to Combat Terrorism.
24	EU–Russia Summit in Helsinki.
26	Referendum in Switzerland approved its contribution to EU social and economic cohesion.

December

4	Commission communication 'Strengthening the European Neighbourhood Policy'.
6	Commission Green Paper 'Global Europe: Europe's trade defence instruments in a changing global economy.'
6	Finland ratified the Constitutional Treaty.
11	The Council partially suspended the accession negotiations with Turkey.
12	Court of First Instance decision in *Organisation des modjahedines du peuple d'Iran*.
15	European Council in Brussels. Confirmed the enlargement process as a key priority. Agreed steps to be taken with regard to migration during 2007.
15	HERA II ended.
18	European Parliament and the Council signed the REACH (registration, evaluation and authorization of chemicals) regulation.
19	New Central European Free Trade Agreement signed in Bucharest.
20	European Parliament and the Council established the European Globalization Adjustment Fund.

© 2007 The Author(s)
Journal compilation © 2007 Blackwell Publishing Ltd

Index

© 2007 The Author(s)
Journal compilation © 2007 Blackwell Publishing Ltd

Printed and bound by CPI Group (UK) Ltd, Croydon, CR0 4YY

13/04/2025

14656463-0003